שמירת שבת כהלכתה

SHEMIRATH
SHABBATH

*a guide to the practical
observance of the Sabbath*

Volume II

Rav Yehoshua Y. Neuwirth

SHEMIRATH SHABBATH

*a guide to the practical
observance of the Sabbath*

the English edition of
שמירת שבת כהלכתה
Sh°mirath Shabbath K°hilchathah

prepared by
W. GRANGEWOOD
in close collaboration with the author

II

*from the second edition of the Hebrew
Volume I, Chapters 23-41*

FELDHEIM
Jerusalem / New York

First published 1989
Hardcover edition: ISBN 0-87306-477-1
Paperback edition: ISBN 0-87306-478-x

Typeset by Astronel

Philipp Feldheim Inc.
200 Airport Executive Park
Spring Valley, NY 10977

Feldheim Publishers Ltd.
POB 6525 / Jerusalem, Israel

Printed in Israel

מצבת זכרון עולמים

אמי מורתי, הרבנית **שרה חיה** ע״ה נויבירט
בת מוהר״ר **יצחק הלוי** זצללה״ה במברגר
אשר עמדה לימין א״א מו״ר
הרה״ג ר׳ **אהרון** בן הרב **שאול צבי** זצללה״ה
לגדלני על ברכי התורה
ואשר היתה ידועה לתהילה ולתפארת בצדקתה ובחכמתה.
פיה פתחה בחכמה ותורת חסד על לשונה.
מצאצאי גדולי אשכנז זיע״א, בעל מלאכת שמים, שו״ת יד הלוי,
אמירה לבית יעקב ועוד,
ומצד אמה בעל ערוך לנר ושו״ת בנין ציון.

נשים במאי זכיין באקרויי בנייהו לבי כנישתא (ברכות יז א)

נפטרה בשיבה טובה ל׳ סיון תשמ״ז

ת.נ.צ.ב.ה.

מוקדש

CONTENTS

23: Housekeeping and use of domestic facilities on Shabbath and Yom Tov
pages 329-344

24: Laws relating to the erection of protective shelters and of partitions on Shabbath and Yom Tov / *pages 345-360*

25: Dangerous nuisances and hazards to health / *pages 361-365*

26: Plants and trees / *pages 366-373*

27: Laws relating to animals on Shabbath and Yom Tov / *pages 374-395*

28: A miscellany including stationery, clocks, noises, baby carriages, remuneration and advance preparations / *pages* 396-424

29: Laws derived from Isaiah: running, walking, commerce, measuring, reading, speaking / *pages* 425-450

CONTENTS

30: General rules relating to actions performed by a non-Jew on Shabbath and Yom Tov / pages 451-485

[xiii]

31: Miscellaneous laws relating to non-Jews, and to Shabbath and Yom Tov outside the land of Israel / *pages* 486-502

32: Laws relating to the saving of human life / *pages* 503-543

1 The supreme importance of saving life. 2 Prolonging life. 3 Lives of adults and children. 4 Violation by the person in danger or someone else. 5 Where person in danger objects to violation of Shabbath. 6 Violation by observant Jew preferable. 7 Violation which proves to have been unnecessary.

33: Laws relating to persons who are ill but whose lives are not in danger / *pages* 544-557

34: Slight indispositions, minor ailments and disabilities / *pages* 558-570

37: Laws relating to babies and small children / *pages* 594-601

38: Caring for the sick and for small children on Shabbath and Yom Tov with the aid of a non-Jew / *pages* 602-614

39: Laws relating to illness, pregnancy, childbirth and breast-feeding on Yom Kippur / *pages* 615-628

40: A medical miscellany, including laws relating to doctors, hospitals, prayers, traveling and Pesach / *pages* 629-675

41: Laws applicable in various emergency situations / *pages* 676-692

The Contents of Volume 1

שמירת שבת כהלכתה

SHEMIRATH
SHABBATH

*a guide to the practical
observance of the Sabbath*

Volume II

Chapter 23

Housekeeping and Use of Domestic Facilities on Shabbath and Yom Tov

CLEANING

1. *a.* 1) a) With the exception mentioned in paragraph 2*b* below, one may use a soft broom to sweep a room covered with tile, wood, linoleum or similar flooring. *circumstances in which sweeping is permitted*

    b) Regarding a carpeted floor see paragraph 4 below.

   2) One may not use a hard broom made of twigs or reeds, and such a broom is *muktzeh*.

   3) Preferably, one should sweep only in a place which was already swept before the beginning of Shabbath or Yom Tov.

b. 1) It is forbidden to reattach a broomstick which has separated from its brush.

   2) It is prohibited to fasten it to the brush even with the aid of a screw which is designed for that purpose.

   3) Even if the stick is still attached to the brush, one may not strengthen the connection with the assistance of a nail.

2. *a.* It is forbidden to sweep a floor which is not paved or otherwise covered. *where sweeping is forbidden*

b. 1) In a place where most of the floors are not paved or covered in some other way, it is forbidden to sweep even a covered floor.

   2) By way of illustration, in a camp consisting mainly of tents or huts with uncovered, earthen floors, it is forbidden to sweep even in the few huts which do have wooden or concrete flooring.

[329]

polishing
floors

3. One may neither apply polishing cream to, nor polish, a wooden floor or linoleum.

carpets

4. *a.* One should not brush a carpet vigorously nor clean it with a specially designed carpet-sweeper, not even with a sweeper which is not electrically operated.

   b. It is also prohibited to shake the dust out of a carpet vigorously.

   c. One may lightly shake a carpet to remove some of the surface dust, but not if the carpet
   1) is dark in color **and**
   2) is new or looks new.

   d. One is allowed gently to sweep even a dark-colored, new carpet with a soft broom in order to collect rubbish lying on its surface.

spraying
water on
floor

5. It is permitted to spray water on the floor of a room, even if it consists of bare earth, to prevent the dust from rising (for instance during dancing on Simchath Torah).

washing
the floor

6. *a.* Washing even a tiled floor is forbidden, whether one uses a rag or a squeegee (a non-absorbent, rubber-bladed wiper especially intended for the purpose).

   b. 1) Where it is essential to wash the floor, it is possible to relax the strictness of the prohibition and permit the washing of tiled and other covered floors, provided that only a squeegee, and not a cloth, is used.

   2) An example is the case of a hospital, where particular attention must be paid to cleanliness.

spilled
liquids

7. *a.* Small quantities of water, wine or other liquid spilled on the table or on the floor may be wiped up with a cloth intended for the purpose, as long as one is careful not to squeeze the cloth. (See also Chapter 12, paragraphs 37 to 39).

   b. Large quantities of liquid may not be wiped up with a cloth, because one is more likely to squeeze it out, but one may wipe them away with the aid of a squeegee.

   c. It is forbidden to remove the cover of a drain in the floor, to allow the liquid to flow away, unless the cover has a handle.

8. *a.* One may use a cloth to dust furniture or other articles.   *dusting*

   b. One may not polish them, either with a cream or a   *furniture* liquid, nor even shine them by vigorous rubbing with a dry cloth.

9. *a.* Cobwebs on furniture or some other movable article   *cobwebs* may be removed, provided that this is done not with one's hand but with a broom or some other instrument.

   b. One should not remove cobwebs from the walls, the ceiling or any other part of the house, both

     1) because the cobwebs themselves are *muktzeh* and

     2) because doing so is analogous to the forbidden activity of detaching something which is connected to the ground.

   c. If one finds a spider, one is of course not allowed to kill it on Shabbath or Yom Tov.

HYGIENE

10. *a.* Where rainwater is unable to flow away, because of a   *draining* blockage in a gutter or drainage pipe, and is causing a   *away* flood, one may clear the stoppage with the assistance   *rainwater* of an article which is not *muktzeh*.

   b. However, where a yard is flooded by rainwater, one may neither

     1) dig a channel through which the water could flow away nor

     2) clear an existing channel which has become filled with earth or debris.

blocked
11. A domestic rubber plunger (but not the larger variety   *sinks and* used by professional plumbers) may be employed to   *toilet bowls*

unblock a clogged sink or toilet bowl, if there is an important need for it.

emptying garbage bins

12. A domestic garbage bin may be emptied if
   a. it gives off a smell which it is difficult to bear **or**
   b. it is full and one has nowhere else to dispose of the rubbish which has collected in the house.

air purifiers

13. a. One is allowed to hang up cartons or other containers of a chemical material designed to act as an air freshener. (But see Chapter 9, paragraphs 1 to 6 and 12, for problems which may arise in opening or perforating such a carton or container on Shabbath or Yom Tov.)
   b. It is also permitted to use an air-purifying spray.
   c. With regard to spraying insecticides, see Chapter 25, paragraph 5.

disinfectant and deodorant in a toilet

14. a. One may put disinfectant or deodorant, either liquid or solid, into the flushing cistern or into the bowl of a toilet on Shabbath or Yom Tov, but
   b. one should not use disinfectant or deodorant which colors the water.
   c. Indeed, disinfectant or deodorant which colors the water should be removed from the cistern or bowl before Shabbath or Yom Tov begins.
   d. The lid of a cistern which is held on by screws may be neither unscrewed nor screwed down on Shabbath or Yom Tov.

cleaning a toilet bowl

15. a. One may flush a toilet bowl on Shabbath or Yom Tov.
   b. One may also clean off dirt adhering to its sides, using for the purpose a brush with synthetic bristles which are not close enough together to hold water.

toilet paper

16. a. It is forbidden to tear toilet paper on Shabbath or Yom Tov, whether one tears along the perforation or not.
   b. 1) If there is no cut or already torn toilet paper and one

has no other practicable substitute, one may use clean sheets of writing paper in its place, notwithstanding the fact that they are *muktzeh*, as stated in Chapter 20, paragraph 5.

2) It is permitted to take more writing paper into the bathroom (toilet) than one needs at the time, since what is left over could be of use later, either to oneself or to another person.

c. One should not use paper with writing or patterns on it as toilet paper on Shabbath or Yom Tov, unless one has neither cut or torn toilet paper, nor writing paper, which one could use instead.

d. 1) In a case where none of the above possibilities are available, and one is in need of toilet paper, considerations of human dignity would justify a relaxation of the usual rule, but only if one tears the paper in a way which one would not normally employ.

2) For example, one could hold the roll down with one elbow, while tearing the paper off with the wrist of the other arm.

3) If one has to tear toilet paper, as above, one should tear it off a roll, rather than tear one sheet into two parts, both of which one then uses.

4) When one has to tear toilet paper, as above, one should try not to tear along the perforation.

e. 1) Sealed cartons containing cut toilet paper should be torn open in such a way that they are no longer fit for use.

2) See also Chapter 9, paragraph 8.

17. a. It is not permitted to scatter sand over a puddle which has formed in the yard.

b. One is, however, allowed to cover the puddle with a board or some other item, provided

1) the board or other item is not *muktzeh* and

2) one does not have the intention of leaving it there permanently.

c. 1) One may scatter cinders or sand to prevent people

covering puddles or ice

from slipping on an icy patch of ground.

2) If one knows in advance that it is likely to be icy, one should prepare the cinders or sand before Shabbath or Yom Tov.

3) Where none has been prepared, one may use such cinders or sand as are available, despite the fact that they are *muktzeh*. (See Chapter 25, paragraphs 8 and 9.)

CENTRAL HEATING

turning on taps

18. *a.* 1) On Shabbath, it is forbidden to turn on the taps of central-heating radiators or of the pipes which conduct hot water from the boiler to the radiators.

2) This is prohibited because the cold water in the pipes and in the radiators would, as a result, flow into the boiler, where it would be heated. (Compare Chapter 1, paragraph 39*a*.)

3) The taps must not be turned on even if the heating system is not yet operating but will be turned on during Shabbath, for example by means of a timer (time-switch) or by a non-Jew. (Regarding the latter, see paragraph 24 below.)

b. On Yom Tov, these taps may be turned on even when the heating system is operating, and it is the custom to permit this even if the weather is not particularly cold.

turning off taps

19. *a.* On both Shabbath and Yom Tov, one is allowed to turn off the taps of central-heating radiators and of the pipes which conduct hot water from the boiler to the radiators.

b. 1) However, on Shabbath it is proper to refrain from doing so as long as the water inside the radiators or inside these pipes is in the process of being heated and has not yet reached a temperature of 45 degrees centigrade (113 degrees Fahrenheit).

2) This is because turning off the taps causes the

water in the boiler to reach a temperature of 45 degrees centigrade more quickly than it otherwise would.

20. *a.* The thermostat which regulates a central-heating system may be turned to a lower marking on Shabbath or Yom Tov only when the system is not operating. *regulating the thermostat*

 b. 1) It is forbidden, both on Shabbath and on Yom Tov, to turn the thermostat to a higher marking while it is preventing the system from operating.

 2) Turning up the thermostat while the system is operating

 a) is permitted on Yom Tov, but

 b) should be avoided on Shabbath.

21. *a.* There is nothing wrong with opening and closing the doors or windows of a centrally heated apartment or house on Shabbath or Yom Tov. *opening and closing doors and windows*

 b. That is to say, one need not worry that one will thereby accelerate the ignition or extinction of the thermostatically operated heating system.

22. *a.* Subject to the very important limitations set out in Chapter 13, paragraph 25, a timer which was set before Shabbath to turn the central heating on or off at a predetermined hour may be adjusted on Shabbath *adjusting a timer*

 1) to turn it on or off at a later time, but

 2) not to turn it on or off at an earlier time.

 b. Subject to those same limitations, a timer may be adjusted on Yom Tov

 1) to turn the heating on or off at a later time, or

 2) to turn it on earlier, but

 3) not to turn it off earlier.

23. *a.* Where a Jew has turned on the central-heating system of an apartment building, even in deliberate violation of the Shabbath, one need not leave the building or turn *heating turned on by a Jew on Shabbath*

[335]

off* the radiators to avoid benefiting from the transgression, but

b. it is certainly forbidden to come nearer to the radiators or lean against them in order to warm oneself.

c. If at all practicable, one should bring polite but firm persuasion to bear, in an attempt to have a timer installed so that the heating can be operated automatically in the future.

d. See Chapter 30, paragraph 53 regarding buildings in which the central-heating system is operated by a non-Jew.

requesting a non-Jew to turn on the heating

24. a. In countries with a cool climate, one may on Shabbath ask a non-Jew to turn on the heating, if one is troubled by the cold, since a person who is suffering from the cold is placed in the same category as someone who is ill. (See Chapter 38, paragraphs 4 and 8.)

b. 1) Where there are small children in the house, one may request a non-Jew to turn on the heating even when the cold is not intense enough to bother the adults, since small children are naturally more sensitive to cold.

2) Once the heating is on, it is permissible for the grown-ups also to avail themselves of its benefit.

c. In any case, one should prepare, before Shabbath, any implements or materials needed for turning on the heating, so that the non-Jew can take them himself, as they are *muktzeh* and one will not be able to handle them on Shabbath.

releasing air from a radiator

25. a. It is forbidden to release air from a radiator on Shabbath by loosening the screw fitted for that purpose.

b. One should take care not to do this even after the heating system has turned itself off.

---

*See paragraph 19 above.

26. *a.* On Shabbath, one may not place on a radiator anything to which the prohibition against cooking applies (as described in Chapter 1, paragraphs 5 to 11), if indeed it could reach 45 degrees centigrade. *placing on a radiator things one may not cook*

    b. This is prohibited

      1) even if one intends to leave it there only for a short time in order to remove the chill **and**

      2) even if the heating system is not operating at the time, but will be activated later (by a non-Jew or a timer).

27. *a.* Humidifiers (containers filled with water and intended to prevent the air in the room from becoming too dry) may be hung on radiators, provided (if it is Shabbath) that the water inside will not reach a temperature of 45 degrees centigrade. *humidifiers*

    b. The fact that the water will evaporate is in itself irrelevant.

28. *a.* One should not hold one's wet hands near a warm radiator on Shabbath, even if its temperature is less than 45 degrees centigrade. *warming wet hands*

    b. There is, however, nothing wrong with warming them at the radiator after they have been dried.

29. One is not permitted to spread or hang wet laundry on or near a radiator, even if its temperature has not reached, and will not reach, 45 degrees centigrade. (See Chapter 15, paragraph 9.) *wet laundry*

30. While wearing wet clothes, one may not stand or sit near a radiator in a position where the temperature reaches 45 degrees centigrade, even if one's sole intention is to warm oneself and not one's clothes. *wearing wet clothes near a radiator*

31. *a.* A pot containing warm food, wrapped on all sides in a cloth, may not be placed on top of a radiator, even before the beginning of Shabbath. (See Chapter 1, paragraphs 65 and 66.) *standing wrapped pots on a radiator*

b. If, however, the pot is not covered on all sides, one may put it near or on top of a radiator, even on Shabbath, so long as it is in a position where its temperature will not reach 45 degrees centigrade.

REPAIRS

removal of doors and windows

32. *a.* 1) It is forbidden to take off the door of a house or of a large cupboard, or to take off a window, on Shabbath or Yom Tov.

2) A door or a window which has come off may not be reinstalled and is *muktzeh*. (But see Chapter 20, paragraph 43.)

handles and locks

b. 1) Similar prohibitions apply to the removal and replacement of door handles,* although

2) a handle which is made to be inserted in, and withdrawn from, a door as and when necessary may be used on Shabbath and Yom Tov and is not *muktzeh*.

c. There is nothing wrong with using a "keyhole lock" (a lock that is inserted into a keyhole, where it is locked into position), even if it is made in two pieces, one of which is detached, leaving the other locked into the keyhole.

shutters

33. *a.* A shutter which becomes defective or comes out of its track may not be repaired and is *muktzeh*.

b. One is not allowed to open or close the lid of a shutter-box (the box into which a shutter rolls up when it is raised).

putty around window-panes

34. One must not spread putty around the edges of a pane of glass in order to fix it into the window or to make it fit more firmly.

---

*If the handle has come out of a door and one is unable to open and close it, one may use a screwdriver or some other *k^eli she-m^elachto l^e-issur* for the purpose, but not, of course, to effect any repair. (See Chapter 20, paragraphs 5, 7 and 8.)

35. *a.* Fragments of a broken windowpane may be removed from the floor, to prevent someone being injured by them, but one should take them away with the assistance of a broom or some similar object, and not move them with one's hands, as they are *muktzeh*. (See Chapter 22, paragraph 35.) *removing broken window-panes*

    b. 1) Pieces of broken glass which remain in the window frame should not be taken out on Shabbath or Yom Tov, since this would be an infringement of the prohibitions that fall under the general heading of "Building."

        2) Where there is a danger that someone might cut himself,

            a) one may ask a non-Jew to remove the glass remaining in the frame, or

            b) if there is no non-Jew available, one may remove it oneself, using a method which one would not normally employ, for example by kicking it out.

36. *a.* One is not allowed to repair a smashed window. *covering a broken window*

    b. It is also prohibited to fill the gap with a piece of plywood in order to keep the wind out or to stop people from looking in, since one might leave it there permanently.

    c. One is permitted to cover the hole with a cloth or a piece of cardboard so long as

        1) one does not attach it with nails or thumbtacks (drawing pins) nor stick it down **and**

        2) one intends that it should be there only temporarily.

37. *a.* One must not write letters or draw patterns in the condensation which has formed on a windowpane. *fogged-up windows*

    b. One may wipe condensation off a windowpane, provided this does not involve wiping off writing or patterns.

squeaky doors

38. It is forbidden to oil the hinges of a squeaky door.

nails, thumbtacks and hooks

39. *a.* One is not allowed to drive in or extract a nail or a thumbtack on Shabbath or Yom Tov.

b. One may likewise not attach or detach a hook which is fixed to the wall by means of suction or an adhesive backing.

c. One may hang a picture on a hook which has been fixed in the wall since before Shabbath or Yom Tov. (See, however, Chapter 20, paragraph 22.)

cistern lids

40. A problem may arise in connection with the domestic water cisterns commonly installed on the roofs of buildings in Jerusalem and other high-altitude areas in Israel.

a. If the lid of such a cistern has a handle or fits onto a protruding rim which stands out from the body of the cistern, one may open it.

b. A lid which has no handle and fits flush into the opening in the cistern may not be opened unless it is attached by a hinge.

removing chair seats

41. A chair seat that is not attached may be removed from its chair and may be put back.

furniture legs

42. One may not fix rubber or plastic noise-absorbers to the legs of chairs or tables, nor may one detach them.

watering concrete or plaster

43. *a.* One may not water freshly poured concrete or plaster either on Shabbath or on Yom Tov.

b. One ought to have the foresight not to pour concrete or plaster shortly before Shabbath or Yom Tov, so as not to put oneself into a position where one might be tempted to violate the Shabbath.

c. See also Chapter 30, paragraph 13.

other references

44. *a.* For the use of scrapers to remove mud from shoes see Chapter 15, paragraph 39.

b. 1) The circumstances in which one may use or move broken items of furniture are set out in Chapter 20, paragraph 42.

2) See also Chapter 28, paragraph 45 concerning broken baby carriages (perambulators).

BELLS AND KNOCKERS

45. *a.* One should not use a bell either on Shabbath or on Yom Tov. *use of a bell*

b. As will be seen from Chapter 28, paragraphs 32 and 34, there is a Rabbinical prohibition extending even to the use of an ordinary bell which is not electrically operated.

c. 1) If
   a) there is no other way in which one can enter one's house, and
   b) one really does need to enter,
   one can rely on the authorities who relax the severity of the rule in such circumstances and may ring the bell, provided that it is not electrically operated.

2) Where at all possible in such a case, one should operate the bell in a manner which one would not adopt on another day, for instance by using one's elbow.

46. *a.* One may not, on Shabbath or Yom Tov, knock on a door with a knocker which is used on the other days of the week, but one may knock with one's hand. *use of a knocker*

b. One may use a knocker which is especially intended for use only on Shabbath and Yom Tov.

47. If one has mistakenly rung an electric bell and, while one is still pressing it, remembers that it is Shabbath, one may take one's finger off the button, unless this would turn on or off a control light which is designed to show whether or not the bell is operating. *pressing a bell by mistake*

[341]

bell
activated
by opening
door

48. *a.* A bell which rings with the opening of a door should be removed from it before Shabbath or Yom Tov starts.

b. If one has forgotten to remove it, one may, nonetheless, open the door on Shabbath or Yom Tov, as long as the bell is not electrically operated.

ELEVATORS*

when use
permitted

49. *a.* It is forbidden to use an elevator on Shabbath or Yom Tov, unless all of the following conditions are fulfilled:

1) the elevator operates automatically, that is to say it goes up and down by itself at fixed intervals or continuously;

2) the elevator stops by itself at the required floors, without the need for any human interference, whether by way of pressing buttons or otherwise;

3) the doors open and close automatically, likewise without the need for any human interference;

4) no prohibited act is involved in entering or leaving the elevator. (See paragraph 53 below.)

b. 1) There are some who permit the use of an elevator only for ascending, and not for descending, even

a) when all the above conditions are fulfilled or

b) when the elevator is being operated by a non-Jew for his own purposes.

2) Their reasons are outlined in paragraph 50 below.

c. There are, however, eminent authorities who allow the use of an elevator (subject to the above conditions) even for descending.

d. One should not touch the electrically operated door of an elevator, either with one's hand or with one's body, when it is about to close. (See paragraph 53 below.)

e. It is highly advisable to publish, on every floor of the

---

*Due to the complicated technicalities involved and the differences of opinion among the authorities, one would be well advised not to use an elevator on Shabbath or Yom Tov without consulting a properly qualified rabbi.

building, detailed instructions on the use of the elevator on Shabbath and Yom Tov, in order to avoid the violation of prohibitions through ignorance.

50. *a.* 1) The objections to descending in an elevator on Shabbath or Yom Tov stem from the way in which most modern elevators operate. *effect of passenger weight*

 2) The weight of the passengers can
 a) cause the elevator to descend more quickly and
 b) affect the amount of current passing through the motor.

 3) It is argued that a Torah prohibition (and not just a Rabbinical restriction) is involved when lights are turned on or powered as a result of these factors.

 b. This is of course disputed by the eminent authorities referred to in paragraph 49*c*, above, who permit the use of an elevator for descending (subject to the conditions set out in paragraph 49*a*).

51. *a.* It is not permitted to benefit from the transgression of a Jew who is operating an elevator on Shabbath or Yom Tov. *elevator operated by a Jew*

 b. For the use of an elevator operated by a non-Jew on Shabbath and Yom Tov, see Chapter 30, paragraph 54.

ESCALATORS, AUTOMATIC DOORS AND COMBINATION LOCKS

52. *a.* One may use automatic escalators and moving sidewalks (pavements) that operate continuously or at fixed intervals. *escalators and moving sidewalks*

 b. One may not use them if they are put into motion by one's approach.

53. *a.* It is prohibited, both on Shabbath and on Yom Tov, to pass through an electrically operated automatic door which is opened *automatic doors*

 1) by means of a photo-electric cell or
 2) when one treads on the floor in front of it.

  b. In both of these cases, by approaching the door, one would be activating an electrical current.

combina-
tion locks

54. *a.* There are two types of combination locks.

  1) One type is opened by rolling individual digits around to compose a predetermined, multi-digit number.

  2) The other type is opened by turning a dial in accordance with set instructions as to the numbers and the direction of rotations.

 b. Both types may be used on Shabbath or Yom Tov.

Chapter 24

Laws Relating to the Erection of Protective Shelters and of Partitions on Shabbath and Yom Tov

PROTECTIVE SHELTERS: GENERAL PRINCIPLES

1. *a.* The Torah prohibits the erection of a permanent, protective shelter on Shabbath or Yom Tov.
   b. The prohibition includes the erection of any permanent roof or covering
   1) intended to provide shelter, for example against the sun or the rain, **or**
   2) designed to furnish a usable space underneath.
   c. It should be noted that a protective shelter intended to last for as little as a few days is regarded as permanent.
   d. The prohibition is applicable even where there are no walls, as where a mat or blanket is spread over some poles to give shelter.
   e. The Torah also forbids the addition on Shabbath or Yom Tov of a permanent extension to an already existing permanent, protective shelter.

prohibited by the Torah

2. *a.* The Rabbis prohibited the erection of a temporary, protective shelter also, for fear that one might come to erect a permanent one.
   b. One is, however, allowed to add a temporary extension to an existing protective shelter, even to a permanent one, as will be explained below.

Rabbinical prohibition

3. *a.* A protective shelter which does not have a roof measuring at least one *tefach* by one *tefach* is treated as temporary and falls only within the Rabbinical prohibition referred to above.

very small, protective shelters

[345]

b. As this situation occurs only infrequently in practice, its intricacies will not be further discussed here.

taking down a protective shelter

4. *a.* Any protective shelter which may not be erected on Shabbath or Yom Tov — whether the source of the prohibition is the Torah or a Rabbinical injunction — may likewise not be taken down on Shabbath or Yom Tov.

b. A protective shelter which may be erected may also be taken down.

TEMPORARY PROTECTIVE SHELTERS

the prohibition: typical examples

5. *a.* The Rabbinical prohibition against erecting a temporary protective shelter applies
   1) even if one intends to take it down that same day and
   2) even if one puts up merely a covering, as where
      a) the walls were put up before Shabbath or Yom Tov **or**
      b) there are no walls and one simply spreads a mat or blanket over poles.

b. 1) It follows that it is, in general, forbidden to spread any kind of canopy, whether hard or soft, as a protection against
      a) the sun,
      b) the rain **or**
      c) mosquitoes, flies and so forth.
   2) It is likewise forbidden to make a tent out of blankets and the like, with the object of using the space underneath, whether one does so
      a) on a balcony,
      b) in a garden or yard or
      c) even indoors.
   3) It goes without saying that it is forbidden to erect an actual tent, notwithstanding that one intends to dismantle it the same day. (See also paragraph 16 below.)

6. *a.* As already mentioned, one may add a temporary *temporary* extension on Shabbath and Yom Tov to an already *extensions* existing protective shelter.

   b. Thus, where a canopy has been open since before Shabbath or Yom Tov to the width of at least one *tefach*, it is permitted to add to it by opening it to its full extent.

   c. If the canopy can be opened from both sides, it should be extended from the side which has already been opened to the extent of a *tefach* and not from the other side.

7. *a.* One may not put a roll of matting or blanket into *rolled up* position on Shabbath or Yom Tov to form a protective *matting or* shelter, even in its rolled state, if the diameter of the *blanket* roll is one *tefach* or more.

   b. Furthermore, a roll may not be opened out on Shabbath or Yom Tov to form a protective shelter, even if
   1) one placed it in position before Shabbath or Yom Tov with the object of unrolling it and
   2) its diameter is more than a *tefach*.

   c. However, if a roll was put in position and one *tefach* of it was unrolled before Shabbath or Yom Tov, one may unroll more of it on Shabbath or Yom Tov, thereby extending the protective shelter already formed by the first *tefach*.

8. *a.* The prohibition against making a protective shelter *minimum* on Shabbath and Yom Tov applies only if an empty *height* space of at least one *tefach* in height is left underneath.

   b. A cover may be put up if the space underneath it will be less than a *tefach*, since it is not regarded as a protective shelter.

net or canopy
9. *a.* One is not allowed to place a net or a canopy over a *over carriage* baby carriage (perambulator), a bed or a crib (cot), as *or crib*

a protection against the sun or against flies. (See, however, paragraphs 11, 13 and 14 below.)

b. 1) Where a net or canopy was already spread over the carriage, bed or crib before Shabbath or Yom Tov, to the width of a *tefach* (excluding the diameter of any roll, as in paragraph 7 above), one is allowed to spread it out to its full extent.

2) When removing a net or canopy which one has extended in these circumstances, one should leave in position the *tefach* of covering which was spread before the beginning of Shabbath or Yom Tov and with which one started.

waterproof covering on a sukka

10. *a.* One is permitted to add a temporary covering to an existing shelter on Shabbath or Yom Tov, even if the additional cover is intended to provide protection from something against which the original shelter is of no avail.

b. 1) One is, therefore, allowed to put a waterproof cover over a *sukka* when it is raining (to prevent the decorations from being spoiled).

2) Nevertheless, one should take care, in doing so, not to move the *s^echach*, as it is *muktzeh*.

wide-mesh netting

11. The spreading of wide-mesh netting over a chicken coop or a baby carriage, to keep birds out, is permissible and does not infringe the prohibition against making a protective shelter.

extending a notional shelter

12. *a.* In defined circumstances and for certain purposes, the Halacha regards a gap of less than three *tefachim* as being nonexistent, that is to say, as being filled by solid matter.

b. As a result of the application of this rule, a protective shelter is considered to have been in place since before Shabbath or Yom Tov in the following two cases:

1) where two cords were strung out, side by side, with

a distance of at least one *tefach*, but less than three
tᵉfachim, between them;

2) where one cord was strung out parallel to a wall or
other partition, at a distance from it of at least one
tefach, but less than three *tᵉfachim*.

c. One may put a temporary covering over the notional
shelter formed by these cords or by the single cord in
conjunction with the partition.

d. 1) One may add a temporary extension to a notional
shelter, just as one may add to any other already
existing protective shelter. (See paragraph 6*a*
above.)

2) a) The extension should be commenced adjacent to
the existing (notional) shelter and spread
outwards from it.

b) That is to say, one should not commence at a
distance from the existing (notional) shelter and
spread the extension to meet it. (Compare
paragraph 6*c* above.)

13. *a.* 1) A covering which   *attached*

     a) forms part of a structure or of an article and   *hoods and*

     b) has been fixed to it since before Shabbath or *roofs*
Yom Tov

may be laid or spread over it on Shabbath or Yom
Tov.

2) This is so

     a) whether the covering is attached by means of
hinges, press-studs, screws, slots or another
equally effective method, and

     b) whether the covering is required for protection
against sun, rain or any other element.

b. 1) One may accordingly open the hood of a baby
carriage, provided it has been attached since before
Shabbath or Yom Tov.

2) Once the hood is opened to the extent of a *tefach*
(measured horizontally), one may also spread a net

or a canopy over the whole baby carriage, although one should begin to spread it from the end where the hood is.

3) If one has attached the hood to a baby carriage on Shabbath or Yom Tov, even in a permitted manner, for example by means of press-studs or slots, one should not open it that day.

4) One may open a sunshade that has been attached to a baby carriage since before Shabbath or Yom Tov.

c. The roof of a *sukka* which is attached to its sides by hinges may be opened and closed on Shabbath and Yom Tov. (See also paragraph 10 above.)

net or canopy tied to a bed or a crib

14. *a.* 1) Some beds, especially cribs, are made with an overhead rod or frame intended to support a canopy or net.

2) Subject to two conditions, the canopy or net may be drawn across to cover the bed or crib even if
   a) it is not at present spread open to the extent of a *tefach* and
   b) its purpose is to provide protection against flies or mosquitoes.

3) The two conditions are
   a) that the canopy or net has been tied to one side or end of the bed or crib since before Shabbath or Yom Tov **and**
   b) that it has cords attached for drawing it across.

b. When removing such a net or canopy, one may take it off the crib or bed altogether, provided this does not involve any violation of the prohibition against untying knots, described in Chapter 15, paragraph 54.

c. 1) A canopy which merely needs to be opened out and is intended purely for decorative or ceremonial purposes, and not as a protective shelter, may be spread on Shabbath or Yom Tov, even if it has no cords attached.

2) An example is a canopy on supporting poles, if not intended for protection.

15. *a.* 1) Our greatest halachic authorities saw fit to extend the prohibition against the erection of a protective shelter to the opening of umbrellas or parasols on Shabbath or Yom Tov. *umbrellas and sunshades*

2) Just as one should not open them, so should one not fold them up.

3) Moreover, one should not use an umbrella or a parasol,

a) even if it has been open since before the beginning of Shabbath or Yom Tov and

b) even in a place where there is an *eiruv.*

b. On the other hand, one may open and close

1) a garden sunshade which has been fixed into the ground since before Shabbath or Yom Tov or

2) an awning over a balcony, a porch or a shop window. (Compare paragraph 13*a* above.)

16. *a.* As we have seen in paragraph 5 above, it is forbidden to erect a tent on Shabbath or Yom Tov. *tent walls*

b. Nevertheless, if a tent has been standing since before Shabbath or Yom Tov, one may sometimes go so far as to

1) let down its walls and

2) secure* them at the bottom, to prevent them from flapping about in the wind.

c. This may be done only if it is usual for the walls in question to be unfastened and raised at frequent intervals.

d. If they are liable to be unfastened and raised only once every few days, it is forbidden to lower and secure them on Shabbath or Yom Tov.

---

*The walls may, of course, be secured only in a manner which is allowed, for example by tying a bow or by slipping a loop over a hook.

COVERING WITHOUT INTENDING TO PROVIDE SHELTER

general rule 17. *a.* The previous paragraphs of this chapter have dealt with the erection of a covering intended either
   1) to shelter or protect or
   2) to furnish a usable space underneath.
   b. One is allowed to spread or erect a covering not intended for either of these purposes,
   1) if it has no walls at all or if the walls it has are less than a *tefach* wide,
   2) if the walls were already standing before the commencement of Shabbath or Yom Tov and one now merely wishes to place the covering over them **or even**
   3) if one holds the covering in place while someone else puts up the walls underneath.
   c. The erection of a covering intended for neither of the above purposes is forbidden only if
   1) the way in which one proceeds is
      a) *first* to erect walls which have a width of at least one *tefach* each and
      b) *then* to place the covering over them, **and**
   2) the conditions set out in paragraph 18 below are fulfilled.

relevance of 18. The prohibition referred to in paragraph 17c above
number of   applies only if
partitions   *a.* 1) one erects walls on two or three of the four sides, **and**
covered
   2) one has in mind to make some use, albeit a secondary use, of the space underneath, or
   b. one erects walls on all four sides, whatever one's intentions as to use are, since a covered space enclosed within four walls is intrinsically usable.

placing
tabletop on 19. *a.* If one wishes to erect a table which, at both ends, has
legs   supports with legs a *tefach* or more wide, one would do

well **not** to put the supports into position first and then put a plank or boards on top of them (because one uses the space underneath for one's legs when sitting at the table). (See paragraph 18a above.)

b. One should reverse the order, that is one should first bring the top to the position where the table is to be set up and hold it in midair, and then the supports of the table should be brought and placed underneath.

20. a. 1) One should not bring an open barrel, stand it in position and then make a table by putting a plank across its opening, since one will thereby have placed a covering over a space surrounded by walls on all four sides. (See paragraph 18b above.) *making a table from a plank and a barrel*

    2) What one should do is to turn the barrel over and lay the plank across its base.

b. If one wishes to make a table out of a plank with upside-down barrels at both ends, the considerations explained in paragraph 19 above are applicable.

21. a. The situation is different if one has put the open barrels into the required position before the commencement of Shabbath or Yom Tov. *placing plank over barrels already in position*

b. In that case, there is nothing wrong with placing the plank over them on Shabbath or Yom Tov. (See paragraph 17b2 above.)

22. When dismantling a table of the kind described, made of a board laid over legs or supports at least a *tefach* in width, or over barrels, the order of procedure should be *dismantling a table*

a. to hold the board in one's hands, then

b. to remove the legs, supports or barrels or have them removed, and finally

c. to take away the board.

23. a. 1) One may both open and close *folding furniture*

    a) a folding chair,

    b) a folding bed,

    c) a folding table and

    d) a folding playpen.

2) This is because each of these items is opened and closed as a matter of course and its moving components are integral, connected parts of the one unit.

b. 1) One may not attach a sunshade to a deck chair.

    2) One may open and close a sunshade which has been attached to a deck chair since before Shabbath or Yom Tov. (See paragraph 13 above.)

c. One may not spread a net over a folding playpen, unless

    1) it has been tied to the side of the playpen since before Shabbath or Yom Tov **and**

    2) it has attached cords for drawing it across (as in paragraph 14 above).

d. One may extend and decrease the size of a table by

    1) raising or lowering flaps or

    2) inserting or extracting an additional leaf, even if, in so doing, one inserts pins protruding from the leaf into corresponding holes in the table, or withdraws them.

e. By contrast, it is forbidden, on Shabbath or Yom Tov, either to assemble or dismantle

    1) a child's crib (cot) made up of separate sections or

    2) a camp-bed which is held together or kept taut by means of pegs or pins which have to be driven into position.

taking out and inserting a drawer

24. A drawer one *tefach* or more deep, fitted under a table,

a. should not be pulled completely out of the table and,

b. if it is completely out, should not be replaced.

tablecloths and blankets

25. *a.* One is allowed to spread a cloth on a table, even if it overlaps the table and hangs down at the sides.

b. It is likewise permitted to spread a blanket over a bed.

ERECTION OF PARTITIONS

26. *a.* The Torah prohibits the erection of a permanent *permanent* partition on Shabbath or Yom Tov. *partitions*

b. Even fixing both the top and bottom of a curtain on to the frame of a portable screen is forbidden, if it is done in order to last for a few days or longer.

c. The size of the partition is not important.

27. *a.* It is permitted to erect a temporary partition (provided *temporary* there are no other prohibitions involved), for example, *partitions*

1) as a shade from the sun,

2) as a windbreak or

3) so that a person who is not feeling well can rest without being disturbed.

(See paragraphs 30, 32 and 34 below for examples where the erection of even a temporary partition is forbidden.)

b. One may even put up four such partitions around the bed of someone who is ill.

c. One is allowed to fix a curtain at both its top and bottom ends to a frame, for example, where it is intended temporarily to fill the place of a door which has come off its hinges, provided that

1) the curtain will indeed remain in the frame for only a short time **and**

2) the curtain is not attached with nails or tacks.

d. One is also allowed to cover a shattered windowpane with a cloth, since it is not usual to leave a window covered in such a makeshift manner for any length of time, but one must of course not attach the cloth with nails or tacks.

28. There are differing opinions as to whether one is *hanging a* permitted to hang a curtain in place of a door in a case *curtain in* where one intends it to remain in position for a few days *place of a* or more. *door for a* *few days or* *more*

a. According to one view, one may do so, but

[355]

1) one may attach it only at the top (and not also at the bottom) **and,**

2) a) if the curtain is a large one, one should not hang it by oneself, but should avail oneself of the assistance of another person.

   b) This is because the curtain might otherwise fold over to form a covering,* which, as we have seen, is forbidden on Shabbath and Yom Tov.

b. According to the other view, to do so would involve the infringement of a prohibition laid down by the Torah.

hanging curtains in front of a window

29. *a.* 1) a) It is forbidden to hang a curtain in front of a window if one attaches it both at the top and at the bottom.

   b) The reason is that curtains are often left hanging in front of windows for a considerable period.

2) If one attaches the curtain only at its top end, whether and how one may hang it depends on the considerations set out in paragraph 28 above.

hanging a curtain on a wall

b. 1) a) According to those who hold the first view expressed in paragraph 28 above, a curtain may be hung on a wall for decorative purposes.

   b) It may even be attached both at its top and bottom ends, but not of course with nails or tacks.

2) a) According to those who hold the second view, hanging the curtain on the wall with the intention that it should remain there for a few days or more involves the infringement of a prohibition laid down by the Torah.

   b) This is so, even if one does not attach it at both ends but merely hangs it from the rail.

---

*It should be noted that, in this exceptional case, one should not form the covering, in spite of the fact that there is no intention to provide either shelter or a usable space below and that there are no partitions.

PARTITIONS ERECTED FOR THEIR HALACHIC EFFECT

30. *a.* Often a partition has to be erected in order to permit one to do something which would otherwise be forbidden.

definition, examples and general rule applicable

b. The following are illustrations of partitions erected for this purpose:

1) a partition one erects in front of shelves containing books invested by the Halacha with a degree of sanctity,* so that one should be allowed to put a child on a potty, or undress a child, in the same room;

2) a partition put around a hospital bed because the presence of uncovered excrement would otherwise prevent the patient from praying or studying Torah;

3) a partition which is added to complete the minimum number of walls required by the Halacha for a *sukka*;

4) a partition designed to convert an area into a *r*e*shuth ha-yachid* so that one may carry objects about within it.

c. For a partition to be effective halachically,

1) it must be at least ten *t*e*fachim* high,

2) it must extend for a distance of at least four *t*e*fachim* **and**

3) it must be able to withstand the force of a normal wind; thus, if it consists of a curtain, it must be secured both at the top and at the bottom.

d. 1) It is prohibited to erect a partition on Shabbath or Yom Tov for the purpose mentioned in *a* above.

2) However, an existing partition which is not secured may be secured at its upper and lower ends on Shabbath or Yom Tov (although not, of course, with

---

*Examples of such books are the Pentateuch, the Prophets, the Talmud, halachic works, prayer books, and commentaries on them.

nails or tacks), to make it effective halachically, as long as

a) such a partition is not normally left in position for more than a short period **and**

b) one indeed intends it to remain standing for only a short period.

failure to meet require- ments

31. *a.* A partition which does not comply with the conditions set out in paragraph 30c above is not effective from the point of view of the Halacha.

b. It may be erected on Shabbath or Yom Tov, provided

1) that one does not secure it at its upper and lower ends with the object of leaving it in position for a few days or more (as in paragraph 26 above) and

2) that there are no other prohibitions involved.

folding screens

32. It is forbidden to open out a folding screen on Shabbath or Yom Tov with the intention that it should serve a halachic purpose (as explained in paragraph 30 above), unless it has been open to the extent of at least a *tefach* since before the beginning of Shabbath or Yom Tov. (See also paragraph 34 below.)

extending a partition

33. *a.* A partition which is attached at its upper and lower ends and has been spread to the extent of a *tefach* since before Shabbath or Yom Tov may be opened out altogether, even if it is intended to serve a halachic purpose (as explained in paragraph 30 above).

b. It is irrelevant whether the strip of a *tefach*

1) runs horizontally along the length of the partition and is a *tefach* wide from top to bottom or

2) runs vertically up the partition and is a *tefach* wide from side to side.

unrolling a partition

34. *a.* It is forbidden to unroll a partition with the intention that it should serve a halachic purpose (as explained in paragraph 30 above), unless it has been unrolled to

the extent of a *tefach* or more since before the commencement of Shabbath or Yom Tov.

b. This is so even if the roll itself is a *tefach* or more in width. (Compare paragraph 7 above.)

35. A partition fixed to the wall, such as a folding door, may be opened to its full extent, *folding doors*

    a. even if it has not been open to the width of a *tefach* or more since before the start of Shabbath or Yom Tov **and**

    b. even if the intention in opening it out is to serve a halachic purpose (as explained in paragraph 30 above).

36. a. One may request a non-Jew to erect a partition which is intended to serve a halachic purpose (as explained in paragraph 30 above), if *when the help of a non-Jew may be sought*

    1) the partition is temporary **and**

    2) one needs it in order to be able to fulfill a mitzva, for example to pray in a place free from the presence of excrement.

    b. It must be remembered that a partition made in order to last for as little as a few days is considered to be permanent and not temporary. (See paragraph 26 above.)

37. a. It is perfectly in order to put up a folding partition if one does not have as one's object the achievement of a halachic effect. *erection of partitions for reasons of privacy*

    b. It makes no difference if one later also makes use of the halachic effect produced by the erection of the partition.

    c. Thus,

    1) a folding screen may be placed between two beds in a hospital ward to provide patients with privacy, and

    2) a patient may subsequently say his prayers, taking advantage of the fact that the screen divides

between him and uncovered excrement on the opposite side (as long as the odor does not reach him).

taking down a partition

38. *a.* Just as it is forbidden to erect a partition on Shabbath or Yom Tov for a halachic purpose (as explained in paragraph 30 above), so it is forbidden to take down a partition while it is serving such a purpose.

b. Nevertheless, once the partition ceases to be used for its halachic effect, it may be removed.

Chapter 25

Dangerous Nuisances and Hazards to Health

INSECTS AND OTHER PESTS

1. *a.* One may, even on Shabbath and Yom Tov, kill an *animals*
animal or insect which is a danger to human life. *and insects*
  b. Different animals and insects fall within this category *which*
  in different places and at different periods of time. *endanger*
  c. Subject to this qualification, the category could *human life*
  include
    1) a mad dog,
    2) a snake which may be venomous,
    3) a scorpion (including the less dangerous black
       scorpion),
    4) even a wasp, when in the vicinity of a child, and
    5) specific types of insects where there is a risk that
       they may be the carriers of a dangerous disease.
  d. One may kill an animal or insect of this kind
    1) even if it is still far away from any human being,
    2) even if it is not pursuing anyone and
    3) even if it is in the process of escaping.

2. Other considerations apply in the case of animals and *animals*
insects whose bite or sting causes considerable pain but *and insects*
is not fatal. *which*
  a. When they are not pursuing anybody but one is afraid *inflict great*
  they may bite or sting someone later, *pain*
    1) one may put some kind of receptacle over them in
       order to catch them.
    2) a) If it is not possible to catch them, one may tread
          on them in the course of walking, even with the
          intention of killing them.
       b) However, one must not kill them in such a way

that other people will realize that this is one's intention.

c) Otherwise people may come to the mistaken conclusion that one is allowed to kill insects or other pests even when there is no fear of their causing injury.

b. When they are pursuing someone and it is not possible to catch them, one may kill them even in the normal way.

insects whose sting causes a lesser pain

3. The rules with regard to insects such as gnats or mosquitoes,* which are liable to bite or sting people but do not cause great pain, are as follows:

a. While they are on one's body, whether or not they are actually in the process of biting one, one may pick them off and throw them aside, if it is impossible to remove them without catching them or picking them up.

b. When they are not on one's body, one may drive them away, but should not catch them.

c. Nevertheless, if they cannot be driven away, one should not object to a person taking a less stringent view and picking them off when they are not actually on his body but on the inner surface of his clothes.

d. 1) In no case may one kill them,

    a) even incidentally, as in paragraph 2a2 above, and

    b) even while they are engaged in biting one.

2) One may likewise not throw them into water, because this will certainly kill them.

harmless insects

4. a. As to ants, flies and other insects which do not bite or sting human beings, one is not permitted

1) to kill them,

2) to catch them,

---

*Where there is a risk of malaria, the rule set out in paragraph 1 above applies.

3) to tread on them in the course of walking, even without intending to kill them,

4) to swill water over them in such a way that they will certainly be killed or

5) to lay down poison in order to kill them.

b. One may

1) sprinkle paraffin (which one had designated, before Shabbath or Yom Tov, for this or some other permitted use) near such insects, so that the smell will drive them away, or

2) put down poison before the commencement of Shabbath or Yom Tov.

5. a. One is allowed to spray insecticide in the room of a *insecticide* person who is sick (even if he is not seriously ill) or in a *sprays* room where there is a child, in order to drive insects out, but one should make sure

1) to leave a door or window open, so that the insects can escape **and**

2) not to spray the insects themselves, since to kill them is forbidden (except as mentioned in paragraphs 1 and 2 above).

b. An aerosol spray may be used for the purpose.

c. For the circumstances in which one may rub one's body with insect repellent see Chapter 14, paragraph 31.

6. a. It is forbidden, on Shabbath or Yom Tov, *traps and*

1) to set a trap to catch mice, rats and similar pests or *poison*

2) to put down poison in order to kill them.

b. One may set a trap or put down poison before the beginning of Shabbath or Yom Tov.

7. As explained in Chapter 22, paragraph 42, a dead mouse *dead mice* or rat which one finds on Shabbath in a place where it disturbs one may be removed and thrown out, despite the fact that it is *muktzeh*.

ELIMINATION OF DANGEROUS NUISANCES
OR OF HAZARDS TO HEALTH

general rule　**8.** *a.* One is allowed, indeed there is a positive obligation, to remove hazards from a place where people are liable to come to harm, but a distinction must be made between
　　1) risks of injury involving only one or two people and
　　2) risks of injury involving several persons.
　b. 1) In a place where only one or two people are present, and they run a risk of physical injury,
　　　a) one may, in averting the danger, move a *muktzeh* object—preferably in an unusual or indirect manner, as explained in Chapter 22, paragraphs 34 and 35—but
　　　b) one may not otherwise violate any prohibition.
　　2) a) On the other hand, the rule is different in a place where more than two people are present (even if it is in a private house) and there is a risk of injury to one or more of them.
　　　b) Here, one is permitted to violate Rabbinical prohibitions in the course of averting the danger.
　c. If there is any risk of danger to the life of even one individual,
　　1) one may, in obviating that danger, violate even prohibitions laid down by the Torah, and
　　2) the faster one acts the better.
　　3) See also Chapter 32, paragraph 16 and Chapter 41, paragraph 1.

dangerous　**9.** *a.* 1) It follows that one is permitted to remove glass
nuisances　　　splinters, a needle, a nail or any other *muktzeh* object from a place where people are liable to be injured by them. (See also Chapter 23, paragraphs 35 and 36 regarding broken windows.)
　　2) A *muktzeh* object may be removed in such a case even if it is in the street in a place where there is no *eiruv*, so long as the street does not actually come

within the definition of a *reshuth ha-rabbim*, as set
out in Chapter 17, paragraph 3.

b. One may likewise scatter even *muktzeh* cinders or
sand over patches of ice or oil in the street, to prevent
passers-by from slipping on them.

c. See Chapter 41 with regard to the extinguishing of
fires on Shabbath and Yom Tov.

10. a. One may spray water on the floor during a heat wave *low*
to increase the humidity. *humidity*

b. 1) It may happen that there is no possibility of doing
this, or that the air is so dry that spraying the floor
will not be sufficiently effective.

2) In that event, one may, for a child or for a person
who is ill (even though not seriously), hang sheets
which were made wet before Shabbath or Yom Tov
around the bed or at the window, but

3) one must be extremely careful

a) not to squeeze the sheets on Shabbath or Yom
Tov, and

b) not to shake the water out of them.

c. If the sheets have become dry, or if one did not prepare
any wet sheets before the commencement of Shabbath
or Yom Tov, one may first hang up the sheets and then
spray or splash them, preferably with dirty water, but,
should the water be clean,

1) one must be extremely careful to use sheets which
are spotlessly clean **and**

2) one must not touch the sheets as long as they are
still wet, lest one comes to squeeze water out of
them.

d. Where there is no other choice, one may dip the sheets
into water, even into clean water, but, if the water is
clean,

1) the sheets must, in this case too, be completely
clean **and**

2) one must be especially careful not to squeeze them
or shake them out.

Chapter 26

Plants and Trees

tending
plants and
trees

1. *a.* It is forbidden to tend a plant or a tree on Shabbath or Yom Tov in any way whatsoever.
   b. The prohibition covers not only plants and trees which grow in earth in the normal way, but also those grown by hydroponics or in a pot, even if the pot is not perforated at its base and even if it is indoors.

flowerpots
are
muktzeh

2. A flowerpot is *muktzeh*, whether or not it is perforated at the base, and should not be moved on Shabbath or Yom Tov.

throwing
seeds or
fruit pips
on the
ground

3. *a.* One must not throw seeds or fruit pips onto moist earth.
   b. One must not throw them even onto dry earth, if it will be made wet by rain or other water (whether on Shabbath or afterwards).

fruit pits in
water

4. *a.* One may not put the pit (stone) of an avocado, or of another fruit, into a container of water, so that it should strike root and begin to sprout.
   b. It is also forbidden to take a pit of this kind out of a cup of water into which it has been put.
   c. Not only the pit but also the cup and the water in the cup are *muktzeh*.

watering:
scope of
prohibition

5. *a.* One is not allowed to water any plant, even if it is growing in a pot which is not perforated at its base.
   b. It is likewise not permitted to pour water
      1) onto sown ground or
      2) onto ground which is going to be ploughed or sown, even if nothing is growing there at present.
   c. Consequently, it is as well not to eat in one's garden on Shabbath or Yom Tov when this entails drinking or

using water or some other liquid which, were it to be spilled, would have an effect on the cultivation of the garden.

d. A person who does eat in the garden — a case in point is a person whose *sukka* is in the garden — should take particular care; for example,

1) when washing his hands, he should do so into a receptacle of some kind,

2) dishes should not be washed in the garden, except inside a bowl,

3) drink remaining in the bottom of a cup should not be poured away onto the ground and

4) rainwater which has collected in a receptacle left in the garden should not be poured onto the ground.

6. *a.* It is permissible to urinate on growing grass or other vegetation, but *relieving oneself in the open*

b. one must not relieve one's bowels in a ploughed field which is about to be sown and

c. one should take care not to spit on growing vegetation.

7. *a.* If the outlet pipe of a sink or basin carries the water away until it is discharged over sown ground, one may, nonetheless, wash one's hands in it or pour water into it on Shabbath. *outlet pipe discharging onto sown ground*

b. One need not worry about the watering of the seeds which will be brought about thereby, providing this consequence is unintended.

c. See also Chapter 12, paragraph 18.

8. *a.* Sprinklers may be turned on before the commencement of Shabbath, and left on over Shabbath, in order to irrigate a field or garden. *irrigation sprinklers*

b. Sprinklers may be turned off even on Shabbath.

9. *a.* One must not place a covering over plants in a nursery, or remove such a covering, since this is done to help the plants grow. *nurseries and hothouses*

b. One may, however, open or close a door in order to enter or leave a hothouse or greenhouse.

plucking and uprooting

10. *a.* It is forbidden to pick fruit from a tree which is attached to the ground, even if both the tree and its fruit have completely dried up.

b. One is not allowed to detach something which is growing, even if it has no roots, as in the case of
1) mushrooms or
2) moss growing on a boulder.

c. One is permitted to pick fruit off a branch that was detached from its connection with the ground prior to the commencement of Shabbath or Yom Tov.

touching trees

11. One may touch a tree, but one may not move any part of it, since it is *muktzeh.*

leaning on trees

12. *a.* One is not allowed to lean against a tree, unless
1) one does so only lightly **and**
2) the tree is so firm that one cannot move it.

b. A person who is infirm should not lean against a tree even lightly, since, in spite of himself, he will lean against it with all his weight (and this would be considered as using the tree, which is forbidden by the prohibition set out in paragraph 14 below).

climbing trees

13. *a.* One must not climb a tree on Shabbath or Yom Tov, even if it is so firm that it does not move when one climbs it.

b. 1) If one has climbed it deliberately, knowing that it is forbidden, one may not come down until after Shabbath or Yom Tov.
2) However, if one did not know that what one was doing was forbidden, one is permitted, indeed one is obliged, to come down immediately.

using trees: general rules

14. *a.* There is a Rabbinical prohibition against the use, on Shabbath or Yom Tov, of

1) a tree or
2) anything directly hanging from, attached to, or supported by a tree.

b. The prohibition does not extend to the use of things only indirectly hanging from, attached to, or supported by a tree.

c. Details are contained in the following paragraphs.

15. a. The prohibition against using a tree extends to
1) placing anything on a tree on Shabbath or Yom Tov or
2) removing anything from it,
whether with one's hand or with the aid of a stick.

using a tree itself

b. One may not tie a rope to a tree or hang a basket from its branches on Shabbath or Yom Tov.

c. 1) The Rabbis even forbade one to put an object which is not *muktzeh*, if it is liable to be used on Shabbath or Yom Tov, onto a tree before Shabbath or Yom Tov commences.
2) This is because one might come to "use" the tree by taking the object off it on Shabbath or Yom Tov.

d. An object which was on a tree at the commencement of Shabbath or Yom Tov, and subsequently dropped off or was removed by a non-Jew, is *muktzeh*.

16. The following examples illustrate the prohibition against the use on Shabbath or Yom Tov of objects directly hanging from, attached to, or supported by a tree.

when indirect use of tree is forbidden

a. One must not put anything into, or take anything out of, a basket hanging on the trunk of a tree or on one of its branches.

b. One must not put anything into, or take anything out of, the pockets of a coat hanging on a tree.

c. One must not use a swing which is attached, even if on only one side, to a tree.

d. One must not hang a swing from a pole
1) which is fixed between two trees or

[369]

2) which is fixed at one end to a tree and at the other to a wall.

e. One must not climb a ladder which is leaning against a tree, even if it has been in that position since before Shabbath or Yom Tov.

when indirect use of tree is permitted

17. As shown by the following examples, one may, on Shabbath or Yom Tov, use an article which is only indirectly hanging from, attached to, or supported by a tree, but only if the tree is sufficiently firm not to sway as a result of such use.

a. 1) One may put things into, or take things out of, a basket which, since before the beginning of Shabbath or Yom Tov, has been hanging on a nail driven into a tree.

2) One must not, however, hang the basket itself on the nail on Shabbath or Yom Tov or remove it.

b. 1) One may put things into, or take things out of, the pockets of a coat which, since before the beginning of Shabbath or Yom Tov, has been hanging on a nail driven into a tree.

2) One must not, however, hang the coat itself on the nail on Shabbath or Yom Tov or remove it.

c. One may use a swing which has been hanging from a pole attached to a tree since before Shabbath or Yom Tov.

d. 1) One may dry one's hands on a towel which has been hanging on a line strung between two trees since before Shabbath or Yom Tov.

2) One must not, however, take the towel off the line.

use of tree to enable performance of mitzva

18. a. The prohibitions against the use of a tree, and of items directly hanging from, attached to, or supported by a tree, are applicable even where the performance of a mitzva is involved.

b. It is, thus, forbidden to take a book off a tree, or off an item which is directly hanging from, attached to, or supported by a tree, even if one wants to use it to study Torah and has no other book of the same nature.

19. a. One is allowed to walk on a lawn on Shabbath or Yom Tov, regardless of the possibility that one may thereby pull up or tear off clumps or blades of grass. *walking on grass or thistles*

  b. Nevertheless, any pieces of grass or vegetation which one does find stuck to one's shoes should not be removed in the normal way with one's hand, since they are *muktzeh*.

  c. If the grass is long, one should walk slowly and should certainly not run, as one would be bound to pull up or tear off some of the grass in this way.

  d. One should not tread on dry thistles which are still attached to the ground, because they will definitely break off.

20. a. It is permitted to sit or lie on grass. *sitting or*

  b. One is similarly allowed to spread a blanket or mat on a lawn and sit on that. *lying on grass*

  c. One may even move grass which is connected to the ground to and fro, provided one takes care not to detach it.

21. One may sit on a tree root which is less than three *t^efachim* high from the ground. *tree roots*

22. a. One is permitted to smell flowers, even while they are still connected to the ground. *smelling growing flowers or fruit*

  b. One may even move them to and fro, as long as
    1) they have flexible stalks which do not become stiff if left to grow **and**
    2) one is careful not to detach anything from the ground.

  c. On the other hand, one is not allowed to smell fruit while it is still on the tree, for fear that one may pick it to eat.

fruits and leaves which fall off on Shabbath

23. Fruits, leaves and branches are *muktzeh*
  a. if
    1) they fell off the tree on Shabbath or Yom Tov or
    2) there is a doubt as to whether they fell off the tree on Shabbath or Yom Tov or before, or
  b. if
    1) they were picked off the tree by a non-Jew on Shabbath or Yom Tov, even for his own use, or
    2) there is a doubt as to whether a non-Jew picked them that day or previously.

gathering fallen fruits or leaves

24. a. One must not gather fruits, leaves or branches which have fallen from a tree, even if they fell before Shabbath or Yom Tov began, since this is forbidden under the same heading as making sheaves.
  b. If fruit has dropped in a place other than that in which it grew, for instance, if it has been dropped in a courtyard, then,
    1) where it is scattered, one may pick up a little at a time, for immediate consumption, but should not collect it all together at once, as one would do on another day of the week; however,
    2) if the fruit did not scatter, but fell together on one spot, it may all be collected at the same time.
  c. If the fruit became mingled with sand or fallen leaves, one should pick up only one fruit at a time and eat it right away. (See also Chapter 3, paragraph 21.)

moving vases

25. Vases are not *muktzeh* and may be moved, even if they contain flowers or twigs and water.

putting flowers and twigs into water and removing them

26. a. Flowers or twigs may not be put into a vase of water on Shabbath or Yom Tov,
    1) even though they are not *muktzeh* (as where twigs were put aside before Shabbath or Yom Tov for decorating the house) and
    2) even if the water has been in the vase since before Shabbath or Yom Tov began.

b. 1) On Shabbath, one may not add to the water which has been in a vase full of flowers since before Shabbath.

2) On Yom Tov, water may be added (unless of course it is also Shabbath).

c. 1) On both Shabbath or Yom Tov, one is permitted to take flowers or twigs out of water, as long as they have not put out roots into the water.

2) The twigs may afterwards be replaced (in the same water), but not the flowers.

27. *a.* The rules set out in the previous paragraph with regard to twigs apply also to *lulavim*, so that, on Yom Tov, *care of a lulav*

1) one may put a *lulav* back into the water from which it was taken and

2) one may add water to that which is already in the receptacle containing the *lulav*, but

3) one may not change the water.

b. 1) One is allowed to wrap a wet towel around a *lulav* on Yom Tov, provided that

a) the towel was made wet before Yom Tov **and**

b) one normally would not bother to wring it out if it became wet, but

2) one may not wet the towel on Yom Tov.

c. On Shabbath a *lulav* is *muktzeh*, as mentioned in Chapter 22, paragraph 30.

28. It is forbidden to walk in one's garden or field with the object of checking the state of the plants so as to determine what work has to be done there on the following day. (See Chapter 29, paragraph 14.) *inspecting a garden or field*

Chapter 27

Laws Relating to Animals on Shabbath and Yom Tov

*general
principles*

1. *a.* In certain cases, the Torah prohibited the performance by animals of activities which are forbidden on Shabbath or Yom Tov.

   b. Details appear in the following paragraphs, but, broadly speaking, the prohibitions relate to two sets of circumstances:
   1) the performance by an animal of a forbidden activity while being led by a Jew, and
   2) the performance of a forbidden activity by an animal belonging to a Jew.

*leading an
animal:
general
scope of
prohibition*

2. *a.* 1) In the Ten Commandments (Exodus 20:10) we are told that, on Shabbath, "you shall not do any work, neither you... nor your animal...."

   2) The intention of the verse—as explained in the tradition handed down to us by the Rabbis and dating back to the receipt of the Torah on Mount Sinai—is to prohibit the performance of a forbidden activity jointly by a human being and an animal.

   b. Consequently, a Jew may not lead an animal if, through this, the animal performs an act which falls within one of the thirty-nine categories of activity forbidden to a Jew on Shabbath.

   c. The prohibition applies
   1) with regard to any animal or bird or, indeed, to any kind of living creature,
   2) whether it belongs to the person leading it, another Jew, a non-Jew or no one at all and

3) whether one leads it with one's hand, with a stick or just by using one's voice.

3. *a.* The Torah (in Exodus 23:12) expresses the intention that not only the Jew, but also his animals, should rest on Shabbath.

b. 1) Consequently, a Jew is generally under an obligation to ensure that an animal which belongs to him does not perform an act which falls within one of the thirty-nine categories of activity forbidden to a Jew on Shabbath.

2) Certain exceptions to this rule are referred to in the succeeding paragraphs.

c. The obligation applies with regard to any animal or bird or, indeed, to any kind of living creature which belongs to a Jew, or to a Jew in partnership with a non-Jew.

d. It does not matter whether the act is performed while the Jew himself is working with the animal or while a non-Jew is working with it.

e. The obligation is breached

1) even if somebody is working with the animal without its Jewish owner's consent,

2) even if the animal started performing the act before Shabbath and continues after Shabbath has begun and

3) even if the animal is performing the act of its own accord.

forbidden activity performed by an animal: general scope of prohibition

4. *a.* Both the prohibition against leading an animal and the obligation to prevent one's animal from performing a forbidden activity are applicable only with reference to activities which would be forbidden *by the Torah* if one performed them oneself.

b. Neither is applicable with reference to activities which would only be subject to a *Rabbinical* prohibition if one performed them oneself.

c. Nonetheless, one should not let one's animal go out

activity forbidden by Rabbinical prohibition

into *carm^elith* with a burden on its back, despite the fact that carrying in *carm^elith* is forbidden only by a Rabbinical prohibition. (See paragraph 7 below.)

Yom Kippur and Yom Tov

5. The prohibition against leading an animal and the obligation to prevent one's animal from performing a forbidden activity are applicable not only on Shabbath, but also on Yom Kippur and Yom Tov.

forbidden activity for animal's benefit

6. *a.* There is nothing wrong with an animal's performing a forbidden activity for its own benefit.

b. One is, thus, allowed to put an animal out to pasture on Shabbath, with the intention that it should pull up and eat grass growing from the ground, in spite of the fact that pulling up grass growing from the ground is a forbidden activity.

c. Were this not so, Shabbath would be a day of suffering for the animal, and not a day of rest as prescribed by the Torah.

d. When putting an animal out to graze, one should not do so with the intention of improving the land.

what an animal may wear in r^eshuth ha-rabbim: general rule

7. *a.* 1) Because of his obligation to prevent his animal from performing a forbidden activity, an owner must ensure that it does not go out into *r^eshuth ha-rabbim* or into *carm^elith* carrying a burden.

2) This is the case even if the burden has been on the animal since before Shabbath.

b. 1) The term "burden" includes any item which is not designed to protect the physical well-being of the animal to the normal extent required.

2) a) An item which is designed to protect the physical well-being of the animal to the normal extent required is to the animal what an article of clothing is to a human being.

b) Accordingly, subject to the exceptions mentioned in paragraphs 10 and 12 below, one may let the animal go out with it.

c. 1) An item is considered as protecting the physical well-being of the animal if it directly
 a) protects it against the cold,
 b) protects it from any other form of suffering,
 c) guards against its running away and becoming lost, or even
 d) keeps its wool clean.

 2) a) An item which is designed to prevent an animal from causing damage is considered to be a burden, and one must not permit one's animal to go out wearing it.
 b) An example is a muzzle placed over the animal's mouth to stop it from biting, or from grazing in a field that does not belong to its owner.

8. An animal which needs to be kept on a leash to prevent it from running away may be taken out on a leash in *r^eshuth ha-rabbim*, but

animal on a leash

a. the person holding it should take care that the section of the leash between the animal and his hand does not hang down to within a *tefach* of the ground,

b. the other (free) end of the leash must not protrude a *tefach* or more from his hand, and

c. he should beware not to lean against the animal when attaching a leash on Shabbath or Yom Tov.

9. *a.* 1) a) An identification tag suspended from the neck of an animal is not regarded as an item which protects the physical well-being of the animal to the normal extent required.

identifica- tion tags and discs

 b) This is because the tag itself does not directly protect the animal, but merely enables one to identify it.

 2) One may not, therefore, allow an animal to go out into *r^eshuth ha-rabbim* wearing such a tag.

b. 1) It follows that, where there is no *eiruv*, a dog owner must be careful not to take his pet out with a disc hanging from its neck.

2) This must be borne in mind in places where dogs wear discs issued by a governmental authority to show that the licence fee has been paid or that the animal is not a stray.

c. Likewise, a cattle owner should take care that his animals have no identification discs around their necks or legs when putting them out to graze on Shabbath in a place where there is no *eiruv*.

d. 1) On the other hand, one may allow an animal to go out, even into *r^eshuth ha-rabbim*, with a tag stapled to its ear, bearing an identity number and other particulars.

2) Such a tag is in a different category, since it cannot be removed.

items which might fall from an animal **10.** a. One must not let one's animal go out into a place where there no *eiruv*, wearing even an item which is designed to protect its physical well-being, if that item is liable to fall off.

b. The reason is that, if the item does drop off, one might forget oneself and carry it for a distance of four *amoth* or more.

carrying a burden on Yom Tov **11.** a. On Yom Tov, too, one should not allow one's animal to go out into *r^eshuth ha-rabbim* or *carm^elith*, in a place where there is no *eiruv*, carrying a burden, as defined in paragraph 7 above.

b. This is so notwithstanding the fact that one may oneself be permitted to carry the article on Yom Tov. (See Chapter 19.)

animal wearing a bell **12.** a. An animal which is put out to pasture with a bell around its neck so that it does not become lost should not be allowed to go out with its bell on Shabbath or Yom Tov, even where there is an *eiruv*.

b. There are two reasons for this Rabbinical prohibition:
1) One is not permitted to sound a bell on Shabbath or Yom Tov. (See Chapter 28, paragraph 34.)

2) People may be given the impression that the animal is being taken to market.

13. *a.* Generally speaking, one should not go more than two thousand *amoth* beyond the boundary of the *eiruv*, or, if there is no *eiruv*, more than two thousand *amoth* beyond the last house of the town or other place where one was when Shabbath or Yom Tov commenced. *animal walking a long distance*

b. One may not physically take an animal beyond the limit to which its owner is permitted to walk.

c. Nevertheless, one is not obliged to prevent an animal (which is not carrying a burden, as defined in paragraph 7 above) from going farther than this limit.

d. One may even encourage the animal to go farther by calling it, so long as one does not physically take it there.

e. One may hand the animal over to a non-Jewish attendant and need not be concerned if he rides it beyond the permitted distance (provided it is not carrying a burden* as defined in paragraph 7 above).

14. *a.* 1) It is forbidden to lend or hire out an animal to a non-Jew, even a horse intended for riding, if there is a fear that he will work with it on Shabbath or carry a burden on it in *reshuth ha-rabbim* or *carmelith*. *lending or hiring an animal to a non-Jew*

2) It is irrelevant when one delivers the animal to the non-Jew, even if it is on the previous Sunday.

b. 1) One may lend or hire out an animal to a non-Jew, notwithstanding the fact that he will not prevent it from going out with a burden (as defined in paragraph 7 above) in a yard which is a *reshuth ha-yachid*.

2) This is so even if the yard is owned in common by two or more Jews and there is no *eiruv*. (See Chapter 17, paragraphs 11 to 13.)

---

*A person who can walk by himself is not considered to be a burden which one may not let an animal carry. (In connection with riding an animal, see paragraph 17*b* below.)

3) The animal may be lent to the non-Jew even on Shabbath.

animal borrowed or hired from a non-Jew

15. A Jew should not permit even an animal which he has hired or borrowed from a non-Jew to perform a forbidden activity, as long as the animal is in his custody.

animal owned jointly by Jew and non-Jew

16. *a.* As explained in paragraph 3 above, the obligation to prevent an animal from performing a forbidden activity applies also in the case of an animal owned in partnership by a Jew and a non-Jew.

b. Simply to allow the non-Jewish partner to work with the animal on Shabbath or Yom Tov, even solely on his own behalf, is prohibited.

c. 1) It may, however, be possible to arrange matters in such a way that the Jew can allow his non-Jewish partner to work with the animal on Shabbath or Yom Tov.

2) A duly qualified halachic authority should be consulted as to the manner in which such an arrangement can be made.

USING AN ANIMAL

scope of prohibition

17. *a.* One is not permitted to use an animal on Shabbath or Yom Tov,

1) even if the use does not involve an infringement of the prohibition against leading an animal,

2) even if it does not involve a breach of the obligation to stop one's animal from performing a forbidden activity and

3) even if it does not involve the animal in performing a forbidden activity at all.

b. Consequently, one must not

1) ride on an animal,

2) hang on the side of an animal,

3) climb onto an animal, even without any intention of riding it,

4) place on an animal an item of which it has no need, even if the item is tied on and stays in place, or

5) sit in a cart harnessed to an animal, even if it is being driven by a non-Jew, as this in itself is included in the prohibition against riding.

c. On the other hand, one may

1) remove from an animal an item which one needs, provided one does not move the animal in doing so,

2) remove from an animal an item which is causing it pain or suffering, even if one moves the animal in doing so, and

3) place on an animal an item which it needs, as in the case of

a) the rope of a halter* worn by a horse,

b) a saddle cushion put on a donkey to keep it warm or

c) a nose-bag worn by small calves who find it difficult to eat off the ground,

but one must take care not to lean on the animal when putting the item on it.

18. a. One should not use an animal to carry a burden, *carrying a*

1) even in a place where there is an *eiruv*, so that the *burden on* animal is not performing a forbidden activity, and *an animal*

2) even for the purposes of Shabbath or Yom Tov.

b. There are two reasons for this:

1) One would thereby be using the animal.

2) Using an animal to carry a burden is a workaday activity inconsistent with the sanctity of the Shabbath.

19. a. 1) There is nothing wrong with allowing one's animal *use by non-* to be ridden by a non-Jewish employee (who can be *Jewish* expected to obey the instructions referred to below), *employee* even in a place which is a *reshuth ha-rabbim* in the full sense of the expression.

---

*See paragraph 7c1c above.

    2) This is because a person who can walk by himself is not considered to be a burden that one must not let one's animal carry.

b. 1) One must, however, instruct him not to put a burden (as defined in paragraph 7 above) on the animal in a place where carrying articles about is prohibited, and one must prevent him from doing so.

    2) Otherwise one will be in breach of one's obligation to stop one's animal from performing a forbidden activity. (See paragraph 3 above.)

taking a dog for a walk   **20.** When taking an animal such as a dog for a walk in a place where there is no *eiruv*, one should be careful not to put any article on it which is not required for the protection of the animal's physical well-being. (See also paragraphs 8 and 9 above.)

FEEDING AND OTHERWISE ATTENDING TO ANIMALS

on Shabbath: general rule   **21.** *a.* 1) One may on Shabbath put food in front of animals or birds which are dependent on one for their food.

    2) Not only their owner, upon whom they are dependent, but any other person may feed them.

b. With the exceptions mentioned in paragraph 23 below, one is not allowed to feed animals or birds which are not dependent on man for their food, even if one's intention is simply to confer a benefit on the Almighty's creatures.

c. In view of this, the custom of scattering grains or the leftovers of *kugel* to the birds on Shabbath Shira is to be disapproved.

d. Nonetheless, it is in order to shake crumbs out of a tablecloth (in a place where there is an *eiruv* or where no *eiruv* is needed), even though birds will eat them.

on Yom Tov: general rule   **22.** *a.* On Yom Tov, too, one may put food in the normal way in front of animals or birds which are dependent on one for their food, if

1) there is no prohibition against catching them on Yom Tov (as to which see paragraphs 31 to 38 below, especially 34), **or**

2) they are of a kind one is not permitted to eat.

b. 1) Food for those animals or birds which one is permitted to eat, but which one is prohibited from catching on Yom Tov, should not be put down in its usual place, but a little distance away.

2) The Rabbis required one to make this variation in the usual method of feeding as a reminder, so that one should not come to catch these animals or birds in order to slaughter and eat them.

3) No such fear of course exists

a) in the case of animals or birds which one is not permitted to eat, or

b) on Shabbath, when slaughter is forbidden.

23. a. Dogs are in a special category, and one may put food in front of them, both on Shabbath and on Yom Tov, even if they are not dependent on man for their food. *dogs and hungry animals*

b. Likewise, one is allowed, both on Shabbath and on Yom Tov, to put food in front of any animal which is hungry and cannot find anything to eat.

24. a. As detailed in previous chapters, many activities which are forbidden on Shabbath are permitted on Yom Tov in the course of preparing food. *preparing food on Yom Tov*

b. This is only the case if the food is for oneself or for another Jew.

c. In preparing food for an animal on Yom Tov, one is not allowed to perform an activity which is forbidden on Shabbath.

d. Even transferring food for an animal from one place to another is forbidden, where there is no *eiruv* and an *eiruv* is necessary.

[383]

putting food in an animal's mouth

25. *a.* One may put food into the mouths of animals which have difficulty in taking food by themselves, but

b. one must beware not to move animals incidentally to feeding them, since, as mentioned in Chapter 20, paragraph 40, all animals are *muktzeh*.

stuffing geese

26. *a.* Geese which are being stuffed and are no longer capable of eating by themselves may be caused suffering by a failure to stuff them.

b. Whenever possible, they should be stuffed immediately before the commencement of Shabbath or Yom Tov and immediately after its termination, so as to avoid stuffing them on Shabbath or Yom Tov.

c. 1) Where this is not sufficient for them, and they will be caused suffering if not fed on Shabbath or Yom Tov, one should have them stuffed by a non-Jew, but he should only stuff them once, in the middle of Shabbath or Yom Tov.

2) There are those who, when there is no non-Jew available, have the geese stuffed by a Jew, and some authorities would support this lenient view, but, if a Jew is employed,

a) the machine used should be hand-operated or activated by a timer (time-switch),

b) it is advisable for the Jew to be a boy aged less than thirteen or a girl aged less than twelve **and**

c) the geese should, of course, be stuffed only once, in the middle of Shabbath or Yom Tov.

changing and adding water in an aquarium

27. *a.* It is forbidden to change the water in an aquarium containing fish on Shabbath or Yom Tov.

b. If, however, it is necessary to add water every day, one may do so, even if the aquarium also contains aquatic plants.

c. The reason why it is permitted to add water on Shabbath and Yom Tov is that the fish are dependent on man for their food, and adding water is in the same category as feeding them, since, without additional water, they are liable to die.

d. There are good grounds for adopting a strict approach in treating an aquarium, together with the water and fish it contains, as *muktzeh*.

e. If one fears that the fish are liable to die without a change of water, one may request a non-Jew, even on Shabbath, to change the water, provided that, in the process, he does not allow the fish to be without water even for an instant.

28. a. A fish which has jumped out of an aquarium on Shabbath or Yom Tov may be put back to prevent it from suffering, so long as there is reason to suppose that it will continue to live when returned to the water. *fish jumping out of an aquarium*

b. There are, however, authorities who forbid this.

29. a. A fish which has died may be removed from an aquarium, so that the other fish should not die, if a considerable financial loss is involved. *removing dead fish from an aquarium*

b. Taking out the dead fish is not a breach of the prohibition against selection (dealt with in detail in Chapters 3 and 4), since the dead fish cannot be said to be mixed together with the live fish.

30. a. One is allowed to feed birds in a cage, because they are dependent on one for their food. (See paragraph 21 above.) *birds in a cage*

b. The cage must not be moved (except in the circumstances referred to immediately below), as it is *muktzeh*.

c. If the cage is so positioned that the birds are suffering, for example, due to strong sunlight, then

1) one should, where possible, eliminate the cause of the suffering by some permitted means, as by drawing the curtain across the window through which the sun is shining, but,

2) where this possibility does not exist, one may move

the cage to a position where the birds will be more comfortable, for instance, from the sun into the shade.

CATCHING ANIMALS

scope of
prohibition

31. *a.* Subject to a few exceptions, to which reference is made in the ensuing paragraphs, it is forbidden to catch any animal (in the broadest sense of the word, including birds, fish, insects and any other living creature) on Shabbath or Yom Tov.

b. The prohibition covers any activity executed with the object of depriving an animal of its liberty, by any means whatsoever, including

1) catching it in a trap, a snare or a net,

2) catching it with one's hand,

3) closing the door of the house while an animal is inside, even though one's intention in so doing is merely to secure the house, and

4) setting a dog on an animal in order to catch it.

different
categories
of animals

32. The nature of the prohibition depends on the kind of animal one wishes to catch.

a. 1) A person who catches an animal, bird or fish of a type which is commonly caught for use infringes a prohibition laid down by the Torah.

2) An example is an animal which is caught for slaughtering and eating or for the use of its skin.

b. 1) A person who catches a creature of a type which is not commonly caught for use infringes a Rabbinical, but not a Torah, prohibition.

2) An example is flies, which, even if they are caught, are not caught because one needs them, but to prevent them from causing annoyance or harm.

definition
of
"catching"

33. *a.* 1) The Torah prohibition is infringed only if the animal is held or if it is confined within a space

small enough for one to be able to catch it easily.

2) The prohibition includes, by way of example,

   a) chasing a deer into a small building, fenced-off garden or enclosed yard in which it can easily be caught and shutting the door or gate on it,

   b) chasing a bird into a cage and closing its door and

   c) taking a fish out of the sea inside a container.

b. 1) A Rabbinical prohibition is infringed if the animal is confined inside a space within which one cannot catch it easily.

2) Examples of the Rabbinical prohibition are

   a) chasing a deer into a large, spacious building, fenced-off garden or enclosed yard, in which it cannot easily be caught, and shutting the door or gate on it,

   b) chasing a bird into a house and closing the door and

   c) chasing a fish into a pool which one then shuts off from the main body of water.

34. *a.* The prohibition against catching animals does not apply to those domestic animals, such as cows and sheep, which are not in the habit of trying to escape when one catches them. *domestic animals one may catch*

  b. One is permitted to drive such an animal into its pen, and one may then close the gate.

  c. Nowadays, hens also fall within this category, as they are not in the habit of escaping from someone who tries to catch them.

  d. At all events, one should not take an animal of this kind with one's hand to put it into its pen or cage, since animals are *muktzeh.*

35. *a.* A Rabbinical prohibition is applicable to the catching of domestic animals *domestic animals one may usually not catch*

  1) which are in the habit of escaping when one tries to catch them, but

2) which, if they leave their pens or cages during the course of the day, return to them at night.
b. Nevertheless, one is allowed to catch such an animal if
1) there is risk of loss or suffering to the animal **and**
2) one cannot wait until after the conclusion of Shabbath or Yom Tov.
c. Even in these circumstances, one should, if possible, not take the animal with one's hand and put it in its pen or cage, since animals are *muktzeh*.

runaways and poultry in new quarters

36. Notwithstanding the contents of the two preceding paragraphs, it is forbidden to catch
a. even a domestic animal, if it has bolted and will not return to its pen or cage at night, and
b. poultry that has been transferred to a new location to which it has not yet grown accustomed.

entering a chicken coop or cattle shed

37. a. It follows from the above that one must take special care on entering or leaving a chicken coop or cattle shed containing birds or animals which one is not allowed to catch (as above).
b. If the situation is such that they have a possibility of escaping, one should avoid any act which traps them.
1) One can prevent such a situation from arising by filling the doorway with one's body before opening the door.
2) In this manner, the birds or animals inside will remain trapped even after the door is opened.
3) Similarly, one should close the door behind one while one's body still blocks the opening.
c. It is recommended that entrances to chicken coops and cattle sheds be constructed in such a way that one
1) must pass through two doors in succession and
2) can close the first before opening the second.

closing the door of a bird cage

38. a. If the door of a cage containing birds opens, one should beware not to close it again, because the act of closing the door traps the birds.

b. There are grounds for relaxing this rule in the case of birds whose nature is to return to their cage after leaving it, provided one's concern in closing the door is
1) to prevent the birds from causing damage if they leave their cage **or**
2) to prevent the birds from being stolen.

c. See also paragraph 42 below.

39. *a.* There is nothing wrong with locking the already closed door of a chicken coop. *locking a chicken coop*

b. This is so even when the chickens have only recently been transferred to the coop and are not yet used to it (that is to say, if they escaped they would not return to it).

40. *a.* It sometimes happens that a cow escapes from the cow shed and runs away into the fields, in such circumstances that one does not expect it to return at night and is afraid it will become lost. *rounding up a runaway cow*

b. 1) In such an event, provided one does not completely trap the animal, one may chase it into a fenced-off area.

2) a) An example would be driving the animal into a farmyard, one gate of which is left open and unguarded.

b) It is sufficient if the open gate is at the far end of the farmyard, even if all the other gates are closed or are guarded so that the animal cannot escape again through them.

41. If a bull escapes from its pen and runs wild, or if one fears it will run wild, one may return it to its pen, since leaving it loose involves a danger to human life. *rounding up a runaway bull*

42. *a.* If a wild bird such as a sparrow flies into the house, one ought not to trap it by closing the window. *sparrow flying into the house*

b. Should one wish to close the window to protect oneself

from the cold, one should, if possible, drive the bird out of the house first.

c. 1) Where there is no such possibility, one may, nonetheless, close the window.

2) This is because one does not intend to trap the bird, and it is in fact not confined in a space so constricted that it can easily be caught. (See paragraph 33 above.)

animals which are sleeping or physically unfit

43. *a.* The prohibition laid down by the Torah against catching an animal on Shabbath or Yom Tov may be applicable even if the animal is sleeping, since it generally tries to escape as soon as it feels it is being caught.

b. On the other hand, if one catches an animal which is ill, old or very young and which cannot move away or walks only slowly and with difficulty, one infringes only a Rabbinical prohibition.

trapping flies in a box

44. *a.* One must not completely close a box in which one knows there are flies, because they will be trapped inside.

b. If one drives off those flies one can see, one may close the box and is not obliged to examine it to make sure there are no more left inside.

c. If one is in doubt whether or not there are flies inside a box, one may close it without examining it, provided one has no intention of catching flies by doing so.

freeing trapped animals

45. *a.* It is perfectly in order to free a trapped animal, although one must not take it with one's hand, as animals are *muktzeh.*

b. 1) See Chapter 25, paragraphs 1 to 3 concerning the catching and killing of pests.

2) See Chapter 25, paragraph 5 concerning the use of insecticide sprays.

MILKING

46. *a.* Subject to the exceptions to which reference is made *general rule* below, it is forbidden to milk an animal on Shabbath.

b. It is forbidden to milk even directly into food.

c. 1) One may have an animal milked by a non-Jew, in order to save it suffering.

2) Indeed, the surest way to avoid a desecration of the Shabbath, in the event that one has to milk an animal, is to have it done by a non-Jew, rather than to adopt the other possible methods described in the following paragraphs.

3) See Chapter 30, paragraph 28 for further details regarding milking through the agency of a non-Jew.

d. 1) Milk which has been extracted on Shabbath, even in a permitted manner, whether by a non-Jew or by means of a milking machine or as described below, may not be drunk on that Shabbath and is in fact *muktzeh.* (See further on this subject Chapter 20, paragraph 32, Chapter 33, paragraph 6 and Chapter 37, paragraph 3.)

2) It may, however, be drunk as soon as Shabbath has terminated.

47. *a.* In the absence of a non-Jew, one should milk to waste, *milking to* that is to say in such a way that the milk will not be *waste* drinkable, for instance

1) into a receptacle which would give one an aversion to drinking its contents,

2) into a receptacle containing paraffin or some similar substance which spoils the milk and which one has had ready since before Shabbath or

3) onto the floor.

b. As mentioned in the preceding paragraph, the resulting milk is *muktzeh.*

c. One should not milk into an ordinary receptacle, even if one's intention is to pour the milk away afterwards.

d. Although one may find it difficult to throw money down the drain as it were, one should trust the Almighty in His goodness to compensate one for sacrifices made in the course of upholding our holy Torah.

use of a milking machine

48. *a.* A farm which has a milking machine may use it on Shabbath, but
   1) the machine must be controlled by a timer (time-switch) set before Shabbath to turn it on and off at predetermined times, **and**,
   2) if the milk is to be used (after Shabbath of course), the connection of the machine to the udder of the animal should be made during an interval when the machine is switched off.

b. 1) A serious practical difficulty arises from the fact that most milking machines are designed in such a way that they cannot be connected to the udder unless they are operating.

2) Most authorities agree that, when the connection has to be made while the machine is on, one should milk to waste, for instance onto the floor. (See paragraph 47 above.)

3) Nonetheless, many Shabbath-observant farmers rely on an opinion whereby, if serious loss would otherwise result, one may connect a machine to the udder while the machine is operating, and yet keep the milk for use, provided
   a) the first milk extracted goes to waste **and**
   b) the subsequent milk, which is to be kept, is made to flow into the clean container by a separate action and does not merely flow into it automatically after the initial drops have run to waste.

c. As mentioned in paragraph 46 above, the milk produced on Shabbath is *muktzeh*.

49. *a.* A person wishing to milk an animal should clean its *cleaning*
teats by spraying water on them. *the teats*
  b. If this is not possible, he should at all events not clean
  them with a wet cloth, but
  1) with a dry cloth or
  2) with a non-absorbent, synthetic material (either
     wet or dry) whose fibers are not close enough
     together to hold water.

50. One should not grease one's hands with an ointment *greasing*
before milking, but one may oil them. *one's hands*

51. *a.* Sometimes one has to test milk, and to that end one *testing milk*
milks the animal into a strip-cup in order to determine,
according to the appearance of the milk, whether or
not it is fit to be drunk.
  b. It is proper to refrain from this kind of milking on
  Shabbath or Yom Tov.
  c. If the test milking cannot be brought forward and
  performed before the commencement of Shabbath or
  Yom Tov or delayed until after Shabbath or Yom Tov,
  one should consult a properly qualified rabbinical
  authority as to the course one should adopt.

52. All the rules which apply to milking on Shabbath are *Yom Tov*
also followed on Yom Tov.

53. Each and every detail relating to the care of milking *care of*
machines on Shabbath and Yom Tov, such as oiling, *milking*
cleaning and changing parts, should be checked with a *machines*
competent halachic authority who is well versed in the
laws of Shabbath and Yom Tov.

VETERINARY TREATMENT

54. *a.* As mentioned in Chapter 20, paragraph 40, animals *moving*
are *muktzeh* on Shabbath and Yom Tov. *animals*

[393]

b. Nevertheless, there are cases in which the Rabbis permitted one to move an animal to prevent it from suffering.

c. See further in this connection paragraphs 25, 26, 28, 29, 30 and 47 above.

d. One should consult a competent halachic authority and obtain detailed instructions as to how, in the particular circumstances prevailing, one should proceed when an animal gives birth on Shabbath or Yom Tov.

administering medication

55. a. Except as mentioned below, one may not, in treating an animal, perform any act which is forbidden on Shabbath or Yom Tov, even if it is only the subject of a Rabbinical prohibition.

b. One may, for the purpose of providing an animal with medical treatment, move an object which is *muktzeh*.

c. 1) As will be seen in Chapter 34 (in particular, paragraph 3 there), the Rabbis restricted the taking of medicine or medical treatment by a human being on Shabbath or Yom Tov.

2) These special restrictions do not apply to the treatment of animals.

3) One may, therefore,
   a) feed medicine to an animal,
   b) administer an intramuscular injection to an animal and
   c) put ointment on an animal's wound.

4) One must be careful, however, not to spread the ointment, in view of what is stated in *a* above.

d. In general, one should take the advice of a properly qualified rabbi as to what one may or may not do for an animal.

assistance by non-Jews

56. One is permitted to request a non-Jew to perform activities which are forbidden on Shabbath or Yom Tov even by the Torah, if one's purpose is to save an animal from danger or to alleviate its suffering.

57. *a.* A dog which has been run over and is barking with *dogs which*
pain may be treated in the manner referred to in *have been*
paragraphs 55 and 56 above, but *run over*
b. one is not allowed to kill it.

58. *a.* It is prohibited to remove newly spawned fish from an *newly*
aquarium to prevent the larger fish from eating them. *spawned*
b. Yet it is permissible to ask a non-Jew to transfer them *fish*
(together with some water) to another receptacle
containing water.

Chapter 28

A Miscellany Including Stationery, Clocks, Noises, Baby Carriages, Remuneration and Advance Preparations

BOOKS AND STATIONERY

separating pages of a book

1. *a.* 1) One is not permitted to cut or tear apart pages of a book which were not properly cut through in binding.

2) In this connection, there is no distinction between a new book and a book which has already been partly read but in which there remain pages that are still not altogether cut through.

b. Concerning pages that have become stuck together with glue or some other material, either at the time of binding or on some other occasion, the situation is as follows:

1) if the pages are stuck together where there is no lettering, they may be separated;

2) if they are stuck together where there is lettering, they may not be separated, since in so doing, one would inevitably erase some of the letters, and this is forbidden on Shabbath and Yom Tov.

books with writing on the edges of their leaves

2. The views of the halachic authorities differ with regard to the use of books which, on the edges of their leaves, have written or printed inscriptions or pictures that are broken and re-united when the books are opened and closed.

a. Many authorities take a lenient approach and allow such books to be opened and closed.

b. It is, however, proper to adopt a stricter attitude and not to use a book of this kind if one has another available.

c. Certainly, the problem would best be avoided by not

writing inscriptions or drawing pictures on the edges
of book leaves in the first place.

3. *a.* It is the practice to allow the two halves of a torn page   *torn pages*
to be placed side by side to enable one to read what is
written, if one has no other copy of the same book.
  b. This is the case even if there is lettering where the page
is torn.
  c. One may not stick the torn parts of the page together
with adhesive tape.

4. *a.* One should not open a sealed envelope containing a   *opening*
letter on Shabbath or Yom Tov, nor should one open a   *letters*
letter which is itself sealed shut (that is to say, not
inside an envelope).
  b. It is also forbidden to steam envelopes or letters open.
  c. One should not even tear the envelope open in such a
way that it cannot be re-used.
  d. For the opening of letters or envelopes through the
agency of a non-Jew see Chapter 31, paragraph 22.

5. *a.* One may open an envelope by removing the staples   *staples*
with which it is sealed.
  b. The same applies to a magazine or booklet which has
been stapled together for transmission by post.
  c. On the other hand, it is prohibited to remove the
staples from pages which have been permanently
stapled together.
  d. It is also prohibited to use a stapler to seal an envelope
or to join pages together.

6. *a.* It is generally forbidden to move the following   *commercial*
documents since they are *muktzeh*:   *papers and*
  1) business letters;   *official*
  2) building plans;   *documents*
  3) accounts;
  4) passports;
  5) identity certificates.

    b. If one is accustomed to using one's identity certificate, as in a time of emergency, one may handle it on Shabbath or Yom Tov. (See also Chapter 18, paragraph 22.)

documents secured in file by cord

7. *a.* One must not, on Shabbath or Yom Tov, tie a knot in cords which are threaded through documents to hold them in place inside a file.

    b. Nevertheless, one is permitted to tie the ends of such cords together with a bow, that is to say by making a loop or a pair of loops over a single knot, but only if one has the intention to untie it again within twenty-four hours.

    c. The general rule is that knots or bows which one may not tie on Shabbath or Yom Tov may also not be untied on Shabbath or Yom Tov.

    d. For additional details see Chapter 15, paragraphs 49, 51, 53, 54, 55 and 56.

loose pages

8. *a.* One is not allowed to sort into their correct order loose pages which have fallen out of a book, unless one intends to read them immediately. (See Chapter 3, paragraph 84.)

    b. See paragraph 3 above with regard to torn pages.

loose-leaf files

9. *a.* One may open and close the metal rings of a loose-leaf file holding documents that are not *muktzeh*.

    b. Nevertheless, sorting the documents into a particular order is prohibited, unless one is about to peruse them in that order.

    c. One is permitted to leaf through a file in search of a required document, and this is not an infringement of the prohibition against selection.

    d. Blank sheets of paper in a file are *muktzeh*.

        1) If the other papers in the file are of some importance to one and one sometimes reads them, then

a) the presence of the blank sheets does not prohibit one from handling those other papers,
b) one may move the whole file and
c) one may even turn over the blank sheets in order to reach a document one requires.
2) If the other papers are not of any importance to one and one does not read them, one should treat the whole file as being *muktzeh*.
e. A file whose contents consist of commercial documents and letters, accounts and other *muktzeh* papers of the kind referred to in paragraph 6 above should not be handled at all.

10. a. An empty notebook (exercise book) is *muktzeh*. (See Chapter 20, paragraph 5.) *notebooks*
b. Where a notebook is only partly empty, then
1) if the written pages are of some importance to one and one sometimes reads them,
a) it is not prohibited to move the notebook on account of the blank pages it contains, yet,
b) it is best to refrain from leafing through the unused sheets, whereas,
2) if one attaches no importance whatever to what is written and does not read it, one should not handle the notebook at all.

11. a. It is permissible to use a card index, if its subject matter is not of the type mentioned in paragraph 6 above, in which case it would be *muktzeh*. *card indexes*
b. Taking a wrong card into one's hand, in the course of looking for the card one needs, and putting it back in its place do not amount to a violation of the prohibition against selection.
c. Where one has taken a card out, one may search for its proper place in the index in order to replace it.

12. a. It is forbidden to sort books with the object of putting them in their proper places in the bookcase. *replacing books*

b. 1) However, if one desires to clear the table of books, one is allowed to pick them up one by one, as they come to hand, putting each into its place in the bookcase.

2) This is because one's object is only to clear the books off the table, not to sort them.

printer's proofs

13. *a.* Printer's proofsheets are *muktzeh* under the category of *k^eli she-m^elachto l^e-issur.*

b. One may not read them so as to find out where they require amendment, because there is a risk that, in the course of reading, one may also correct errors.

c. It is perfectly in order to read them with the intention merely of understanding their contents, in the same way as one would read or study an ordinary book.

telephone directories

14. *a.* A telephone directory is *muktzeh* under the category of *k^eli she-m^elachto l^e-issur.*

b. Nonetheless, one may look up in it an address one needs for Shabbath.

marking a page

15. One must not make any mark on a page, even with one's fingernail, to indicate up to where on the page one has read or to denote a word which requires correction after Shabbath or Yom Tov.

folding paper

16. *a.* Letters and other documents may be folded, either into their original folds or into new folds, but

b. one should not fold paper to make toys or other objects. (See Chapter 16, paragraph 19.)

c. Similarly, paper table napkins must not be folded into special shapes, as is often done when setting a table for guests, but they may be folded in half, or into quarters, for the sake of neatness.

wrapping a book

17. *a.* One is not allowed to wrap the binding of a book in paper, folding the paper around each cover to make it fit.

b. One is allowed to wrap a book in paper in the way one is accustomed to do when wrapping a gift or when packing for dispatch (but one must, of course, not stick it down).

18. *a.* With regard to reading books other than those *reading* invested by the Halacha with a degree of sanctity, see Chapter 29, paragraph 47.

b. With regard to opening and reading letters which have reached one on Shabbath, see Chapter 29, paragraph 45 and Chapter 31, paragraph 22.

CLOCKS AND WATCHES

19. *a.* Winding up a watch or a clock is, subject to the *winding:* exceptions mentioned below, forbidden, since this *general* amounts to putting the finishing touches to an *prohibition* instrument which would otherwise be unusable for its intended purpose.

b. One should not wind up a watch or a clock even while it is still going.

20. *a.* Nevertheless, one may wind up a watch or a clock *winding:* where the following conditions are **all** satisfied: *when*

1) one needs it in order to attend to the requirements of *permitted* a person who is ill, for instance, to know when to feed him at regular intervals;

2) there is no non-Jew available who could wind it;

3) it is still going at the time of winding.

b. In addition, there are authorities who permit a watch or a clock to be wound up where the following conditions are **all** satisfied:

1) one needs it in order to perform a mitzva, for instance to know when it is time to go to the synagogue or to study Torah;

2) there is no non-Jew available who could wind it;

3) it is still going at the time of winding.

c. On *yom tov sheini shel galuyoth*, it is permitted to

wind up a watch or a clock
1) which is still going,
2) so long as one is winding it for use on that same day.

winding by a non-Jew

21. *a.* One may ask a non-Jew to wind up a watch or a clock to be used for the purposes of a person who is ill (as mentioned in paragraph 20 above) even if it has stopped going.

b. One may ask a non-Jew to wind up a watch or a clock, if it is still going, for the purposes of any mitzva.

shaking a watch or clock which has stopped

22. *a.* It is forbidden to shake a watch or a clock which has stopped, since it will probaby start going again, and this is tantamount to winding it up.

b. See also paragraph 24 below.

setting

23. *a.* One may adjust the hands of a watch or a clock to set it to the correct time, but,

b. if it is a chiming clock or an alarm clock, only in the event that one is certain it will not chime or ring while being reset.

c. Subject to the same condition, the hands of a wall clock may be adjusted, although the clock itself should not be moved. (See paragraph 27 below.)

becoming muktzeh

24. *a.* 1) A wristwatch, a pocket-watch and an alarm clock are not *muktzeh* while they are going and may be handled, even if they are battery-operated.

2) However, a watch or a clock which is not working is *muktzeh*, whether it has stopped
a) due to a defect in its mechanism or
b) because it was not wound up before Shabbath or Yom Tov.

3) a) Nevertheless, a gold watch which one does not normally remove from one's hand, even when it is not working, is considered to be an ornament.

b) It may be handled in the usual way, even if it

has stopped going (but see paragraphs 22 above and 28 below).

b. 1) One must not press the buttons of an electronic watch. *electronic watches*

2) An electronic watch on which one cannot tell the time without pressing a button that causes it to light up is *muktzeh*.

25. If a wristwatch stops on Shabbath while one is wearing it, and one is in a place where it is liable to be stolen if left, one may take it to a safe place and put it down there (provided, of course, that the rules concerning carrying, set out in Chapters 17 and 18, permit one to do this). *watch stopping while being worn*

26. With regard to wearing a wristwatch where there is no *eiruv* and where carrying items from one place to another is forbidden, see Chapter 18, paragraph 27. *wearing a wristwatch where there is no eiruv*

27. Wall clocks are *muktzeh* and may not be moved even when they are going. *wall clocks*

28. a. A wristwatch which is wound automatically by the natural movement of the hand may be worn, provided it is going. *automatic watches*

b. 1) One must not put it on while it is not going.

2) This applies even to a gold watch which serves as an ornament, since, in putting it on, one is bound to wind it up by the movements one makes.

3) Consequently, an automatic watch which stops working is *muktzeh*, even if it is made of gold.

29. a. It is forbidden to wind up the alarm mechanism of a clock on Shabbath or Yom Tov. *alarm clocks*

b. Should one wish to wake up at a particular time in order to perform a mitzva, for example to study Torah or to pray, one may proceed as follows:

1) one may, before Shabbath or Yom Tov commences,

wind up the alarm mechanism and depress the appropriate button, lever or catch to prevent it from operating before it is required, and

2) one may, on Shabbath or Yom Tov, release this button, lever or catch, so that the alarm will operate at the desired time.*

c. One is permitted, on Shabbath or Yom Tov, to adjust the hands which determine at what time the alarm will operate, as long as one is sure it will not ring in the course of adjustment.

d. One is allowed to stop the ringing or buzzing of an alarm clock on Shabbath or Yom Tov, unless it is electrically (including battery) operated, in which case stopping the alarm would break an electrical circuit.

e. In those cases where it is permissible to wind up a clock which is still going, as set out in paragraph 20 above, one may do so even if one thereby also winds up an alarm mechanism.

stopwatches and sandglasses

30. *a.* 1) Stopwatches and sandglasses may not be used on Shabbath or Yom Tov, except when one needs them for a person who is ill (even if he is not dangerously ill).

2) This need could arise if, for instance, one has to feed a patient at regular intervals or to measure his pulse.

b. These instruments (unless they form part of an ordinary clock or watch) are *muktzeh* under the heading of *k^eli she-m^elachto l^e-issur*.

timers

31. See Chapter 13, paragraphs 23 to 27 for the use of timers (time-switches).

---

*If the clock is electrically (including battery-) operated, a duly qualified halachic authority should first be consulted.

PRODUCING MUSICAL AND OTHER SOUNDS
ON SHABBATH OR YOM TOV

32. There is a general prohibition, the scope of which will *general* become apparent below, on the production of a noise on *prohibition* Shabbath or Yom Tov, whether
    a. by means of a musical instrument,
    b. by means of any other instrument or,
    c. in some cases, even with one's hand.

33. For the purposes of the rules relating to this prohibition, *categories* a distinction must be made between *of*
    a. instruments or devices designed for producing a *instruments* sound, such as musical instruments, bells, toys that emit noises, whistles and so forth, and
    b. instruments or devices not designed for producing a sound.

34. a. One must not produce any sound, even a sound that is *instruments* not musical, with an instrument which is designed for *designed* that purpose. *for*
    b. Such an instrument is *muktzeh*, under the heading of *producing a* k*e*li she-m*e*lachto l*e*-issur. *sound*
    c. One is, therefore, prohibited from using instruments such as whistles, tuning forks or bells on Shabbath or Yom Tov, and they are all *muktzeh*.
    d. 1) On Shabbath, and on every Yom Tov except for Rosh Hashana, a *shofar* may not be sounded and is *muktzeh*.
       2) On Rosh Hashana (when it does not fall on Shabbath), the *shofar* is sounded in performance of a mitzva, and one may handle it even after one has fulfilled the mitzva.
    e. Concerning the use of doorbells and knockers, see Chapter 23, paragraphs 45 to 48.

instruments **35.** *a.* 1) An instrument that is not designed for producing a
not   sound may be used to produce a sound which is not
designed   musical or rhythmic.
for
producing a   2) One must not produce a musical or rhythmic sound,
sound   even with such an instrument.

           3) The same rule applies in relation to any other item
which is not designed for producing a sound, but
with whose assistance one can make a noise, such
as a door, a window or a hard floor.

  b. It follows that, as long as one does not beat out a
specific rhythm, one may

    1) tap a bottle or glass with a spoon, to silence a party
of guests,

    2) rap on the door with a key, to attract the attention
of someone who will draw the bolt on the inside, or

    3) bang two pots together, to wake up somebody who
is sleeping.

  c. One should not

    1) bang the top of the table, either with an instrument
or with one's hand, in time to a tune nor

    2) tap one's foot on the floor to add to the melody of a
song.

clapping **36.** *a.* One may not produce a musical or rhythmic sound,
hands   even if one uses not an instrument or other object, but
merely one's own limbs, as where one claps one's
hands or snaps one's fingers.

  b. By way of exception, one may produce such a sound
with one's limbs

    1) in celebration of a mitzva **or**

    2) in a manner which one does not usually adopt on a
weekday, as where one claps one hand on the back
of the other.

  c. One may clap one's hands, even in the usual way (but
not to a specific rhythm), where the aim is, for
example,

    1) to wake up someone who is sleeping or

    2) to silence a talkative assembly.

37. One is allowed to whistle even a tune through one's lips *whistling*
(unaided by any instrument) on Shabbath or Yom Tov.

38. One should not dance on Shabbath or Yom Tov, except in *dancing*
celebration of a mitzva (as on Simchath Torah).

39. *a.* The bells attached to the silver ornaments with which *bells on*
it is customary to adorn a *sefer Torah* are designed to *sefer Torah*
produce a sound.
b. 1) Nonetheless, one should not protest against those
who place ornaments with bells on the *sefer Torah*
on Shabbath or Yom Tov.
2) This is because there are some authorities who hold
that their action is justified by the mitzva element
involved.

40. *a.* A whistling kettle may be put on the fire on Yom Tov, *whistling*
despite the fact that it will whistle when the water *kettles*
inside it boils.
b. This should, however, only be permitted in a place
where it is common to use such kettles and everyone
recognizes the sound of its whistle.
c. Furthermore, a whistling kettle should not be put on
the fire when the water inside it is already boiling,
because it will begin to whistle right away, as a direct
and immediate result of one's action.

41. The production of noises to amuse a baby, either by an *babies*
adult or by the baby itself, is dealt with in Chapter 16,
paragraphs 2 and 3.

THE USE OF BABY CARRIAGES ON SHABBATH AND YOM TOV

42. *a.* One may push a baby carriage (perambulator) on *pushing a*
Shabbath or Yom Tov (subject to the contents of *baby*
paragraph 43 below), not only along a paved road, but *carriage*
also over a sandy path.

b. 1) It does not matter that tracks are formed by the weight of the baby carriage pressing down on the sand, or

2) that one directly moves sand aside with the wheels when turning the baby carriage.

where the transfer of objects is forbidden

43. *a.* One is not allowed to push a baby carriage in a place where it is forbidden to transfer objects from one spot to another.

b. See also Chapter 18, paragraphs 50 and 51.

converting a baby carriage into a stroller

44. *a.* It is prohibited

1) to convert a baby carriage into a stroller (pushchair), or vice versa, or

2) to fit a seat onto a baby carriage for an older child, if this is done by means of screws which are fastened tightly and are not meant to be frequently unscrewed and screwed down again.

b. If it is done by an arrangement or combination of springs, clips, hinges or slots, then it is allowed.

c. For the attachment and opening of hoods, canopies and sunshades on Shabbath or Yom Tov, see Chapter 24, paragraphs 9 and 13.

repairs

45. *a.* 1) It is forbidden to repair a defective baby carriage on Shabbath or Yom Tov.

2) This must be borne in mind if, for example,

a) a tire comes off a wheel,

b) a wheel drops off or

c) a spring becomes detached from its permanent position.

b. 1) A defective baby carriage which can easily be repaired is *muktzeh* if

a) the defect occurred on Shabbath or Yom Tov **or**

b) the baby carriage has not been used in its defective state.

2) It may not be used, nor indeed handled, since one might come to repair it on Shabbath or Yom Tov. (See, however, Chapter 22, paragraph 34).

46. *a.* A combined high chair and baby walker, composed of *baby* a detachable upper part designed for sitting on and a *walkers* lower part designed for helping a baby learn to walk, may be put together or taken apart on Shabbath or Yom Tov.

    b. This is permitted, even if the two sections are joined by screws, since they are made to be frequently screwed together and unscrewed, in accordance with the needs of the child.

47. Squeaky wheels may not be oiled.   *squeaky* *wheels*

REMUNERATION FOR SERVICES RENDERED ON
SHABBATH OR YOM TOV

48. *a.* There is a Rabbinical prohibition against receiving *general rule* remuneration for work done on Shabbath.

    b. The prohibition is applicable even if there is nothing wrong with the actual performance of the work on Shabbath.

    c. It is forbidden to receive the remuneration even if, before the commencement of Shabbath, one agreed to carry out the work on Shabbath and to take payment for it after Shabbath.

    d. The reason for the prohibition is that accepting payment in such circumstances has an affinity with the execution of a commercial transaction, which is itself forbidden on Shabbath or Yom Tov.

49. *a.* While it is the person accepting payment who violates *who* the prohibition against receiving remuneration for *trans-* services rendered on Shabbath, *gresses?*

    b. the person making the payment is also guilty of a transgression, in leading his fellow Jew into sin.

50. The rules relating to the receipt of remuneration for *Yom Tov* services rendered on Yom Tov are identical, in all respects, with the rules relating to the receipt of remuneration for services rendered on Shabbath.

rental payment distinguished from purchase price

51. *a.* The prohibition against receiving remuneration for services rendered on Shabbath extends in principle
1) not only to a reward for the physical performance of work, but also
2) to rent due for a room or apartment (as to which see paragraphs 62 and 63 below) and
3) to charges for the hire of any object (as to which see paragraph 60 below).

b. It does not extend to the payment, after Shabbath, of a debt incurred on Shabbath, as, for example,
1) where one has taken food or drink, on Shabbath, from a shopkeeper, in the circumstances set out in Chapter 29, paragraph 17, or
2) where one has taken medicines, on Shabbath, from a pharmacy, in the circumstances set out in Chapter 33, paragraph 4.

gifts

52. *a.* The receipt of any consideration, whether monetary or otherwise, even food, due in payment for services rendered on Shabbath is forbidden (subject to some limited exceptions referred to in paragraphs 54, 55 and 67 below).

b. Nevertheless, one may accept a voluntary gift presented in return for such services.

c. Something one would be entitled to claim by right (if the services were rendered on a weekday) is not a gift, but remuneration, and may not be accepted.

d. Consequently, one may not receive a "gift"
1) which it was agreed should be given in return for the services or
2) which it is the accepted practice to give in return for such services.

e. On the other hand, one may voluntarily return a favor for another one has received on Shabbath.

53. The prohibition against receiving remuneration is infringed *time of payment*

a. whether the payment is made after the performance of the services, as is usual in the case of a fee paid for work done, or

b. whether it is paid in advance, before Shabbath, for services to be performed on Shabbath, or even

c. when no payment is made at all, but a previously owed debt is written off against the services rendered. *cancellation of debt*

54. a. An arrangement to perform services for a person on Shabbath, in consideration for services which that person will perform for one on that or another day, is likewise not permitted. *work in return for work*

b. 1) It is, however, allowed where the consideration consists merely of looking after something in order to prevent loss or injury, and no direct, material gain is conferred.

2) A person may, thus, babysit for a neighbor on the understanding that the neighbor will babysit for him on another occasion.

55. a. If one has to be on duty on Shabbath, for example in a hospital or in the kitchen of a kibbutz, one may exchange one's turn for a different spell of duty on a weekday or on Shabbath. *changing position on duty roster*

b. This is because neither party obtains a direct, material gain over and above his release from having to be on duty at the time originally appointed.

c. In connection with hospital duty, see further Chapter 40, paragraph 23.

56. It is forbidden to receive remuneration, even from a non-Jew, for services rendered on Shabbath. *receipt from non-Jew*

57. a. One may remunerate a non-Jew for services which he has performed on Shabbath (and which one was allowed to have performed by him on Shabbath). *payment to non-Jew*

b. See also Chapter 30, paragraph 29.

services over a period including Shabbath

58. *a.* The prohibition against receiving remuneration for work done on Shabbath applies to

1) a separate payment made for that work, and even to

2) a payment covering that work together with work done on a day other than Shabbath, if the latter work is not connected with the former.

b. It does not apply to, and one may receive, payment for work performed over a period of time which includes Shabbath.

c. 1) It should be noted that payment may be received in the last-mentioned case only if work is performed under a firm arrangement which the parties

a) regard as binding on themselves and

b) expect to last.

2) a) It is otherwise if the parties regard the arrangement as a temporary one, which either of them is perfectly free to terminate at will, the amount owing up to the date of termination being calculated on a daily basis.

b) In that case, it is forbidden to accept remuneration for the work done on Shabbath, even when it forms part of one payment covering the total number of days worked.

3) a) In other words, what is important is not whether the payment covers work over a period, but whether, in the eyes of the parties, the arrangement was genuinely for employment over a period.

b) Calculation of remuneration on a daily basis, not within the context of a previously envisaged period of employment, gives an *individual* importance to *each day*, including Shabbath.

c) That being so, payment cannot be *generally* attributed to the total number of days *as a period*.

d. 1) It follows that a babysitter or a tutor giving private lessons may receive payment including remuneration for work done on Shabbath, provided there is a firm arrangement for his employment over a period, as described above.

2) Since payment is genuinely for an overall period of employment, the sum due may even be calculated on an hourly basis, including hours worked on Shabbath.

e. 1) Nevertheless, one may not, on Shabbath itself, hire someone, even to do work which is allowed to be done on Shabbath, and even if one promises terms which make payment permissible, as described above.

2) If one hires someone before Shabbath, one should not speak with him on Shabbath about the remuneration he will receive for his work, even though it will be paid in a permissible manner together with remuneration for work done on other days of the week.

3) Even to ask someone if he wishes to do paid work for one after Shabbath is forbidden. (See also Chapter 29, paragraphs 51 to 53.)

59. a. Owing to the prohibition against the receipt of remuneration for work done on Shabbath, it is forbidden to hire a watchman, or any other Jewish employee for that matter, to work just on Shabbath. *hiring for work to be done on Shabbath*

b. 1) Where one does require work to be performed specifically on Shabbath, one should make it a condition of the employment that some work should also be done before or after Shabbath.

2) Thus, the employee will be able to receive payment for all of his work together, including that not done on Shabbath, as permitted by the rule discussed in paragraph 58 above.

c. 1) Such a situation can arise when one employs waiters or helpers to assist at a party to be held on Shabbath.

[413]

2) One ought to stipulate that they should commence preparations before Shabbath or should help with the cleaning up after Shabbath.

renting eating utensils   60. *a.* The position is similar when one rents eating utensils for use at a dinner to be given on Shabbath.

       b. One should ensure
         1) that the rental period starts a number of hours before Shabbath begins, or continues after Shabbath has terminated, and
         2) that there is an overall fee for the whole period.

work requiring preparation   61. One may accept remuneration which covers both work done on Shabbath and preparations one had to make before Shabbath.

hotels   62. *a.* It is permissible to pay a hotel bill, even if one slept and ate at the hotel only on Shabbath.

       b. This is because the payment also covers the hotel proprietor's expenses for such things as
         1) buying and cooking food before Shabbath,
         2) cleaning and maintenance of the hotel before and after Shabbath and
         3) laundry.

renting a room   63. *a.* 1) The prohibition against receiving payment for services rendered on Shabbath forbids the receipt of rent for the bare use of a room which is let only over Shabbath.
           2) Rent may be received if it includes payment for some additional facility, such as the use of the landlord's linen.

       b. If no additional facility is provided, one ought to stipulate that the period of the rental should begin some while before Shabbath commences or should end some while after it terminates.

       c. There is, of course, nothing wrong with the payment of

rent for a period covering several days and including Shabbath.

64. *a.* Where the use of a warm *mikveh* is permitted on Shabbath,* one may pay the entrance charge either before or after Shabbath. *use of mikveh*

    b. The reason for this is that the charge covers the cost of heating and cleaning the *mikveh* prior to Shabbath, so that it will be in a fit state to be used on Shabbath.

65. *a.* One is allowed to pay, before Shabbath, for admittance on Shabbath to zoological gardens or to similar attractions which one may visit on Shabbath.** *ticket for zoological gardens*

    b. The relevant factor here is that the price of the ticket includes such expenses as the maintenance of cleanliness, both before and after Shabbath, and the cost of feeding the animals.

66. *a.* There is a difference of opinion among the authorities as to whether the prohibition against receiving remuneration for work done on Shabbath applies also when the performance of the work is a mitzvah. *payment for performance of mitzva*

    b. Examples occur where a person is engaged as a cantor on Shabbath or Yom Tov or to sound the *shofar* on Rosh Hashana.

    c. Even those authorities who adopt the lenient view do not dispute the assertion, based on a Talmudic source, that, in general, a person does not profit from a reward he accepts for fulfilling these functions.

    d. Bearing in mind the conflicting views on the subject, it is as well, where payment is made, to arrange for the

---

*See Chapter 14, paragraph 1.
**This is only allowed where one does not infringe a prohibition by carrying a ticket and where it is usual to pay in advance, so that other people will not think one has paid on Shabbath or otherwise violated the Shabbath.

remuneration also to cover
1) at least one service conducted by the cantor on a day other than Shabbath or
2) the sounding of the *shofar* during the month preceding Rosh Hashana (Elul).
e. See also paragraph 61 above.

medical attention

67. A doctor or a nurse who is called upon to give medical attention on Shabbath may request a fee for that attention, but the matter should not be mentioned on Shabbath.

remuneration received

68. If a person has transgressed the rules set out in the preceding paragraphs and has accepted remuneration for services rendered on Shabbath or Yom Tov, neither he nor anyone else may at any time derive any benefit from such remuneration.

MAKING PREPARATIONS ON SHABBATH AND YOM TOV FOR A SUBSEQUENT DAY

general prohibition

69. a. It is, in general, forbidden to make preparations
1) on Shabbath or Yom Tov for an ordinary day of the week,
2) on Yom Tov for the intermediate days of the festival,
3) on Shabbath for Yom Tov,
4) on Yom Tov for Shabbath (except as mentioned in paragraph 85 below),
5) on the first day of Yom Tov for the second, whether it be the second day of Rosh Hashana or *yom tov sheini shel galuyoth*, or
6) on one Shabbath for another.
b. The prohibition is applicable even if the preparation is necessary for the purposes of a mitzva which is to be performed immediately after Shabbath or Yom Tov ends.

70. *a.* Preparations which are forbidden comprise anything one does that is not required for the same day, *"prepara-tions" defined*
    1) even if it involves only a minimal effort and
    2) even if it consists merely of saying a few words to achieve a halachic effect (as in paragraph 71*e* below).

  b. There is nothing wrong with the performance of an act which, without the expenditure of any additional effort, serves a purpose both on Shabbath and on the following day.

71. The examples below serve to illustrate the rule.
  a. One may not prepare food on Shabbath, to be consumed after Shabbath has terminated. *preparing food*

  b. 1) One may not wash dishes or cutlery which will no longer be used that day. *washing dishes*
    2) See, however, Chapter 12, paragraph 1.

  c. 1) One may not fold an article of clothing on one Shabbath for use on the following Shabbath, even if it is specifically intended for use only on Shabbath. *folding clothes*
    2) For rules regarding the folding of clothes in general, see Chapter 15, paragraphs 44 to 46.

  d. One may not roll a *sefer Torah* on Shabbath to the portion that is to be read the next day, even if that next day is Yom Tov. *rolling a sefer Torah*

  e. 1) One may not release a person from a vow, unless the release is required for that day. *release from a vow*
    2) For additional details, see Chapter 29, paragraph 58.

  f. 1) When the day before Passover falls on Shabbath, one may not wash the dishes after the last meal at which *chametz* is eaten, since they will certainly not be required that day. *cleaning chametz off dishes before Passover*
    2) One should clean them of *chametz*, as one is obliged to do, by wiping it off with one's finger, with a paper napkin or in some similar permissible manner.

3) Should this not be possible, one should try to find a non-Jew to wash the dishes.

4) If no non-Jew is available, one should rinse them oneself, but only to the extent needed to remove actual *chametz*.

sleeping on Shabbath

72. *a.* One is allowed to sleep on Shabbath, even if one's sole purpose in doing so is to enable one to stay up late after Shabbath.

b. Nevertheless, a person should not say, on Shabbath, that he is going to sleep so that he will not be too tired to work after Shabbath.

preparing the wine for havdala

73. It is forbidden, before Shabbath has ended, to prepare the wine for *havdala*, but

a. one is permitted (provided there is an *eiruv* and carrying articles about is allowed) to bring a bottle of wine to a place where one intends to drink it at the third Shabbath meal as well as to use it subsequently for *havdala*, and,

b. if it will be difficult to obtain wine for *havdala* afterwards, one may bring it before Shabbath terminates (provided there is an *eiruv*, so that carrying articles is allowed), but not so late that it becomes obvious that one is bringing it for after Shabbath.

taking a prayer book to the synagogue

74. One should not take a prayer book to the synagogue on Shabbath (even in a place where there is an *eiruv*) with the intention of praying from it after Shabbath, unless one also makes some use of it before Shabbath is over.

Purim

75. When Purim occurs on Sunday, one should not bring the scroll containing the Book of Esther to the synagogue while it is still Shabbath, even where there is an *eiruv*, unless one also reads from it a little during Shabbath.

preparing clothes for Av

76. *a.* Generally speaking, as a sign of mourning for the destruction of the Temple, it is forbidden to wear newly

washed clothes during the first nine days of the month of Av.

b. If the clothes were washed and worn, even for only a short period, before the first of Av, they may be worn afterwards.

c. It is also customary to wear newly washed clothes on Shabbath occurring during these nine days.

d. Many people prepare clothes for use during these nine days by wearing them for a short while before the first of Av.

e. If one has forgotten to do so, one should not, on the Shabbath occurring during the nine days, put on washed clothes and then take them off after a short while, since this amounts to making preparations on Shabbath for a weekday.

f. What one may do in such a situation is to change, on Shabbath, out of the clean clothes one put on before Shabbath and into other, clean clothes, which one will leave on until after Shabbath, so that one will be left with two sets of reasonably clean clothes to wear during the week.

77. When the Fast of the Ninth of Av, which marks the anniversary of the destruction of the Temple, falls immediately after Shabbath, one should note the following:

Ninth of Av

a. one may eat and drink more than usual at the third Shabbath meal, even though one's intention is to make it easier to fast the next day, but one should not say that that is why one is eating;

b. the leather-free shoes or slippers one is going to wear on the fast should not be brought to the synagogue on Shabbath;

c. one should not bring the Book of Lamentations to the synagogue while it is still Shabbath, even where there is an *eiruv*, unless one reads from it a little during Shabbath;

[419]

d. one should not change out of one's Shabbath clothes before nightfall;

e. if possible, one ought to wait at home until the termination of Shabbath and then remove one's Shabbath clothes, change one's shoes and go to the synagogue;

f. if this is impracticable, one should not take off one's ordinary shoes until after the intonation of *Bar*^e*chu* at the commencement of the evening service (and, when one does take them off, one should be careful not to touch them with one's fingers, so as to avoid the necessity for washing one's hands on the fast day).

making beds **78.** *a.* One is allowed to make the beds on Shabbath so that the house will look tidy.

b. One is also allowed to make a bed or shake out bedclothes for use on Shabbath.

c. One is not allowed either to make a bed (where tidiness is not a consideration) or to shake out bedclothes for use after Shabbath will have ended.

clearing the table **79.** *a.* Dishes and cutlery may be cleared off the table, even after the last meal of the Shabbath or Yom Tov,

 1) so that the room should look clean and tidy **or**

 2) to avoid attracting insects.

b. 1) Since it is permissible, in these circumstances, to take the dishes and cutlery into the kitchen, there is nothing wrong with leaving them there in an orderly fashion (taking care, of course, not to violate the prohibition against selection on Shabbath detailed in Chapter 12, paragraph 23).

 2) This is so, even if one's object is that they should be ready for washing immediately upon the termination of Shabbath or Yom Tov.

c. It is, however, forbidden to clear the table

 1) in the last few minutes of Shabbath or Yom Tov, during which one no longer needs the room to be tidy, or

2) even in the middle of the day, if one intends to leave the room and not enter it again until after Shabbath or Yom Tov is over.

80. *a.* 1) One may light candles on Yom Tov (in a permissible manner) close to the end of the day, provided *lighting candles*
a) one can enjoy their light before nightfall **and**
b) one would otherwise have to spend that time sitting in the gathering darkness.
2) It makes no difference
a) that one's principal intention is to use the candles after nightfall or
b) whether the ensuing day is a second day of Yom Tov or an ordinary weekday.
b. Nevertheless, one is not permitted to prepare candles in candlesticks on Yom Tov for lighting after Yom Tov has ended.

81. *a.* Any otherwise permissible act *acts not*
1) which is done without the involvement of any *involving*
special bother **and** *any special*
2) which one is used to doing without thinking about *bother and*
the benefit that will result from its being done, *done as a*
may be done on Shabbath, even if one will derive a *matter of*
benefit from it after Shabbath, as long as one does not *course*
expressly say that one is making preparations for after Shabbath.
b. Consequently,
1) if one takes a *tallith* to the synagogue (in a place where there is an *eiruv*), one may carry it home again;
2) one may return a book to its place in the bookcase after use (but see paragraph 12 above);
3) one may put the *arba'a minim* back into water after use on the Yom Tov of Sukkoth, despite the fact that one will derive an advantage therefrom in that they will not dry up and so will be fit for one to use on the following day;

4) one may put food which has been left over after a meal back into the refrigerator;

5) one may stand a dirty dish in water on Shabbath if the remains of food will otherwise dry hard and stick to its sides (but, if the food has already dried on to its sides, the dish must not be stood in water on Shabbath, since, in that event, the dish is soaked with the specific thought in mind of making it easier to clean after Shabbath than it is at present, as explained in Chapter 12, paragraph 3);

6) a) a person may leave home on Shabbath afternoon, even on a very hot day, taking with him (in a place where there is an *eiruv*) a pullover to be worn when he is out in the evening (after Shabbath), although

   b) it is better if he does not say he is taking it for the evening;

7) one may leave the house, even shortly before nightfall, carrying a key in one's pocket—where there is an *eiruv*—so that one will be able to enter one's house after Shabbath.

acts not involving any special bother and performed preparatory to something which could be done in a permissible manner

82. *a.* An act may be done on Shabbath preparatory to an activity one intends to perform after Shabbath, provided that

1) the act itself is otherwise permissible,

2) the act is done without the involvement of any special bother, **and**

3) the activity for which one is preparing could conceivably be performed in a permissible manner on Shabbath.

b. 1) One may accordingly

   a) walk to the extreme limit permitted on Shabbath (two thousand *amoth* beyond the last house in the town or the same distance beyond the boundary of the *eiruv* of the place where one happens to be) and

   b) wait there until after Shabbath,

so that one can then go further in order to perform an activity which is allowed on Shabbath.

2) This is so even though walking as far as the place where the activity is to be performed is itself forbidden on Shabbath. (See Chapter 29, paragraph 11.)

83. *a.* A person may perform an otherwise permissible act whose purpose is not required until after Shabbath, if
1) it does not involve any special bother,
2) failure to perform the act on Shabbath will be, or is liable to be, detrimental **and**
3) performance after Shabbath, even where possible, will be ineffectual.

acts not involving any special bother and which are necessary to avert loss

b. Consequently,
1) a person may annul his wife's vows on Shabbath, even if the annulment is not required for the purposes of Shabbath (since failure by a husband to annul his wife's vow on the day on which he hears of it precludes him from doing so in the future);
2) a person may rinse and soak raw meat on Shabbath, to prepare it for salting after Shabbath in accordance with halachic requirements, if
a) Shabbath is the third day after the slaughter of the animal (including the day of slaughter),
b) he forgot to salt or rinse the meat prior to Shabbath **and**
c) there is no non-Jew available who could do the rinsing and soaking
(since failure to salt or rinse the meat before the end of the third day would preclude one from eating it cooked in a pot in the normal way, as explained in Chapter 11, paragraph 5);
3) an object which is not *muktzeh* may be moved on Shabbath to avoid its being stolen or broken, even if one has no use for it until after Shabbath;
4) one may take in clothes from the yard or balcony

(subject to compliance, where relevant, with the rules set out in Chapter 17), if one fears that they will be made wet by the rain and one will be unable to wear them in the evening, after Shabbath.

learning 84. *a.* One is permitted to learn things on Shabbath which one is not required to know until the following day.

b. This is not an infringement of the prohibition against preparing on Shabbath for another day, since the actual acquisition of knowledge is an everyday need.

c. See also Chapter 29, paragraph 47.

eiruv 85. Where one has set aside an *eiruv tavshilin* before Yom
tavshilin Tov, one may make preparations for Shabbath on the Yom Tov which falls on the previous day, as specified in Chapter 2, paragraphs 10 to 16.

Laws Derived from Isaiah: Running, Walking, Commerce, Measuring, Reading, Speaking

SCRIPTURAL SOURCE OF THE PROHIBITIONS

1. *a.* Certain things are prohibited on Shabbath or Yom Tov despite the fact that they neither resemble any activity forbidden by the Torah nor lead to the performance of such an activity. *Isaiah 58:13 and 14*

b. These prohibitions are derived from verses 13 and 14 in Chapter 58 of Isaiah:

"If you draw back your foot because of Shabbath, [if you restrain yourself] from doing that which you desire on My holy day, [if you] call Shabbath a joy, [if you call] God's sanctified [day] honored, and respect it by not following your [usual] ways, by not pursuing your business and [by not] speaking about [forbidden] matters, then shall you rejoice in God and I shall make you ride over the heights of the earth and shall feed you the inheritance of Jacob, your father; for the mouth of God has spoken."

c. Since their direct source is one of the Prophets, they are treated with the severity appropriate to Torah (as opposed to Rabbinical) prohibitions.

d. The rules governing them are the same on both Shabbath and Yom Tov.

2. *a.* The above verses have been expounded by the Rabbis in the following manner. *traditional interpretation*

1) "Call Shabbath a joy"—there is a positive commandment to enjoy the Shabbath, to sanctify it and to honor it.

2) "[Call] God's sanctified [day] honored"—just as

there is a commandment to honor and enjoy Shabbath, so is there a commandment to honor and enjoy Yom Tov.

3) "[Call] God's sanctified [day] honored"—on Yom Kippur, since one cannot honor the day with food and drink, one is commanded to honor it by wearing clean clothes, spreading a cloth on the table and kindling lights in the synagogue and the house of learning.

4) "And respect it by not following your [usual] ways"—your manner of walking on Shabbath should not be the same as on other days of the week.*

5) "And respect it by not following your [usual] ways"—your ways are forbidden, but the ways of Heaven are permitted.

6) "And respect it by not following your [usual] ways, by not pursuing your business"—you should not make your way on Shabbath to a place where you will pursue your business.

7) "Not pursuing your business"—your business is forbidden; a person should not pursue his everyday affairs on Shabbath.

8) "Not pursuing your business"—your business is forbidden, but the business of Heaven is permitted.

9) "And [by not] speaking about [forbidden] matters"—your conversation on Shabbath should not be the same as on other days of the week.

10) "And [by not] speaking about [forbidden] matters"—speech about forbidden matters is prohibited, whereas thought is permitted.

b. 1) The laws flowing from the first three interpretations above are dealt with in detail in later chapters.

---

*Another interpretation will be mentioned in Chapter 42, paragraph 32.

2) The laws flowing from the last seven interpretations above are dealt with in detail in the following paragraphs of this chapter.

RUNNING

3. *a.* "And respect it by not following your [usual] *general rule* ways"—your manner of walking on Shabbath should not be the same as on other days of the week.
   b. Consequently, as a general rule, one should not run on Shabbath, or walk with long strides, but should walk in a leisurely manner.

4. It is permissible to run   *when it is*
   a. to escape from the rain,   *necessary*
   b. in a place where one is afraid to walk slowly or   *to run*
   c. in any other comparable case of need.

5. Children are allowed to add to their enjoyment of *running* Shabbath by playing running games. (See also Chapter *games* 16, paragraph 39.)

6. *a.* "Your [usual] ways"—your ways are forbidden, but *running to* the ways of Heaven are permitted.   *perform a*
   b. Consequently, it is permitted, indeed it is a mitzva, to *mitzva* run
      1) to the synagogue,
      2) to a Torah study session or
      3) to any other place where one is going to perform a mitzva.

GOING TO A PLACE IN PREPARATION FOR AFTER SHABBATH

7. "And respect it by not following your [usual] ways, by *when* not pursuing your business"—it is forbidden to go to a *forbidden:* place on Shabbath when the three following conditions *the rule* are **all** present:

a. One wishes to perform an act there after Shabbath which is prohibited on Shabbath.

b. There are no conceivable means whereby the act could be performed on Shabbath in a permissible manner.

c. It is recognizable from one's actions that one wishes to perform the prohibited act after Shabbath.

examples of prohibition

8. Consequently, it is forbidden

a. to go into one's place of work on Shabbath, with the object of beginning to work immediately upon the termination of Shabbath,

b. to go to a bus stop on Shabbath and wait there, with the object of boarding a bus immediately upon the termination of Shabbath (except in the circumstances mentioned in paragraph 10 below),

c. to go on Shabbath to an apartment one is thinking of buying or renting, and inspect it with the object of seeing whether it is suitable, or what repairs have to be carried out, and

d. to go for a stroll on Shabbath in a market which is normally frequented only by those buying or selling (for instance, a wholesale market), with the object of finding things one will be able to buy after Shabbath.

looking for a shop

9. a. 1) On the other hand, it is permitted, while walking along the street, to look for a particular shop, even if one's object in so doing is to be able to locate it and go into it immediately upon the termination of Shabbath.

2) One may not, however, wait at the shop entrance for Shabbath to end.

window-shopping

b. 1) One may look at merchandise displayed in a shop window, even if one's intention is to find something one wishes to buy after Shabbath.

2) One may not, however, pay attention to the prices. (See paragraph 44 below.)

bus stop shelters

10. One may wait under a bus stop shelter in order to take refuge, for instance from the rain or the sun, even if one intends to board a bus as soon as Shabbath ends.*

11. a. One is allowed on Shabbath to walk to the farthest permissible point** and to wait there, so that as soon as Shabbath ends one will be able to go beyond this limit, with the object of

walking as far as allowed and waiting there

1) starting a hike,
2) fetching an object which is not *muktzeh* or
3) doing something which is allowed on Shabbath.

b. 1) It is also permitted on Shabbath to go and see if animals which one is allowed to feed on Shabbath (as explained in Chapter 27, paragraphs 21 and 23) have enough to eat for the next day.

2) This is so, even if there is no *eiruv* and one would not be allowed to bring them the food on Shabbath.

c. 1) The fact that,

a) in *a* above, one may not on Shabbath walk as far as the place one needs to reach (because it is beyond the permitted limit), and that,

b) in *b* above, one may not on Shabbath take the food to the animals (due to the absence of an *eiruv*)

is not a consideration.

2) If certain, not unusual prerequisites had been present, these acts *could* have been performed on Shabbath in a permissible manner. (See condition *b* in paragraph 7 above.)

a) It is sufficient that, if the town had been built up to within two thousand *amoth* of the place one wants to reach, one would have been able to go there on Shabbath, even though it is not in fact so built up.

---

*One must, of course, make suitable arrangements to avoid carrying a ticket or money on Shabbath.

**In general terms, the limit to which one may walk is two thousand *amoth* beyond the boundary of the *eiruv* or, if there is no *eiruv*, two thousand *amoth* beyond the last house of the town.

b) It is likewise sufficient that, if the relevant areas had been surrounded by a suitable partition or if there had been any *eiruv*, one would have been permitted to fetch the object one needs or take food to the animals on Shabbath, even though there is in fact no partition or *eiruv*.

d. 1) It is essential that one's main intention should be to do something which is allowed on Shabbath (or which would be permitted if certain prerequisites were present, as explained above).

2) It does not matter that, in the result, after one has walked beyond the permitted limit on the termination of Shabbath, one also does something there which is forbidden on Shabbath, such as
   a) picking fruit off trees,
   b) handling fruit which is *muktzeh* or
   c) hiring workers.

e. 1) It is, however, prohibited to walk on Shabbath to the farthest permissible point and wait there, so that as soon as Shabbath expires one will be able to walk past this limit, with the sole object of
   a) picking fruit off trees,
   b) fetching fruit which is *muktzeh* or
   c) hiring workers.

2) This is because no means exist whereby one would be allowed to perform these acts on Shabbath.

going to perform a mitzva

12. *a.* "And respect it by not following your [usual] ways, by not pursuing your business"—you should not make your way on Shabbath to a place where you will pursue your business, but the business of Heaven is permitted.

b. Consequently, one may, towards the end of Shabbath,
   1) walk to a bus stop and wait there, with the object of boarding a bus to go and perform a mitzva immediately on the termination of Shabbath,* and

---

*See note to paragraph 10 above.

2) walk to the farthest permissible point and wait there, so that as soon as Shabbath ends one will be able to go beyond this limit, with the object of
a) picking an *ethrog* off the tree or
b) buying a *lulav* to make up *arba'a minim* for the festival of Sukkoth.

CARRYING ON ONE'S EVERYDAY AFFAIRS

13. a. "Not pursuing your business" — your business is forbidden; a person should not pursue his everyday affairs on Shabbath. *general prohibition*
   b. A considerable number of detailed laws stem from this general prohibition, as will be explained in the following paragraphs.

14. It is forbidden on Shabbath to check, in a shop, a field or any other place of work, or even in one's home, to see what is lacking and will need to be done there once Shabbath has terminated. (See, however, the limitations on this prohibition expressed in paragraph 7 above and paragraph 65 below.) *checking what will have to be done after Shabbath*

15. One may not hire a workman on Shabbath, even if
   a. the workman is a non-Jew,
   b. the work is to be done after Shabbath **and**
   c. one does not speak to him about payment. *hiring for work to be done after Shabbath*

BUYING AND SELLING ON SHABBATH AND YOM TOV

16. a. One is prohibited from engaging in trade on Shabbath or Yom Tov. *general prohibition*
   b. This prohibition is applicable both to selling and to buying.
   c. It applies even if the "trading" is motivated by halachic considerations, as where

1) one wishes to sell one's *chametz* to a non-Jew on a Shabbath which is the day preceding Passover, or
2) one wishes to sell to a non-Jew an animal which is about to give birth for the first time. (Such a sale would prevent sanctity, with its attendant complications, from attaching to the firstborn.)

when goods may be taken from a shopkeeper

17. *a.* Despite the above prohibition, the Rabbis have ruled that one may take goods* from a shopkeeper on Shabbath (where there is an *eiruv* and the goods may be carried about) or Yom Tov, provided
1) the goods are required for Shabbath or Yom Tov **and**
2) one is careful not to mention expressions of "buying" or "selling" (as will be explained in the paragraphs below).**

b. One may promise the shopkeeper that one will come to an arrangement with him after Shabbath or Yom Tov with regard to the merchandise one has taken.

c. One may even give the shopkeeper some object as security, but one should not expressly say to him that that is why one is leaving it with him.

mentioning cost, measures and quantities: general rule

18. *a.* As a result, one may go to one's usual shopkeeper and take from him whatever* one needs for Shabbath or Yom Tov.

b. However (subject to the fuller explanation given in the succeeding paragraphs), one must not
1) quantify the amount one requires, by cost, weight or measure, or
2) add it to previous purchases and specify the cumulative amount, by cost, weight, measure or number.

---

*See, however, paragraph 26 below.
**Of course the shop may not be kept open as if for regular business.

19. *a.* One should not ask a shopkeeper for a quantity of food *mentioning*
by money's worth, for instance fruit costing a total of *cost*
so-and-so much, if one's intention in mentioning the
price is to state the limit of what one wants to spend, so
as to ascertain how much the shopkeeper is willing to
sell for this amount.

b. It is as well to avoid referring to cost even when the
items have a fixed price and one's intention is, by
stating the total cost, to indicate to the shopkeeper the
quantity one requires.

c. One may indicate the desired commodity even if one
has to mention money for this purpose, as where there
are two kinds of apples and one wants those costing so-
and-so much.

20. *a.* 1) It is as well not to ask a shopkeeper for a specific *quantifying*
quantity of a commodity which needs to be weighed *amount*
or measured. (Contrast paragraph 21 below, where *required*
the commodity is already packed and is merely
identified by quantity.)

2) Actual weighing or measuring is of course
forbidden. (See paragraph 32 below.)

b. One may

1) request the shopkeeper to fill a bag or container
with a commodity and

2) promise him to weigh an identical bag or container
filled with the same commodity after Shabbath,
one's intention in doing so being to ascertain how
much one has to pay him.

c. It is also permissible for the shopkeeper to fill a vessel
designed for measuring and to hand it to the customer
together with its contents, that is to say without
emptying it into another vessel.

d. If the shopkeeper is not precise as to the amount he
puts into the measuring vessel, but pours in a little
more or a little less than the exact measure, he may
even empty it into vessels belonging to the customer.
(See paragraphs 34 and 35 below.)

identifying **21.** One may indicate to the shopkeeper the kind of item one
by quantity   would like to acquire from him, even if one has to mention
weight or measure for this purpose, as where one
identifies the desired goods by the size of the package.
(See, however, paragraph 23 below.)

specifying **22.** One may ask the shopkeeper for a particular number of
number   articles, as is common, for example, in the case of bottles,
so long as one's intention is to let him know how many
one needs (and not to enable him to work out the cost).

stating a **23.** *a.* A person who takes merchandise from a shopkeeper
balance   on Shabbath, in the ways mentioned above, and still
owes him money for purchases made before Shabbath,
should not specify the new cumulative balance on
Shabbath.

    b. The cumulative balance may be stated neither in
weight, in measure, in money nor in number.

    c. For instance, it is prohibited to tell the shopkeeper
    1) that one now owes him such-and-such a sum,
including the previous debt, or
    2) that one now owes him altogether for goods
aggregating in weight, measure or number to
whatever the total is of the new and previous
transactions.

recording of **24.** *a.* Although the Rabbis permitted a shopkeeper to supply
cost by   goods, as explained above, it is forbidden for him to
shopkeeper   talk about payment.

    b. Even hinting at the price of the merchandise is
prohibited.

    c. It is also forbidden on Shabbath to attach variously
numbered slips to cards bearing customers' names, in
order to show the value of goods purchased.

    d. It is likewise forbidden to insert slips bearing the
names of the customers into a book at pages whose
numbers correspond with the values of their respective
purchases.

25. *a.* Subject to the remaining contents of this paragraph, a person may

buying vouchers in advance

1) purchase special vouchers, before Shabbath, corresponding to the goods he will need on Shabbath, and hand them over to the shopkeeper on Shabbath, in exchange for the goods he receives, and
2) pay before Shabbath for meals he will eat at a restaurant on Shabbath, receiving, in return, vouchers which will enable whoever is serving in the restaurant to know what items he has to provide.

b. These vouchers may not carry any mention of a price, but each may bear an inscription that, in exchange for it, one may obtain a particular food or meal.

c. Better still, the shopkeeper or restaurateur should furnish a different-colored voucher for each product or course, so that the items can be identified according to color, without the necessity for reading the vouchers on Shabbath.

26. *a.* With the exception of food, all items (including eating utensils)

goods intended for sale

1) which are intended for sale **and**
2) whose owner is particular not to use them, for example for fear that they may be spoiled,

are *muktzeh* and may not be moved. (See Chapter 20, paragraph 21.)

b. On the other hand, items intended for lending out or for hire do not thereby become *muktzeh* and may be moved.

27. *a.* One is not allowed to buy something from an automatic vending machine,

buying from an automatic vending machine

1) even if it is activated, not by a coin, but by a token which can be purchased before Shabbath,
2) even if it is not electrically operated,

> 3) even if one is in need of the items one wishes to purchase for Shabbath and
> 4) even if one requests a non-Jew to activate the machine and take out the desired items.
> b. The same prohibition applies to the use of a coin-operated scale. (See also Chapter 14, paragraph 37.)

selling from an automatic vending machine

28. The position with regard to corporations which market their products through automatic vending machines is as follows:

> a. If one can assume that the machines would be used by Jews in violation of the Shabbath, it is proper for the proprietors of the corporation to see to it that the machines are not left in an operational state over Shabbath.
> b. In a place where the users of the machines are non-Jews, the machines may be left in working condition over Shabbath.

GIFTS AND TRANSFERS OF OWNERSHIP ON SHABBATH AND YOM TOV

gifts

29. a. It is forbidden to give or receive a gift on Shabbath or Yom Tov, except for the purposes of Shabbath or Yom Tov or in the manner described below.

> b. One is, therefore, allowed to give someone an *ethrog* or a *lulav* on the first (or second) day of Sukkoth so that he can perform the mitzva of taking the *arba'a minim*.
> c. 1) a) If one wishes to present a gift on Shabbath or Yom Tov, one should transfer its ownership to the recipient prior to Shabbath or Yom Tov.
>   b) One can do this by handing it to a third person, who accepts it on his behalf.
>   c) The presentation can then take place on Shabbath or Yom Tov.
>   2) Where this has not been done, the presentation may nonetheless take place on Shabbath or Yom Tov, but the recipient should have the intention not

to acquire ownership of the gift until Shabbath or Yom Tov is over.

3) This situation commonly occurs when a public presentation is made on Shabbath or Yom Tov to a bridegroom who delivers a discourse, or to a bar mitzva boy.

30. *a.* 1) a) One should not formally abandon the owner- *abandoning* ship of property on Shabbath or Yom Tov, *ownership* except for the purpose of a mitzva.

b) An example of the exception is where one abandons the ownership of *chametz* on a Shabbath which is the day preceding Passover.

2) Notwithstanding this rule, one may throw something out into the street, despite the fact that it thereby becomes ownerless, provided

a) there is an *eiruv* and

b) the item in question does not constitute a nuisance to the public.

b. 1) One may acquire ownerless property on Shabbath *acquiring* or Yom Tov. *ownerless*

2) A person finding lost property on Shabbath or Yom *property* Tov may, thus, pick it up and keep it (unless this is forbidden for other reasons).

31. It is prohibited to perform the mitzva of redeeming the *redemption* firstborn on Shabbath or Yom Tov, even if the period of *of the* thirty days following the birth expires on that day. *firstborn*

MEASURING AND WEIGHING ON SHABBATH AND YOM TOV

32. *a.* There is a Rabbinical prohibition (subject to excep- *general* tions specified in the paragraphs which follow) *prohibition* against measuring and weighing on Shabbath or Yom Tov.

b. It applies even to measuring with a vessel which is not specially designed for that purpose.

c. Measuring and weighing are forbidden whether they are done
  1) for the purpose of buying or selling or
  2) for one's own personal use, and not in any way in connection with buying or selling.
d. One may consequently not weigh or measure
  1) for the purpose of preparing food on Shabbath or
  2) to ascertain the amount of flour one needs when baking a cake on Yom Tov.
e. See also paragraphs 40 to 42 below.

counting floor tiles

33. a. The prohibition against measuring is not transgressed by counting the number of standard-size floor tiles in a room.
  b. One may count the tiles even if one's intention is to ascertain the size of the room for the purpose of planning the furniture layout.

approximate measurement

34. One is also allowed to measure, even with a vessel designed for the purpose, if one does not measure precisely, but puts in a little more or a little less than the exact quantity.

use of scales for weighing

35. Scales should not be used for weighing at all, even if
  a. one does not weigh precisely, but puts on the scales a little more or a little less than the exact weight, or
  b. one does not use weights made for the purpose, but substitutes for them some other item (whose weight one knows or which one intends to weigh after Shabbath).

weighing in one's hand

36. An experienced tradesman is also prohibited from estimating the weight of an item by picking it up in his hand, except in the following situation:
  a. his purpose is not for trading, but for use at home, and
  b. he does not hold weights in his other hand for comparison.

37. *a.* One must not weigh oneself or another person.

b. Similarly, one must not measure a person's height or any of his other dimensions.

c. For the weighing of a baby when one has to know if it has gained after a feed, and how much, see Chapter 37, paragraph 5.

weighing and measuring people

38. *a.* It is permitted to measure and weigh for the purposes of a mitzva.*

b. Consequently,

1) one may measure a drinking cup to make sure it contains a sufficient quantity for making *kiddush*,

2) one may, on the first (or second) evening of Passover, measure or weigh the amount one has to eat to fulfill the mitzva of eating matza, and

3) one may measure the distance of two thousand *amoth* beyond the last house of the town, to ascertain how far one is allowed to walk on Shabbath.

measuring and weighing for a mitzva

39. *a.* It is permitted to measure and weigh for the purposes of a person who is ill.

b. Consequently,

1) one may measure and weigh the quantity of food needed for a sick person who has to eat on Yom Kippur (but see Chapter 39, paragraph 19),

2) one may take a sick person's temperature (and see further Chapter 40, paragraph 2), and

3) one may make use of a stopwatch** or a sandglass for the purposes of a sick person, as where one has to feed him at fixed intervals or measure his pulse. (See also Chapter 28, paragraph 30.)

measuring and weighing for an ill person

*See, however, paragraph 42 below regarding the separation of *challa*.

**A duly qualified halachic authority should be consulted if one wishes to use an electronic watch.

baby food **40.** *a.* One may weigh or measure baby food, if one has to know how much the baby eats.

b. However, if possible, one should estimate the quantity rather than measure it exactly. (See paragraph 34 above.)

measuring spices and flavorings on Yom Tov **41.** *a.* When preparing food on Yom Tov, one may use a marked measuring cup, in order to ascertain the quantities of the various spices and flavorings one is using, provided that

1) the taste of the food would be adversely affected if one were to use inexact quantities **and**
2) one would normally measure these ingredients if preparing the food on another day.

b. Nevertheless, one should not use scales to weigh the ingredients.

measuring flour on Yom Tov **42.** *a.* Flour and other commodities which can be added in approximate quantities without adversely affecting the taste of the food should not be measured or weighed on Yom Tov.

b. One should not measure or weigh flour, even in order to make certain that one is kneading a dough of a quantity sufficient to require the removal of *challa.*

c. In these cases, the amount of the flour or other ingredients should be estimated.

d. 1) It may happen that one has to be precise as to the amount even of commodities such as flour, so as to avoid spoiling the taste of the food.

2) When baking a cake on Yom Tov, this may sometimes be the case.

3) In that event, one may measure these ingredients too, but one should not weigh them on scales.

handling measuring instruments **43.** *a.* All instruments designed for measuring or weighing, such as scales, rulers and tape measures, are *muktzeh.*

b. They may not be moved, except subject to the restrictions applicable to a *k^eli she-m^elachto l^e-issur.* (See Chapter 20, paragraphs 7 to 13.)

WHAT ONE IS FORBIDDEN TO READ* ON SHABBATH AND YOM TOV

44. *a.* One must not read papers connected with one's day-to-day business.

bills, accounts, price labels and timetables

b. Examples are
1) bills of debt,
2) accounts,
3) price labels on goods displayed in a shop window and
4) travel timetables.

c. Bills of debt, accounts and other documents which a person looks after carefully are *muktzeh mei-chamath chesron kis.* (See Chapter 20, paragraphs 19 and 20.)

45. *a.* 1) There is a prohibition against reading even social correspondence on Shabbath or Yom Tov.

letters

2) a) If, however, a letter in this category has reached one on Shabbath or Yom Tov, and one has not yet read it, one is allowed to read it silently (without moving one's lips).

b) This is permitted because the letter may possibly contain information (of a noncommercial nature) which one needs to know that day.

b. One may not read business correspondence and, if one makes a point of looking after such correspondence, it is *muktzeh.* (See paragraph 44c above.)

c. One may read letters containing a discussion of Torah topics, even if they reached one before Shabbath or Yom Tov commenced.

d. See also Chapter 28, paragraph 4, and Chapter 31, paragraphs 21 and 22.

46. *a.* 1) Strictly speaking, it is permissible to read about current events in a newspaper, although

newspapers

2) it is forbidden to read such items as

---

*Reference to reading in the paragraphs which follow includes reading cursorily or merely glancing through material.

a) business news,
b) advertisements containing offers of sale or purchase, or of employment, or
c) a cookery column.

b. The likelihood of one's reading forbidden material is so great, however, that, in general, it is desirable not to read newspapers at all on Shabbath and Yom Tov.

c. Nevertheless, there is nothing wrong with reading newspaper items which deal with Torah topics, so long as one is careful not to read commercial items or other forbidden material.

professional literature and journals and textbooks

47. *a.* Strictly speaking, one may also permit
1) the reading of professional literature and journals which are not of a business nature, and of textbooks, and
2) even visits to educational exhibitions, although

b. a person may not read professional literature and journals dealing with
1) matters of commerce or
2) his own occupation, if its practice is forbidden on Shabbath or Yom Tov (as where an engineer wishes to read literature on the subject of engineering).

general reading

c. As a general rule, it is desirable to refrain from reading any books or journals whose subject matter is not consonant with the spirit of sanctity which should prevail on Shabbath or Yom Tov.

posters

48. *a.* The same considerations apply to the reading of posters and advertisements, which is permissible (although not necessarily desirable) if one takes care not to read commercial items.

b. One should not, however, read obituary notices, since one should not be sad on Shabbath or Yom Tov.

lists

49. *a.* One may not read a list of guests one has invited to a

Shabbath or Yom Tov meal, and the same applies to any other lists one has prepared.

b. Two reasons have been given for this prohibition:
1) There is a fear that one could come to add to the list or delete something from it.
2) The Rabbis were afraid one might come to read papers connected with one's day-to-day business.

50. For the reading of printer's proofs see Chapter 28, paragraph 13.

printer's proofs

SPEAKING ON SHABBATH AND YOM TOV WITH THE OBJECT OF
CONDUCTING EVERYDAY AFFAIRS

51. a. One must not on Shabbath tell another person, even a non-Jew, to do something for one after Shabbath, if
1) it is forbidden to do that thing on Shabbath itself **and**
2) there is no possibility of doing it in a permitted manner on Shabbath.

asking for something to be done after Shabbath: when forbidden

b. Making such a request would amount to pursuing one's business on Shabbath by means of one's words, contrary to the prohibition based on the verses in Isaiah referred to in paragraph 2 above.

c. As mentioned there, and as will become clearer in the ensuing paragraphs, pursuing one's own business is forbidden, but pursuing the business of Heaven is permitted.

52. a. It follows from the contents of the previous paragraph that one must not on Shabbath tell a taxicab driver, even if he is not Jewish, to call at one's house after Shabbath, unless one needs him for the purpose of a mitzva.

hinting that one wants something done after Shabbath

b. One may, however, indirectly intimate to him on Shabbath one's desire that he should present himself when Shabbath ends, for example,

[443]

1) by asking him whether he thinks he would be free to come after Shabbath or
2) by informing him that one would be happy if he were able to come after Shabbath.

asking for something to be done after Shabbath: when permitted

53. *a.* 1) One may tell a non-Jew, or even a Jew, on Shabbath, to bring fruit for one after Shabbath
    a) even from a place that is beyond the limit to which one is permitted to walk, or
    b) even in a place where there is no *eiruv* and one is not allowed to carry things about on Shabbath.

2) The reason for this is that there could be a possibility of one's bringing the fruit oneself on Shabbath in a permissible manner, namely
    a) if the relevant areas were surrounded by a suitable partition or
    b) if there were an *eiruv*.

b. 1) On the other hand, one may not tell a person on Shabbath
    a) to pick fruit for one after Shabbath and bring it to one, even from within the permitted limit to which one can walk, or
    b) to bring one, after Shabbath, fruit which is *muktzeh*.

2) The reason for this is that no means exist whereby one could make it permissible for these acts to be done on Shabbath.

finding a teacher for one's son

54. *a.* 1) One is allowed to look for a teacher for one's son on Shabbath or Yom Tov, whether it be to teach him Torah, a trade, a profession or a subject one thinks will be useful to him in his career.

2) In all these cases one is regarded as performing a mitzva.

b. One may also promise him a fee, as long as one does not specify any sum.

charity

55. *a.* One may, in general, deal with charitable affairs on

Shabbath and Yom Tov, provided one does not transgress any specific prohibition.

b. One may make calculations (orally, but not of course in writing), for the purposes of a mitzva, or for the public need (dealing with public affairs in itself being considered a mitzva—see also paragraph 57 below).

c. Nonetheless, trading, even for the purposes of a mitzva, is forbidden.

d. It is permissible to allocate (but not, of course, to distribute or handle) charity moneys on Shabbath or Yom Tov for poor people or for the performance of a mitzva.

e. Consequently, it is the practice to permit—indeed, in some places, to require—persons called up to the reading of the Torah

1) to promise donations to charity or for the purposes of a mitzva, and

2) even to mention the amount they undertake to contribute.

56. a. 1) a) Whether or not the practice of "selling" the right to perform mitzvoth in the synagogue is permitted on Shabbath or Yom Tov depends on the custom of the place.

      recording charitable donations

b) One ought not to raise any objection where it is done.

2) a) It is, however, preferable, where an alternative exists, to take a strict view with regard to the recording of the sums which the "purchasers" agree to pay.

b) That is to say, it is better not to make use even of cards or slips of paper on which the suggested amounts to be promised were written before Shabbath or Yom Tov.

c) Yet, those who do use such cards or slips have authority upon which they can rely, since they are acting in furtherance of a mitzva.

b. 1) The same considerations apply to appeals in the

synagogue for charitable causes (for instance, when prayers are being said in memory of the dead).

2) It is a common practice to hand each congregant a card bearing his name, so that he can signify which of the amounts noted on the card he wishes to donate,
a) by attaching a paperclip or
b) by folding down an appropriate tab.

public affairs

57. *a.* As far as restrictions on speech on Shabbath or Yom Tov are concerned, the conduct of public affairs is regarded as a mitzva, provided those affairs indeed have to be dealt with that day.

b. It follows that, where there is a need to do so, one may discuss matters of public importance with government officials on Shabbath.

c. One is not allowed to perform any other forbidden act merely on the grounds of public necessity, even if it entails the violation of a Rabbinical (rather than a Torah) prohibition.

d. See also paragraph 55*b* above.

release from and annulment of vows

58. *a.* The verses from Isaiah referred to in paragraph 2 above are also the source of a prohibition against the release from vows on Shabbath or Yom Tov.

b. A person may be released from a vow on Shabbath or Yom Tov only when it is required for Shabbath or the festival or for the purpose of a mitzva.

c. A person may be released in such a case, even if he could have been released before Shabbath or Yom Tov but, for some reason, failed to attend to the matter.

d. 1) The annulment of the vows of a small girl by her father and of a wife by her husband, on the day on which he hears of it, is always permitted.

2) This is because omission by the father or husband to annul on the day on which he hears of the vow precludes subsequent annulment. (See also Chapter 28, paragraph 83.)

SPEAKING ABOUT THINGS ONE IS FORBIDDEN
TO DO ON SHABBATH AND YOM TOV

59. *a.* "And [by not] speaking about [forbidden] matters" — *general* your conversation on Shabbath should not be the *prohibition* same as on other days of the week.

b. As a result, one should not say that, after Shabbath, one is going to do something which is forbidden on Shabbath, even if the prohibition concerned is only Rabbinical.

c. Thus, one may not say on Shabbath,

1) "I am going to drive into town tomorrow,"
2) "I am going to write a letter tomorrow,"
3) "I shall buy those things tomorrow" or
4) "I shall collect those goods from the shop tomorrow" (when the goods in the shop are *muktzeh*).

d. 1) One may speak about an activity forbidden,
    a) **not** by virtue of the laws of Shabbath or Yom Tov in themselves, **but**
    b) by virtue of other considerations pertaining to a particular Shabbath or Yom Tov.

2) One may, thus, say,
    a) on Yom Kippur, "I am going to eat such-and-such a food tomorrow" or
    b) on Passover, "I am going to eat *chametz* tomorrow."

60. *a.* It is proper, when one can, to take a strict approach *speaking* and not to talk on Shabbath about a forbidden act one *about* intends to do after Shabbath, even if the act is to be *perform-* done in the performance of a mitzva. *ance of*
mitzva
b. An exception occurs where there is a particular need to speak about the act on Shabbath, for example

1) when one wishes to ask a friend one happens to see on Shabbath to accompany one in one's car after Shabbath for the purposes of a mitzva, or
2) when one is afraid of being remiss in the

[447]

performance of the mitzva after Shabbath and wishes to stimulate one's enthusiasm by talking about it.

making calculations

61. *a.* It is forbidden to make calculations (aloud) on Shabbath if there is a possibility that the calculations may be of some use to one.

b. There is no prohibition against making a calculation (not in writing, of course) which can be of no practical use.

c. As explained in paragraph 55 above, one may also make verbal calculations for the purposes of a mitzva.

when permitted to discuss prices

62. One may talk about the price of an article one has bought (except in the circumstances mentioned in paragraph 63 below),

a. when one has already paid for it or

b. even when one has not yet paid for it, if the price is fixed and does not require calculation.

when forbidden to discuss prices

63. *a.* One should not tell another person that one has bought a particular item in a certain shop, or that one has paid a particular amount for it, if one in fact intends the information to be of practical benefit.

b. This could be the case when the person to whom one is speaking is himself thinking of purchasing an article of that kind.

idle talk and worse

64. *a.* One ought to refrain on Shabbath from too much idle, useless talk.

b. It goes without saying that one must not discuss distressing subjects, nor engage in conversation which is in any event forbidden, for example, by making false or defamatory statements.

thought

65. *a.* "And [by not] speaking about [forbidden] matters" — speech is forbidden, whereas thought is permitted.

b. As a result, a person may say on Shabbath that he will go to a particular place on the following day, even if he has in mind to travel there by car.

c. Thinking about one's business on Shabbath is not, as such, forbidden, but

1) this does not extend to the perusal of one's accounts and

2) thoughts of this kind are inhibited by other considerations.

d. 1) Thus, if thinking about one's business will result in a feeling of anxiety or in a sensation of uneasiness, it is forbidden.

2) Worry is inconsistent with the rest for which we pray in the Shabbath afternoon service, "a rest of peace, of calm, of tranquillity and of security, a perfect rest such as You desire."

3) In the Grace after Meals we also pray "that there should be no trouble, grief or sighing on the day of our rest."

e. 1) What is more, it is inherent in one's obligation to enjoy Shabbath that one should not give a thought to one's business, but should rest as if all one's work were done.

2) This is how one should understand the verse in Exodus 20:9, "You should labor for six days and do all your work" — a person cannot always complete all of his work in six days, but, when Shabbath arrives, he should have the same peace of mind as if he had completed everything he had to do.

66. *a.* 1) A person may say, "I am going to such-and-such a place tomorrow," even if the place is beyond the limit to which it is permissible to walk on Shabbath, or even if it is overseas. *forbidden activities one may talk about*

2) a) The reason for this is that the act of going (by foot) is not in itself a forbidden activity;

b) if the houses of the town reached to within two thousand *amoth* of the place to which one wants to go, one would be able to walk there on Shabbath.

3) Similar considerations apply to saying that one wishes, after Shabbath, to bring something from a place where there is no *eiruv*.

4) See also paragraph 11 above.

sanctity in speech and thought

b. 1) The ideal is to have the holiness of the Shabbath so close at heart that one only talks about Torah topics and things one needs.

2) "He rested on the seventh day" (Genesis 2:2). From what did He rest? Every day He had said, "Let such and such happen!" and it was so. Shabbath arrived and all the works of creation were complete. He stopped speaking. He rested from speech. So should we rest from workaday speech, if we wish the sanctity of the Shabbath to permeate us through and through.

3) The Talmud (Yerushalmi Shabbath, Chapter 15, Halacha 3, Bavli Shabbath 150b) tells of a righteous man who went for a stroll in his field on Shabbath and, seeing a break in the fence, thought to himself that he would fill in the gap when Shabbath was over. Aftewards, he said, "Since I thought about it on Shabbath, I shall forever refrain from repairing it." What did the Almighty do for him? He caused a tree to grow in the gap, and from that tree the righteous man derived his and his family's livelihood for the rest of his days.

Chapter 30

General Rules Relating to Actions Performed by a Non-Jew on Shabbath and Yom Tov

1. *a.* It is prohibited, both on Shabbath and on Yom Tov, to tell a non-Jew to perform an act for a Jew which a Jew is himself forbidden to perform. *telling a non-Jew to perform a forbidden act*
   b. It does not matter whether the act
      1) is forbidden by the Torah itself or
      2) is the subject of a Rabbinical prohibition.
   c. It is prohibited not only
      1) to tell a non-Jew on Shabbath or Yom Tov to perform the act on Shabbath or Yom Tov, but also
      2) to tell him on an ordinary weekday to perform the act on Shabbath or Yom Tov, or
      3) to tell him on Shabbath or Yom Tov to perform the act after Shabbath or Yom Tov.
   d. Exceptions to the rule are detailed in this chapter and the next.

2. *a.* In addition, one must not hint to a non-Jew that he should, on Shabbath or Yom Tov, perform a forbidden act for a Jew if *hinting to a non-Jew that he should perform a forbidden act*
      1) the hint is given on Shabbath or Yom Tov **and**
      2) the hint is conveyed by means of expressions or motions which directly indicate to the non-Jew that he should perform the act.
   b. One may, however, hint to him in this way (that is to say, directly)
      1) before Shabbath or Yom Tov that he should perform the act on Shabbath or Yom Tov, or
      2) on Shabbath or Yom Tov that he should perform the act after Shabbath or Yom Tov.

    c. 1) Furthermore, one may hint to a non-Jew, even on Shabbath or Yom Tov, that he should perform the forbidden act on Shabbath or Yom Tov, if one does not use expressions or motions which directly indicate to him what he should do.

    2) One should merely describe the situation to him so that he puts two and two together, understands that the act has to be done and does it of his own accord.

    d. Illustrations of the above may be found in paragraphs 5 to 10 below.

    e. The use of polite language does not turn a statement into a hint; thus, requesting or asking a non-Jew to do something is equivalent to telling him to do it.

benefiting from the act of a non-Jew

    3. *a.* 1) Although there are circumstances in which it is permissible to hint to a non-Jew that he should perform a forbidden activity on Shabbath or Yom Tov (as explained in paragraph 2 above),

    2) there may still be a prohibition against deriving a benefit from that activity on Shabbath or Yom Tov.

    b. Indeed, even if a non-Jew of his own accord performs a forbidden act for a Jew on Shabbath or Yom Tov, it may be prohibited for a Jew to derive from it anything other than an indirect or non-substantive benefit.

    c. See paragraphs 35 to 61 below for further details on this subject, including information as to when a benefit is considered to be direct and substantive.

two prohibitions summarized

    4. *a.* It follows that there are two prohibitions involved in the performance of forbidden activities by non-Jews on Shabbath or Yom Tov:

    1) a prohibition against telling a non-Jew to perform a forbidden act on Shabbath or Yom Tov (even if no benefit is derived from the act by a Jew);

    2) a prohibition against deriving a direct, substantive benefit from a forbidden act performed by a non-Jew on Shabbath or Yom Tov (even if the non-Jew

has not been told by a Jew to perform the act on Shabbath or Yom Tov, but has performed it for a Jew of his own volition).

b. The rules relating to these prohibitions are elucidated by the examples in paragraphs 5 to 10 below.

5. *a.* 1) One may say to a non-Jew on Shabbath, "It is difficult to sleep with the light on," so that he understands himself that he should turn it off. *turning off the light*

2) All one has done is to describe to him the circumstances which make it necessary for the act to be done.

b. 1) One may not say to a non-Jew on Shabbath, "Why didn't you turn off my light last Shabbath?" so that he understands that he should turn it off now.

2) The mention of the forbidden act itself (albeit in relation to the past) gives the language a peremptory tone more in the nature of a request than of an indirect hint.

6. *a.* 1) One may say to a non-Jew on Shabbath, "What a pity all that gas is being wasted," so that he understands himself that he should turn it off. *turning off the gas*

2) Once again, one has merely told him of the situation which makes it desirable to turn off the gas.

b. 1) One may not, however, say to him, "Whoever turns off the gas won't lose by it," so that he understands that he is to turn it off.

2) Here again, the mention of the forbidden act imparts to the hint a directness more in the nature of a request.

7. *a.* 1) Likewise, if there is light in the room, but not enough to make reading easy and comfortable, one may say to a non-Jew, *turning on the light*

    a) "I can't read, because there isn't enough light," or

       b) "It's rather dark, because there's only one light on,"

so that he understands himself that he should switch on an additional light.

2) Here too one is merely stating facts from which it is apparent that the act of turning on the light needs to be performed.

3) a) One is allowed to derive from the additional light the same kind of benefit as one could have derived in that place (albeit with difficulty) from the original light, and this one may do for as long as the original light continues to burn.

       b) The mere improvement in one's convenience of reading is not so substantial a benefit as to fall within the prohibition referred to in paragraph 3 above.

b. 1) On the other hand, one may not say to a non-Jew, on Shabbath, "Do me a favor. There's not enough light in the room."

2) By using this turn of phrase, one is plainly just telling the non-Jew what to do.

3) Nevertheless, prior to the commencement of Shabbath, one may indicate to the non-Jew, even by means of so thinly veiled a hint, that he should do the forbidden act on Shabbath.

c. 1) When there is no light whatsoever in the room, there is a prohibition against benefiting from a light turned on by a non-Jew.

2) There is a prohibition even if the non-Jew turned on the light for a Jew of his own volition, without receiving any hint to do so.

3) For the extent to which the circumstances affect the prohibition see paragraphs 37 and 38 below.

4) Benefit derived from the turning on of a light by a non-Jew where previously there was no light whatsoever is both direct and substantive, since, without any light, one could not see at all.

5) This type of benefit is not allowed, even where a

mitzva is concerned, as where the switching on of the light enables one to study Torah or to pray.

8. *a.* One may say to a non-Jew on Shabbath, "I have no toilet paper," so that he realizes himself that one wishes him to tear sheets off the roll.

   b. Here again he is merely being told a fact from which he can deduce the necessity for the performance of the forbidden act.

tearing toilet paper

9. *a.* One may say to a non-Jew on Shabbath, "Why didn't you call for me with your car last week, after Shabbath?" so that he understands that one wishes him to call for one after the current Shabbath.

   b. Since the act is to be performed after Shabbath, one is permitted to hint in language of a peremptory character.

calling with a car after Shabbath

10. *a.* One may say to a non-Jew, before Shabbath begins, "Why didn't you want to open my mail last Shabbath?" so that he understands that he is to open one's mail on the Shabbath which is just about to start. (See, however, Chapter 29, paragraph 45.)

   b. Peremptory language is permitted because the hint is being given before Shabbath commences.

   c. One must not express oneself in this manner on Shabbath.

   d. See further Chapter 31, paragraph 22.

opening letters

ACTS PERFORMED BY A NON-JEW FOR AN ILL PERSON
OR TO SAVE SACRED WRITINGS OR
TO PREVENT SERIOUS LOSS

11. *a.* Generally, one may tell a non-Jew on Shabbath to do something which is required in the treatment of a person who is ill,

    1) even if it involves an activity prohibited by the

illness and health risks

Torah (as distinct from a Rabbinical prohibition) **and**

2) even if the person in question is not seriously ill. (See definition in Chapter 33, paragraph 1.)

b. For further details, see paragraph 43 below and Chapter 38, paragraphs 4 to 13.

c. It follows that one may tell a non-Jew on Shabbath to put on a light so that one can see to the needs of a person who is ill, even if that person is not seriously ill. (See also paragraph 44 below.)

d. Similarly, one may tell him to put out a light so that the sick person can sleep.

e. Furthermore, one may tell the non-Jew to drive to town and buy medicine for someone who is ill in bed (or any other person who is ill enough to fit the definition in Chapter 33, paragraph 1).

f. 1) A person who is suffering from the cold is placed in the same category as someone who is ill.

2) Consequently, in cold countries, when one is troubled by the cold, or where there are small children in the house, one may tell a non-Jew to turn on the heating.

3) See further Chapter 23, paragraph 24.

g. 1) On a very hot summer's day, one is allowed to tell a non-Jew to turn on a fan or the air-conditioning, in order to alleviate the discomfort of a person who is suffering from the difficult weather conditions.

2) See also Chapter 13, paragraphs 34 and 35.

h. If the weather changes on Shabbath and the cold air produced by the continued operation of the air-conditioning is liable to be injurious to one's health, one may tell a non-Jew to switch off the system.

sacred writings   **12.** *a.* One may tell a non-Jew on Shabbath to save sacred writings from being destroyed, even if, in so doing, he will have to perform an act prohibited by the Torah.

b. It follows that one may tell him to put out a fire in order to save sacred writings, even when there is no danger to life.

c. *Sifrei Torah*, the Pentateuch, the Prophets, the Talmud, halachic works, prayer books and other Torah-study books, as well as extracts from them and commentaries, are all considered to be sacred writings.

d. From this stems the practice of telling a non-Jew to put out a fire, even where there is no danger to life, in order to save the *mezuzoth* fixed to the doorposts (it being forbidden for a Jew to remove the *mezuzoth* from the doorposts on Shabbath).

e. It is also the practice to tell a non-Jew to put out the candles in the synagogue after the Friday night service, for fear of there being a fire which could destroy the sacred writings kept there.

f. A person who finds sacred writings in *reshuth ha-rabbim* on Shabbath, and is apprehensive that they may be destroyed or damaged if left where they are, may tell a non-Jew to bring them to his house.

13. a. 1) One is allowed to hint to a non-Jew that he should carry out some action to prevent a serious loss of property. *preventing serious loss*

2) This is permitted
   a) even if one employs an expression which directly indicates what is to be done and
   b) even when the act involved is forbidden by the Torah (and not only by a Rabbinical prohibition).

3) The reason why hinting to a non-Jew in this way was permitted by the Rabbis in such a case is that
   a) people tend to lose their composure when suddenly faced with the prospect of serious financial damage and,
   b) if not allowed a practical alternative, they might themselves come to perform an action

which is prohibited by the Torah, in an effort to save their property.

b. Consequently, when there is a fire, one may say to a non-Jew,

1) "Whoever puts out the fire won't lose by it," or,

2) in a place where the firemen are not Jewish, "Whoever calls the fire department won't lose by it."

(See also Chapter 41, paragraph 14.)

c. If a freshly poured concrete roof will not harden properly and will be ruined in the event that it is not watered on Shabbath, one may say to a non-Jew, "Whoever waters the concrete won't lose by it." (See also Chapter 23, paragraph 43.)

TELLING A NON-JEW TO DO AN ACT WHICH IS FORBIDDEN
BY A RABBINICAL PROHIBITION

when
permitted

14. a. As mentioned in paragraph 1 above, it is generally forbidden to tell a non-Jew to perform a prohibited act for a Jew.

b. In the following cases, however, one may directly tell a non-Jew (and not merely hint to him) on Shabbath to perform an activity which is forbidden by a Rabbinical prohibition (but not by the Torah itself):

1) for a person who is slightly ill (as explained in Chapter 38, paragraphs 14 to 16);

2) to avoid serious loss;

3) in a case of great need;

4) for the purpose of a mitzva;

5) in honor of unexpected guests;

6) (in some, but not in all, cases) where a change in one of the circumstances would make it permissible for a Jew to perform the same activity.

c. It is important to take note of the contents of paragraph 62 below.

d. The illustrations in paragraphs 15 to 21 below elucidate the application of the above rules in specific
instances.

15. *a.* One may tell a non-Jew to save movable property from
a fire,

saving
property

  1) even if the property includes items which are *muk-*   *from a fire*
  tzeh **and**
  2) even if the property will have to be taken through a
  place where there is no *eiruv* (and carrying objects
  about is forbidden), as long as that place is not
  actually a *r^eshuth ha-rabbim*, as defined in Chapter 17, paragraph 3.

  b. One may not tell him to extinguish the fire where

  1) there is clearly no danger to human life,
  2) there are not three or more people in the vicinity
  who may be exposed to the risk of bodily injury **and**
  3) there are no *mezuzoth* or other sacred writings
  which are liable to be burned.

16. *a.* One may tell a non-Jew to bring

bringing
food

  1) food that is essential for a Shabbath meal (or for
  any other meal which it is a mitzva to eat) or
  2) hot food prepared for a Shabbath meal,
  even through a place where there is no *eiruv*, so long as
  he will not have to take it through an actual *r^eshuth
  ha-rabbim*, as defined in Chapter 17, paragraph 3.

  b. When there is no *eiruv*, however, one should not put
the food into, or take it out of, the non-Jew's hand, but
should ask him to pick it up and put it down himself.

17. *a.* 1) A Jew may tell a non-Jew on Shabbath to bring a

taking a
prayer book
to the
synagogue

  prayer book to the synagogue, even in a place
  where there is no *eiruv*, so long as he will not have
  to carry it through an actual *r^eshuth ha-rabbim*, as
  defined in Chapter 17, paragraph 3.
  2) The non-Jew must, however, take the prayer book
  by himself, without the Jew's putting it into his

hand, and, in the synagogue, the Jew must not take
it from the non-Jew's hand, but the non-Jew should
put it down by himself.

removing   *b.* 1) A problem can arise if a Jew finds *chametz* in his
chametz   house on the Yom Tov of Pesach, on Shabbath
               occurring during Pesach or on Shabbath occurring
               on the day before Pesach.

         2) Despite the fact that the *chametz* is *muktzeh* and
            the Jew may not handle it himself, he may ask a
            non-Jew
            a) to remove it from the house (unless there is an
               actual *r*^e*shuth ha-rabbim* outside) or
            b) to dispose of it in the toilet bowl or in the sea.

winding a   18. *a.* One is allowed to ask a non-Jew to wind up a watch
watch   which is still going, if one needs it for a mitzva.

         b. An example would be if one needed to know when to go
             to a Torah study session or to prayers.

         c. See also Chapter 28, paragraph 21.

putting a   19. *a.* One is permitted to tell a non-Jew to move a *k*^e*li she-*
k^e*li she-*   *m*^e*lachto l*^e*-issur*, such as a hammer, even if one's
m^e*lachto*   purpose is only to prevent its being spoiled or stolen.
l^e*-issur in a*
safe place   *b.* The reason here is as mentioned in paragraph 14*b*6
             above, namely that the Jew himself would be able to
             move it, if he needed to use it for a permitted purpose or
             if he wished to make use of the place which it occupies.
             (See Chapter 20, paragraph 7.)

taking   20. *a.* 1) One may tell a non-Jew that he should remove the
candle-   candlesticks from the table once the candles go out,
sticks off the   so long as one needs to use the space which they
table   occupy.

             2) This is because a Jew may move the candlesticks
                himself for this purpose, if he does so by means of
                another article held in his hands. (See Chapter 22,
                paragraph 35.)

b. If one has stipulated, before Shabbath, that the non-Jew should remove the candlesticks, or if it is the custom of the place for a non-Jew to remove them, one may request him to do so even when one does not need the space they occupy.*

c. See Chapter 20, paragraphs 59 to 61, for the rules applicable to a table or a cloth on which burning candles were standing when Shabbath commenced.

21. It is permissible to ask a non-Jew to transfer a burning candle from one room to another, if it is required for the purpose of a mitzva or in honor of unexpected guests.

moving burning candles

SAVING THE PUBLIC FROM UNWITTING TRANSGRESSION

22. *a.* One is allowed to request a non-Jew on Shabbath to do something which involves a Torah prohibition, if
   1) it will save the public from an unwitting transgression and
   2) the non-Jew could not achieve that object by doing something which involves only a Rabbinical prohibition.

   repairing wire of eiruv

   b. 1) a) One is therefore allowed to tell a non-Jew to repair the torn wire of an *eiruv* (as explained in Chapter 17, paragraph 25) by tying it together with a double knot.
      b) If, however, it is possible for the non-Jew to repair the wire by means of a bow tied over a single knot, then that is the preferred course.
   2) It makes no difference whether the wire was torn on Shabbath or whether it was torn before Shabbath but not repaired in time.

---

*This ruling is based on giving due weight to an opinion (not generally accepted in practice) which goes even further and permits one to remove the candlesticks oneself in these circumstances.

PROHIBITED ACTS PERFORMED IN THE COURSE
OF PERMITTED ACTIVITY

the
principle

23. *a.* 1) One may ask a non-Jew on Shabbath to perform an activity which a Jew is also permitted to perform, even if one knows that the non-Jew will, to that end, do an act which involves a Torah prohibition, but
2) one should not ask such a thing of a non-Jew if one also intends immediately to benefit from, and make use of, the prohibited act oneself, and the non-Jew knows this.

washing
dishes

b. 1) It is, therefore, permitted to tell a non-Jew to wash dishes for a Jew, even if one knows that, in order to wash the dishes, the non-Jew will
a) turn on the light and heat water or
b) operate a dishwasher.
2) One should not, however, ask this of a non-Jew if one's intention is to wash the dishes together with him, once he has turned on the light and heated the water for the purpose.
3) Nevertheless, if the non-Jew has begun washing the dishes by himself,
a) one may help him by the light of the lamp which he has switched on, although
b) one should not wash the dishes in the water the non-Jew has heated on Shabbath. (See paragraph 48 below.)

bringing
something
from a dark
room

c. 1) One may ask a non-Jew to bring something from a dark room, knowing that he will have to turn on the light in order to find the required object.
2) Yet, one should not ask a non-Jew to come with one, if, in so doing, the non-Jew will have to turn on the light.
3) This is because
a) the direct and immediate benefit derived from the light by the Jew, coupled with
b) the fact that the non-Jew is coming for the purposes of the Jew,

[462]

makes it clear that the non-Jew is in reality turning
on the light for his Jewish companion.

THE PERIOD BEFORE THE STARS COME OUT ON FRIDAY NIGHT

24. *a.* During the period between sunset and the time when   *when*
the stars come out on Friday night, one may tell a   *assistance*
non-Jew to perform a prohibited act, if indeed   *of non-Jew*
1) its performance is a matter of importance,   *may be*
2) it is required for Shabbath **or**   *requested*
3) it is done for the purpose of a mitzva.
  b. Consequently, one may, during this period of time, ask
a non-Jew
1) to switch on a light for Shabbath, for example, in
the room where one is going to eat a Shabbath
meal, or even in a bedroom, or
2) to put on a memorial light.

ORDERING WORK FROM A NON-JEW BEFORE SHABBATH

25. *a.* 1) It is forbidden to order work from a non-Jew, even   *the rule*
at the beginning of the week, if, due to the shortage
of time at his disposal for completing the work, he
will be compelled to perform it on Shabbath.
    2) In this connection, it makes no difference whether
the performance of the work involves the violation
of a Torah prohibition or of a Rabbinical prohibition.
  b. 1) One may order work from a non-Jew, even on Friday, as long as one does not lay down a time limit
for completion which would compel him to work on
Shabbath.
    2) If, nonetheless, the non-Jew wishes to work on
Shabbath, this need not concern one (except to the
extent mentioned in paragraph 36 below), subject
to two conditions:
      a) the non-Jew's motivation must be self-interest
(as particularized below);

   b) the non-Jew must not do the work on the Jew's premises, and indeed any items requiring to have work done to them must be removed from the Jew's premises before Shabbath commences.

  3) The non-Jew's motivation is presumed to be self-interest when
   a) the Jew has told him how much his remuneration will be,
   b) a standard charge is payable,
   c) the Jew has promised to reach an understanding with him on the amount of his fee or
   d) the non-Jew, on his own initiative,* volunteers his unsolicited services without charge.

shoe repairs and laundry

26. Hence, one may ask a non-Jew, just before Shabbath, to repair one's shoes or to wash one's laundry, but

 a. one must not require the shoes or the laundry to be ready immediately upon the termination of Shabbath **and**

 b. the shoes or the washing must be removed from one's house before Shabbath begins.

repairs to electricity network

27. *a.* On the other hand, a Jew is not allowed to ask a non-Jew to repair his domestic electricity supply, if the non-Jew will do any of the work on Shabbath.

 b. The reason for this is that the non-Jew will be doing the work in the Jew's house.

 c. It makes no difference whether the Jew speaks to the non-Jew on Shabbath or prior to Shabbath.

 d. The fact that the non-Jew's object in working on Shabbath is to receive payment for the repair does not affect the issue.

 e. For telegrams and express letters, see Chapter 31, paragraph 20.

---

*The assumption is that the non-Jew's initiative is motivated by a desire to free himself of a debt of gratitude which he owes the Jew for past favors.

PREVENTING SUFFERING OF ANIMALS

28. *a.* 1) One may tell a non-Jew on Shabbath to milk one's cows, to save them the suffering they would be caused if they were not milked for a whole day. *telling non-Jew to milk cows*

    2) Nonetheless, one should try, as far as possible, to milk before and after Shabbath, in order to minimize the extent to which one avails oneself of the services of a non-Jew to milk on Shabbath.

    3) For the restrictions on using and handling milk extracted on Shabbath, which is *muktzeh*, see Chapter 27, paragraph 46, Chapter 33, paragraph 6 and Chapter 37, paragraph 3.

  b. A Jew may be present while the non-Jew is milking, to ensure that he does not take any of the milk for himself, but the Jew may not speak to the non-Jew about such matters as remuneration. *presence of Jew when non-Jew milks*

  c. When a non-Jew milks a Jew's cow on Shabbath, he may also clean its teats with a wet cloth, as one would do on any other day, but one must be careful how one intimates to the non-Jew one's wish that he should clean the teats. *cleaning a cow's teats*

    1) One should hint to the non-Jew of the need to clean the teats, by merely describing the situation to him, as explained in paragraph 2*c* above, saying, for example, "This milk won't be any good if the teats of the animal aren't cleaned before milking."

    2) a) Alternatively, one should tell the non-Jew to clean the animal's teats in a way which is permissible for a Jew, as particularized in Chapter 27, paragraph 49.

       b) If the non-Jew nevertheless proceeds to clean them in the usual (forbidden) way, that is not one's concern.

  d. 1) In agricultural settlements where it is the task of a non-Jew on Shabbath to put the milk of the individual farmers into a centralized cold store, he may *centralized storage of milk*

also measure and strain the quantity of milk supplied by each farmer.

2) For a Jew expressly to tell him to do so, even before
the beginning of Shabbath, is forbidden.

3) Yet, one may give him an appropriate hint, before
Shabbath, even in language which directly indicates to him what he should do. (See paragraph 2*a*
and *b* above.)

REMUNERATING A NON-JEW FOR TROUBLE TAKEN BY HIM ON SHABBATH

payment of money **29.** *a.* 1) After Shabbath, one may pay a non-Jew for a service one was allowed to have performed by him on
Shabbath, but

2) one must not give him money on Shabbath itself,
and

3) even to indicate to him where the money is, so that
he can take it himself, is forbidden.

reward other than money *b.* 1) A reward other than money, such as a slice of cake,
may be given to the non-Jew even on Shabbath.

2) It is of no concern to one that the non-Jew subsequently takes the piece of cake out into the street, in
a place where there is no *eiruv* and carrying objects
about is prohibited.

3) However, where this is likely to happen, it is better
not to hand the cake directly to the non-Jew, but to
put it down in front of him, letting him take it by
himself.

HIRING A NON-JEW TO PERFORM A PERMITTED ACTIVITY

hiring and discussing remunera- tion **30.** *a.* One may hire a non-Jew before Shabbath to perform
on Shabbath an activity which a Jew would be
allowed to perform, such as washing dishes.

b. It is forbidden to discuss the non-Jew's remuneration
with him on Shabbath.

c. On Shabbath itself, one must not hire a non-Jew

1) even to perform an activity of this type and

2) even without determining his remuneration.

WORK PERFORMED FOR A JEW

31. *a.* A non-Jewish domestic who works in the house of a *non-Jewish* Jew is not allowed to perform for him on Shabbath any *domestics* activity which the Jew himself is forbidden to perform, for example, darning socks,

1) even if she does it inside her own room **and**

2) even if the Jew does not tell her to do it specifically on Shabbath but benefits from the fact that she is freeing herself to do his other work in the week which follows.

b. She may perform the forbidden activity on Shabbath,

1) if the terms of her employment stipulate a specified number of hours and her purpose in working on Shabbath is to make more free time for herself on weekdays,

2) so long as the Jew has not required her to finish the work on Shabbath (as in paragraph 25 above), **and**

3) provided she does not work outside her own room* (as in paragraph 25 above).

c. See also Chapter 31, paragraph 9.

32. *a.* A Jew is obliged to protest if a non-Jew comes to his *objecting to* house to perform for him there, on Shabbath, an activ- *activity per-* ity which a Jew is not allowed to perform. *formed in a*

b. This is so, even if one does not have in mind to benefit *Jew's house* from the non-Jew's act on Shabbath itself.

c. The reason is that people would be led to suspect that one told the non-Jew to carry out the work on Shabbath.

d. See further paragraph 38 below.

---

*Work done in her own room is not considered to be done in the Jew's house.

TELLING A NON-JEW TO PERFORM
PROHIBITED ACTIVITIES FOR HIMSELF

activities
performed
with the
non-Jew's
property

33. *a.* One may tell a non-Jew to perform an act which is prohibited even by the Torah, if

1) the materials or objects used in the performance of the act belong to the non-Jew **and**

2) the non-Jew performs the act for his own needs.

b. One may, thus, tell a non-Jewish domestic to repair her stockings on Shabbath, even if one's intention in so doing is that she should be free to do one's work when Shabbath terminates.

c. 1) One may also tell her to cook something for herself, provided the basic ingredients she has to use are hers.

2) It does not matter if she uses one's appliances or implements, such as one's matches or stove, so long as one does not expressly tell her to use them.

d. 1) Although, in the circumstances mentioned in paragraph 15*b* above, one may not tell a non-Jew to extinguish a fire in one's house,

2) one may tell him to put out a fire in his (the non-Jew's) house, or in that of another non-Jew, even if one's intention in so doing is to avoid the fire's spreading to one's own house and damaging property there.

activities
performed
with the
Jew's
property

34. *a.* A Jew is generally forbidden to tell a non-Jew to perform a prohibited activity on Shabbath with an article or item which belongs to the Jew,

1) even if he tells him before Shabbath,

2) even if the activity is the subject only of a Rabbinical prohibition,

3) even if the non-Jew performs the activity for his own purposes **and**

4) even if the Jew transfers the ownership of the article or item to the non-Jew with all due formality.

b. A Jew must not, therefore, tell a non-Jew, whether

before or during Shabbath, to use his (the Jew's) car on Shabbath, even if the journey is for the purposes of the non-Jew.

c. 1) One may, however, lend a non-Jew money prior to Shabbath so that he can buy things for himself with it on Shabbath.

2) One may even promise the non-Jew that, after Shabbath, one will buy from him what he has bought and reward him for his trouble.

BENEFITING FROM A FORBIDDEN ACTIVITY PERFORMED BY A NON-JEW
ON SHABBATH OR YOM TOV: THE GENERAL RULE

35. a. As stated in paragraph 3 above, there is a Rabbinical prohibition *nature of prohibition*

1) not only against telling a non-Jew to do a forbidden act on Shabbath, but also

2) against benefiting from a forbidden act performed by a non-Jew in specified circumstances.

b. The reason given for the additional prohibition is that, if one were permitted to benefit from the non-Jew's act, one might come to tell him to do it on Shabbath or Yom Tov.

c. The type of benefit which is prohibited is,

1) in the case of food, eating it and,

2) in the case of something inedible, putting it to its normal use.

d. The rules governing the application of the prohibition vary from situation to situation, as will be explained in the remaining paragraphs of this chapter.

BENEFITING FROM A TORAH PROHIBITION
PERFORMED BY A NON-JEW FOR A JEW

36. a. A Jew is, as a rule, forbidden to derive a direct, sub- *when* stantive benefit on Shabbath or Yom Tov from the *forbidden* performance by a non-Jew for a Jew, on Shabbath or

Yom Tov, of an act which is the subject of a Torah prohibition.

  b. To be forbidden, the benefit must, in general, be both

   1) direct, that is to say, obtained from the actual thing made or produced in contravention of the prohibition, or from something with which the prohibited act is performed, **and**

   2) substantive, that is to say, of a kind which would not have been enjoyed (even to a lesser degree) without performance of the prohibited act.

  c. Even after Shabbath or Yom Tov, the benefit remains forbidden, until such time has passed since the termination of Shabbath or Yom Tov as would suffice for the performance of the prohibited act.

  d. Paragraphs 37 to 42 below contain examples to elucidate the detailed application of these rules.

  e. Regarding Rabbinical prohibitions, see paragraphs 59 to 62 below.

turning on a light 37. a. In general, no Jew is allowed to derive a direct, substantive benefit on Shabbath from a light which a non-Jew has turned on for a Jew on Shabbath,

   1) even if the non-Jew turned the light on of his own volition, without so much as the slightest hint from a Jew,

   2) even if the Jew who desires to use the light is not the Jew for whom it was turned on **and**

   3) even if the intention of the Jew is to use the light for the purpose of performing a mitzva, as where it enables him to pray or to study Torah.

  b. Whether and how the prohibition applies depends on the circumstances in which the light was turned on, as is explained in the following paragraph.

reaction when non-Jew turns on light 38. a. If a Jew has told a non-Jew (either expressly or by a direct hint, as in paragraph 2a above) to turn on the light in a dark room, the prohibition against benefiting from the light is so stringent as to require the Jew to leave the room.

b. 1) If the Jew sees that the non-Jew wants to turn the light on for him

    a) of his own accord, without having been told to do so,

    b) in circumstances where the Jew will derive a direct, substantive benefit from the non-Jew's action,

he must protest, even to the extent of driving him out of the house.

2) Where the Jew has, nevertheless, failed to protest,

    a) he may stay in the room, in order to do something which he would have done even without the light turned on by the non-Jew, such as hold a conversation, but

    b) he must not do something which he would not have done without the non-Jew's light, such as read or eat a meal (if indeed he would not have done so otherwise).

c. If the non-Jew turns on the light against the Jew's will, and despite his genuine protest, the Jew may benefit from it in the normal way, since the non-Jew is regarded as having put the light on for his own purposes.

d. For the situation where there was already light in the room, see paragraphs 7a above and 58b below.

39. a. Food cooked by a non-Jew for a Jew on Shabbath may not, as a rule, be eaten by any Jew on the Shabbath, not even by a Jew other than the one for whom it was prepared. *food cooked by a non-Jew*

b. The cooked food itself is often *muktzeh* and in that case should not be handled. (See Chapter 32, paragraph 79.)

c. Before eating the food after Shabbath, one has to wait for a period of time which would suffice to cook food of the same kind.

d. It should be noted that there is a general prohibition against eating food cooked by a non-Jew, but this is not the place to discuss its scope and a duly qualified halachic authority should be consulted as to its applicability in any given situation.

shoe repairs 40. a. A Jew may not wear shoes which he knows were repaired for him on Shabbath by a non-Jew, until he waits such a period of time after Shabbath as would suffice for repairing them.

b. This is so even if the shoes were delivered to the non-Jew before Shabbath, in a permissible manner, as described in paragraph 26 above.

cleaning shoes 41. A Jew who wrongfully tells a non-Jew to polish his shoes on Shabbath is not allowed to wear them until the elapse of such a period of time after Shabbath as would suffice for polishing them. (Compare paragraph 38a above and contrast paragraph 58a below.)

bringing food through r^eshuth ha-rabbim 42. a. No Jew is allowed on Shabbath to eat food which a non-Jew has brought on Shabbath, for a Jew, through an actual *r^eshuth ha-rabbim*, as defined in Chapter 17, paragraph 3 (despite the fact that, even without the non-Jew's action, the Jew could have eaten the food — by going to the place from which the non-Jew brought it).*

b. 1) After Shabbath, however, it is not necessary to wait, and one may eat the food immediately.

2) The reason for this is that the benefit derived from the non-Jew's action is not all that different from the benefit one could have enjoyed on Shabbath by going to the place from where the non-Jew brought the food and eating it there.

---

*In certain circumstances, it may be otherwise if the non-Jew brings the food because he is a paid deliveryman. (See Chapter 31, paragraph 23, and compare paragraph 11g there.)

c. See Chapter 31, paragraph 7, for the lighting by a non-Jew of a heater on which there is food that will be warmed up.

BENEFITING FROM A FORBIDDEN ACT PERFORMED BY A NON-JEW FOR AN ILL PERSON

43. a. 1) Anyone may derive a benefit, even on Shabbath, *the rule* from a forbidden act performed by a non-Jew on Shabbath for a person who is ill, provided that
  a) (if the act in question is the subject of a Torah prohibition) there are no grounds for fearing* that, in order to serve the needs of the healthy person, the non-Jew has done or will do more than he would otherwise do, **and**
  b) the product of the non-Jew's act is not *muktzeh*.
  2) This applies even if the person for whom the act is performed is not seriously ill (as in paragraph 11 above).
  b. If the conditions set out in *a* above are not met,
  1) a healthy person is not allowed to benefit from the non-Jew's act on Shabbath, but
  2) he may benefit from it immediately after Shabbath ends and need not wait until the passage of such time as would suffice for its performance.

44. a. 1) Therefore, a light turned on by a non-Jew for a *examples* person who is ill (including a person who is not seriously ill) may also be used by a healthy person.
  2) The reason is that the same light can serve one individual or a crowd of a hundred people, and there is no reason for the non-Jew to turn on additional lights.
  b. 1) On the other hand, a healthy person is not permitted to benefit until after Shabbath from food which

---

*This is the case when the result of the act performed by the non-Jew for the ill person can, of its very nature, serve also the needs of others, without any addition on his part.

a non-Jew has cooked on Shabbath for a person who is ill.

2) Here there are grounds for fearing that the non-Jew has cooked, or will cook, more, in order to serve the needs of the healthy person.

3) Furthermore, the food cooked by the non-Jew may be *muktzeh*. (See Chapter 32, paragraph 79.)

4) See Chapter 38, paragraph 11, regarding the use of food left over after Shabbath and of the utensils in which the non-Jew did the cooking.

c. Fruit picked by a non-Jew on Shabbath for a sick person is *muktzeh* and may not be eaten by a healthy person on the Shabbath.

BENEFITING FROM A FORBIDDEN ACT PERFORMED BY A NON-JEW FOR HIMSELF

the rule 45. a. 1) A Jew may derive a benefit, even on Shabbath, from a forbidden act performed by a non-Jew on Shabbath for himself, or for another non-Jew, provided that

a) (if the act is the subject of a Torah prohibition) there is no fear that, in order to serve the needs of the Jew, the non-Jew has done or will do more than he would otherwise do, and

b) the product of the act is not *muktzeh*.

2) The Jew may benefit only

a) where he knows that the non-Jew has performed the act for himself or for another non-Jew **or**

b) where this is clear from the circumstances, as where the non-Jew himself immediately takes advantage of the results of his act.

b. If the conditions set out in a above are not met,

1) a Jew is not allowed to benefit from the non-Jew's act on Shabbath, but

2) he may benefit from it immediately after Shabbath ends, and need not wait for such time to elapse as would be sufficient for its performance.

46. *a.* In the following two cases, it is presumed that the *presump-* non-Jew has not served, and will not serve, the needs *tion that* of the Jew by doing more than he would otherwise do: *non-Jew* 1) when the result of the act performed by the non-Jew *will not do* for himself can, of its very nature, serve also the *more* needs of others, without any addition on his part; 2) when the non-Jew does not at all know the Jew who will later benefit from his act.
   b. The detailed application of these rules is illustrated in paragraphs 47 to 49 below.

47. *a.* 1) A Jew may benefit from a light turned on by a *turning on* non-Jew if there are indications that he has turned *the light* it on for himself or for another non-Jew, as where the non-Jew makes immediate use of the light.
   2) This is because a light which is good for one person is equally good for several people, and there is no reason for any additional activity on the part of the non-Jew.
   b. The same remains true even when the non-Jew turns on the light so that he can do some work (such as washing the dishes) for the Jew.
   c. The Jew may derive a benefit from the light even after the non-Jew has finished what he was doing and has left.
   d. What is more, the Jew may request the non-Jew not to extinguish the light which he (the non-Jew) has switched on for his own use.

48. *a.* 1) A Jew is not allowed to benefit on Shabbath from *boiling* water which a non-Jew has boiled for himself *water* (except in the circumstances specified in *b* below).
   2) This is because there are grounds for fearing that the non-Jew has added, or will add, more water for the Jew.
   3) Water boiled by a non-Jew for himself on Shabbath may be used by a Jew as soon as Shabbath terminates.

b. 1) Where there are no grounds for apprehension, the
Jew may drink the water on Shabbath.
2) That would be the case
a) if the non-Jew does not know the Jew at all, as
where a Jew arrives at a café owned by a non-
Jew, whose usual clientele is non-Jewish, and
finds water already boiled, or
b) if a Jew staying in a guest-house belonging to a
non-Jew tells his host in advance that he does
not want to drink hot water there on Shabbath,
and the non-Jew then boils water for himself or
for other non-Jews on Shabbath.

*milk pro-
duced and
fruit picked
on
Shabbath*

49. a. If a non-Jew milks his animals on Shabbath, a Jew is
not permitted to drink the milk on Shabbath.
b. He may likewise not eat fruit which a non-Jew has
picked on Shabbath.
c. Both the milk and the fruit are *muktzeh*. (See Chapter
22, paragraph 50.)
d. The milk and the fruit are prohibited even if there is
only a doubt as to whether the milking or the picking
took place on Shabbath.

BENEFITING FROM A FORBIDDEN ACT PERFORMED BY A NON-JEW BOTH FOR JEWS AND NON-JEWS

rules

50. How one classifies a forbidden act performed by a non-
Jew on Shabbath in circumstances where it can be of
benefit both to non-Jews and Jews depends on a number
of considerations.
a. 1) An act which the non-Jew would have performed in
any event, regardless of the presence or absence of
Jews, cannot be said to have been performed in any
measure for a Jew.
2) This holds true even if most of those in a position to
benefit are Jews.
3) Consequently, the rules covering acts performed

for a non-Jew (set out in paragraph 45 above) are applicable.

b. 1) An act which the non-Jew clearly has performed for the benefit of a Jew, or for the benefit equally of a non-Jew and a Jew, is governed by the rules set out in paragraph 36 above.

2) This holds true even if most of those in a position to benefit are non-Jews.

c. 1) An act which the non-Jew clearly has performed chiefly for his own benefit, or for that of another non-Jew, is governed by the rules set out in paragraph 45 above.

2) This holds true even if most of those in a position to benefit are Jews.

3) Where the non-Jew takes immediate advantage of the results of his act, one can assume that he performed it chiefly for his own benefit.

d. In the absence of the above considerations,

1) where most of those in a position to benefit are Jews, the act is assumed to have been performed for them, and the rules set out in paragraph 36 above are applicable,

2) where most of those in a position to benefit are non-Jews, the act is assumed to have been performed for them, and the rules set out in paragraph 45 above are applicable, and

3) where those in a position to benefit are evenly divided between Jews and non-Jews, the act is treated as having been performed for a Jew, and the rules set out in paragraph 36 above are applicable.*

---

*Two alternative grounds have been advanced for this ruling, namely that, in such circumstances,

a. the non-Jew is assumed to have acted for the benefit equally of Jews and non-Jews (as in *b* above) or

b. there is no way of telling whether he acted for the benefit of the Jews or the non-Jews.

(For a better understanding of these principles, reference should be made to the examples in paragraphs 51 to 55 below.)

caretaker
turning on
lights in
apartment
building

51. If the non-Jewish caretaker of an apartment building occupied by both Jews and non-Jews turns on the lights, of his own accord, without receiving instructions from any Jewish occupant,* on the common staircase used by Jews as well as non-Jews, the position is as follows:

a. Where the duty of the caretaker is to turn the lights on regardless of whether the Jewish occupants are at home, then Jews may make use of the light. (See paragraph 50a above.)

b. If the caretaker's duties are not defined in this way, then Jews may use the light where most of the occupants are non-Jews, since, in that case, the caretaker presumably had the latter in mind when he turned on the lights. (See paragraph 50d2 above.)

c. Where most of the occupants are Jews, it is forbidden to use the light (when the situation is not as in a above), since, in that case, the caretaker presumably had the Jews in mind when he turned on the lights. (See paragraph 50d1 above.)

d. The same applies if there are the same number of Jewish as non-Jewish occupants, since, there being no preponderance of the one or the other, the caretaker presumably intended to turn on the lights for the benefit equally of Jews and non-Jews. (See paragraph 50d3 above.)

e. When one is forbidden to use the light,
1) this does not mean that one is not allowed to pass through the staircase, or that one may only do so with one's eyes closed, but that
2) one should not use it to do something which one would not otherwise have done there.

---

*See paragraph 38 above.

52. *a.* 1) Lights switched on by a non-Jew to enable him to *lights*
go up or down the stairs may also be used by a Jew. *turned on*
2) Since the non-Jew derives an immediate benefit *by non-Jew*
from turning on the light, it is clear that he has *using*
performed the act for his own purposes. *staircase*
3) It does not matter that the other users of the staircase are Jews.

b. 1) The case would be different if a Jew asked a non-
Jew to accompany him upstairs, intending the non-
Jew to turn on the lights.
2) Were the non-Jew to turn on the lights in these
circumstances, the direct and immediate benefit
obtained by the Jew, coupled with the fact that the
non-Jew is present only in compliance with the
Jew's wishes, would indicate that the lights were,
in reality, turned on for the Jew.
3) Consequently, the Jew would be forbidden to
benefit from the light. (See paragraph 50*b* above.)

53. *a.* 1) In an apartment building occupied both by Jews *operation of*
and non-Jews, one may benefit from the turning *central-*
on, by the non-Jewish caretaker, of the central- *heating*
heating system serving the whole building. *system*
2) This is because it is the duty of the caretaker to turn
on the heating even when the Jewish occupants are
not at home.
3) One is permitted to take advantage of the heating
in these circumstances, even if it is not particularly
cold. (See also Chapter 23, paragraph 24.)

b. 1) Nonetheless, one must not turn on the taps of the
radiators on Shabbath, as the cold water inside the
pipes would thereby be heated. (See Chapter 23,
paragraph 18.)
2) With regard to turning off radiator taps, see Chapter 23, paragraph 19.

operation of
54. *a.* 1) A Jew may ascend in an electric elevator operated *elevator*

by a non-Jewish attendant for both Jews and non-Jews, as long as

   a) the attendant does not set it in motion especially for the Jew **and**

   b) the attendant does not, in fact, perform any particular (forbidden) action for the Jew.

2) It follows that the Jew should enter and leave the elevator only at floors where it is also being entered or left by non-Jews.

b. 1) A person whose sense of responsibility extends even to the remoter effects of his actions should not use an elevator on Shabbath, even in the manner mentioned above, except on the way to or from Torah study sessions or public prayers.

2) The reason for this is the likelihood that other people will follow his example in using the elevator, but without taking care to observe the various laws applicable.

c. At all events, it is as well to use an elevator on Shabbath only for ascending, and not for descending.

d. For the use of an electric elevator in general, see Chapter 23, paragraphs 49 to 51.

ships

55. *a.* 1) One may travel on Shabbath in a ship owned and operated by non-Jews, if it sails at fixed times regardless of whether or not there are passengers.

2) This is because all of the activities involved in the operation of the ship would be performed even if there were no Jewish passengers on board.

3) As a result, it does not matter if most of the passengers are Jews.

b. 1) To eat the food cooked on board such a ship on Shabbath is, however, certainly forbidden (even when halachic considerations not related to Shabbath would otherwise permit its consumption).

2) The reason is that account is taken, when preparing the food, of each and every passenger, and the non-Jews will obviously do more because of the

presence of the Jews than they would have done in their absence.

c. 1) If one's journey is for the purposes of a mitzva, or for business, one may set sail even on Friday, so long as it is not yet Shabbath.

2) On the other hand, if one is traveling for pleasure, one should set sail only during the first three days of the week.*

d. 1) It may happen that one is traveling for the purpose of a mitzva or on business and has no alternative other than to sail on Shabbath.

2) In that event, one should consult a duly qualified halachic authority as to how one should conduct oneself with reference to such matters as the actual departure, taking luggage on board and handling items which are *muktzeh*.

e. 1) A person whose ship reaches its destination on Shabbath should attempt to remain on board until Shabbath ends.

2) a) Should he be unable to do so, he may not disembark his baggage, nor even take his passport ashore, since this would infringe the prohibition against transferring an object from one *reshuth* to another, but,

b) subject to the various considerations discussed in this chapter, he might be able to avail himself of the assistance of a non-Jew in this regard.

3) a) If one knows in advance that one will reach one's destination on Shabbath, one should, if possible, postpone one's departure to another day.

b) Thus one will avoid the multitude of problems which arise over disembarkation on Shabbath and over the various activities connected with such disembarkation.

---

*If the journey is short, one may be allowed to set sail later, but one should first ask a duly qualified halachic authority for his opinion on the matter.

BENEFITS WHICH ARE INDIRECT OR NOT SUBSTANTIVE

the rule **56.** *a.* In a case where a non-Jew performs an act for a Jew on Shabbath of his own volition, the Jew may derive a benefit from it which is indirect or not substantive,
1) even on Shabbath **and**
2) even if the act is the subject of a Torah prohibition.

b. A benefit is generally considered to be indirect if it is obtained neither from whatever is actually made or produced in contravention of the prohibition, nor from an article with which the prohibited act is performed.

c. A benefit is generally considered as not being substantive if it would also have been obtained (even in a lesser degree) without performance of the prohibited act.

d. The following two paragraphs contain examples to illustrate the application of this rule.

opening   **57.** *a.* A Jew may eat the contents of a can of preserves which
cans and   a non-Jew has opened for him on Shabbath (in a pro-
envelopes   hibited manner, as particularized in Chapter 9, paragraphs 2 and 3).

b. He may likewise read a letter whose envelope has been cut open by a non-Jew on Shabbath (but see Chapter 29, paragraph 45).

c. In neither case is a benefit derived directly from the article opened (the can or the envelope), but rather from the contents (the preserves or the letter), which one is enabled to reach as a result of the act of opening.*

---

*a. It should be remembered that one must not tell the non-Jew on Shabbath to open the can or the envelope.

b. One may only hint to him indirectly, by telling him of the situation which gives rise to the need for the can or the envelope to be opened.

c. See paragraphs 1, 2 and 10 above and Chapter 31, paragraphs 3 and 22.

58. *a*. Should a non-Jew polish a Jew's shoes on Shabbath, *polishing* without having been told to do so, the Jew may wear *shoes* them even on Shabbath, and the benefit he derives is not regarded as substantive if he would also have worn the shoes without their having been polished. (See, however, paragraph 41 above.)

b. If a non-Jew turns on an additional light in a room *turning on* which was already lit, one may do by the additional *additional* light (as long as the original light continues to burn) *lights* whatever one would have done, albeit with difficulty, by the original light.*

BENEFITING FROM A RABBINICAL PROHIBITION
PERFORMED BY A NON-JEW FOR A JEW

59. Where a non-Jew performs on Shabbath, for a Jew, an *the rule* activity which is the subject only of a Rabbinical prohibition, the position is as follows:

a. 1) The Jew for whom it is performed is not allowed to derive a direct, substantive benefit from the activity until the elapse, after Shabbath, of such a period of time as would suffice for its performance.

2) The restriction also applies to the members of his household and other persons whom he has invited to be his guests that Shabbath.

3) However, it is permitted to handle items with which the forbidden activity was performed, and they are not *muktzeh*, since other people are allowed to use them. (Compare Chapter 20, paragraph 34, and Chapter 22, paragraph 48.)

b. Other Jews may benefit from the forbidden activity even on Shabbath, and even to the extent of eating food made available as a result of its performance.

---

*From paragraph 7 above, it will be seen that one may do no more than intimate indirectly to the non-Jew that he should turn on more lights, by telling him of the situation which makes additional light necessary.

c. These principles are illustrated in paragraphs 60 and 61 below.

d. The contents of paragraph 62 below should be noted.

bringing food

60. *a.* 1) The following is the position if a non-Jew brings food for a Jew on Shabbath

    a) from beyond the limit to which the Jew is permitted to walk, **but**

    b) not through an actual *r^eshuth ha-rabbim*, as defined in Chapter 17, paragraph 3.

  2) The food is not *muktzeh* and may be moved, even by the recipient himself, but

  3) neither he nor the members of his household nor guests he invited for Shabbath may eat the food, until the elapse of such a period of time after Shabbath as would suffice to bring the food from beyond the limit mentioned.

  4) Other persons may eat the food right away, even on Shabbath.

b. 1) It is otherwise if a non-Jew brings food for a Jew on Shabbath

    a) from within the limit to which the Jew is permitted to walk,

    b) through an area in which carrying items about is prohibited due to the absence of an *eiruv*, **but**

    c) where that area does not fit the definition of an actual *r^eshuth ha-rabbim*, as set out in Chapter 17, paragraph 3.

  2) In such an event, if it is necessary for the purposes of Shabbath, there is room for permitting even the Jew for whom the food was brought to eat it that day.*

---

*a. This is because, in case of need, one relies on the view that the Jew is not deriving a substantive benefit from the non-Jew's action in bringing the food.

  b. The grounds for this view are that the Jew could have eaten the food without the non-Jew's help, by going to the place from which the non-Jew brought it.

c. Contrast the situation in paragraph 42 above, where the bringing of the food involves a Torah prohibition.

d. See Chapter 31, paragraph 4, regarding the delivery of milk on Shabbath.

e. Concerning the delivery of mail, see Chapter 31, paragraphs 21 and 23.

61. *a.* If a non-Jew buys food for a Jew on Shabbath, neither the Jew nor the members of his household, nor guests he invited for Shabbath, may benefit from it, but they may handle it. *buying food*

b. See also Chapter 31, paragraph 16.

62. *a.* Throughout this chapter, it has been apparent that whether or not one may tell a non-Jew to perform a particular act, and whether or not one may benefit from an act performed by him, may depend upon whether that act *distinguishing between Rabbinical and Torah prohibitions*

1) is forbidden by the Torah or

2) is the subject only of a Rabbinical prohibition.

b. Where this distinction is a consideration, a qualified halachic authority should be consulted to ascertain whether a particular act is prohibited by the Torah or by the Rabbis, and what precisely one may or may not do.

Chapter 31

Miscellaneous Laws Relating to Non-Jews, and to Shabbath and Yom Tov Outside the Land of Israel

ASSISTANCE OF NON-JEW IN CONNECTION WITH PREPARATION OF FOOD

refrigerators **1.** *a.* 1) One may, on Shabbath, request a non-Jew to take something out of, or put something into, an electric refrigerator, even if the act of opening the door will
   a) immediately activate the motor of the refrigerator and
   b) switch on the internal light.

2) This is due to the fact that the non-Jew's mind is not directed to either of these forbidden activities, but merely to removing something from the refrigerator or placing something inside it.

3) Similarly, one may ask a non-Jew to close an open refrigerator, even if this will extinguish an internal light.

b. 1) Furthermore, if the internal light of a refrigerator has been turned on by someone opening the door, a Jew may tell a non-Jew that he, the Jew, will not be able to re-open the door if the non-Jew closes it without first extracting or disconnecting the bulb.

2) In doing so, one is merely relating to the non-Jew the circumstances which necessitate the performance of a forbidden activity, and the non-Jew draws his own conclusions as to what is expected of him. (See Chapter 30, paragraphs 2 and 5.)

boilers **2.** *a.* One may tell a non-Jew on Shabbath to use the hot water from a boiler,
   1) even though cold water flowing into the boiler, in

place of the water being extracted, will be heated by
the hot water remaining there, and

   2) even if the heating element will automatically be
turned on and will heat up the cold water.

  b. See Chapter 14, paragraph 2, for a restriction on the
use of water heated on Shabbath.

3. *a.* One is allowed to hint indirectly to a non-Jew on   *cans*
Shabbath or Yom Tov that he should open a can of
preserves which one may not open in the normal
manner oneself.* (See Chapter 9, paragraphs 2 and 3.)

  b. The hint should be given by telling him of the situation
which makes it necessary for the can to be opened (as
explained in Chapter 30, paragraph 2), for instance, by
saying, "I can't eat any of the food in this can as long
as it's closed."

4. *a.* In a case of great need, one may ask a non-Jewish   *milk*
milkman (either before or on Shabbath) to deliver milk
to one's house on Shabbath,

   1) even if his round takes him through places where it
is forbidden to carry objects about,

   2) provided he does not pass through an actual
r^eshuth ha-rabbim, as defined in Chapter 17,
paragraph 3.

  (Compare Chapter 30, paragraph 14.)

  b. One may drink the milk he brings on Shabbath, if one
knows

   1) that it was not milked that day **and**

   2) that it was not brought that day from outside the
limit to which one is permitted to walk.

  (See Chapter 30, paragraphs 49 and 60.)

  c. One should not receive the milk from the non-Jew's

---

*One should not directly tell him to open a can, even though one
could open it oneself if one spoiled it for further use, since he will
understand that he is to open it in the normal manner, without
spoiling it.

hand, but must take care that he brings it into the house and puts it down there.

d. At all events, one is not allowed to prepare money, even before Shabbath, for paying the milkman.

e. One may pay the milkman before Shabbath for the milk he will bring on Shabbath, receiving in return a voucher showing how much milk the milkman owes one.

f. It is none of one's concern if the non-Jewish milkman notes down in his book how much one owes him.

g. One must not, however, let the milkman take empty bottles away, even if they were made ready the previous day, since this is not necessary for Shabbath.*

h. 1) In large cities, where the milkman passes through a *r^eshuth ha-rabbim* fitting the definition in Chapter 17, paragraph 3, one may not drink milk delivered on Shabbath.

2) Nevertheless, one may drink it immediately after Shabbath, without waiting for the lapse of such a period of time as would suffice for its delivery.

meat   5. a. One may ask a non-Jew to rinse and soak meat, if

1) one has forgotten to salt it before Shabbath **and**

2) the third day from the animal's slaughter falls on Shabbath.

b. This is because, unless one takes action before the end of the third day, it will become forbidden to prepare the meat for eating by cooking it in a pot, as one would normally do.

c. See further Chapter 11, paragraph 5.

turning on   6. a. In countries with a cool climate, one may request a
heating   non-Jew on Shabbath to put on the heater, if one is

---

*Where the bottles belong to the dairy, which wants them back, one may make them ready before Shabbath and let the milkman take them on Shabbath.

troubled by the cold, since a person who is suffering from the cold is placed in the same category as someone who is ill. (See Chapter 38, paragraphs 4 and 8.)

b. 1) Where there are small children, one may request a non-Jew to turn on the heater even when the cold is not intense enough to trouble the adults, since small children are naturally more sensitive to cold.

2) Once the heater is on, it is permissible for the grown-ups also to avail themselves of its benefit.

c. 1) At all events, since the implements or materials required for turning on the heater are *muktzeh*, one will not be able to handle them on Shabbath.

2) Consequently, they should be made ready before Shabbath begins, so that the non-Jew will be able to take them himself, without one's assistance.

7. One may tell a non-Jew to put a pot of cooked food to warm on a room heater* which he is going to turn on, even if the food is altogether cold, but the non-Jew must put the pot in position before he turns on the heater to warm the room.

warming food on heater

8. a. One may also tell a non-Jew to put a pot containing cooked food, even if it is cold, onto an electric plate which will subsequently be turned on by a timer.

b. See also Chapter 1, paragraph 26.

electric plates turned on by timer

9. a. One is not required to raise any objection if a non-Jew who is employed to wash one's dishes after Shabbath wishes to do them on Shabbath, so that he will be free in the evening. (Compare Chapter 30, paragraph 31.)

b. One may even let him
1) heat water and
2) turn on the light

washing dishes

---

*This is not permitted if the heater is of a type on which it is usual to cook.

[489]

for the purpose of washing the dishes.

c. Furthermore, one may use the light once the non-Jew has turned it on. (See Chapter 30, paragraph 47.)

d. One may not, however, use the water which the non-Jew has heated, since there are grounds for fearing that the non-Jew has heated, or will heat, more water for one than he would heat just for himself. (See Chapter 30, paragraph 48.)

remunera- 10. Concerning remuneration of a non-Jew after Shabbath
tion for trouble which he has taken on Shabbath, see Chapter 30, paragraph 29.

USING THE SERVICES OF A NON-JEW IN CONNECTION WITH
CLOTHES, COPYING, BUYING OR SELLING

delivery of 11. a. It is permitted to tell a non-Jewish deliveryman who
laundry has brought the laundry on Shabbath, through places where there is no *eiruv* and carrying articles about is forbidden, to put it down in a particular place.

b. One is also allowed to watch over him while he counts the items.

c. One must not, however, talk to him about such matters as payment.

d. To count the items oneself is forbidden.

e. It is prohibited to pay the non-Jew on Shabbath, even if it is by way of letting him take money one has prepared beforehand.

f. It is similarly forbidden to calculate the account with him for subsequent payment.

g. When one has to, that is to say when one has nothing else suitable to wear on Shabbath, one may put on laundered clothing delivered by a non-Jew that Shabbath, even if it has been brought through an actual *r*ᵉ*shuth ha-rabbim*, as defined in Chapter 17, paragraph 3.

h. One should not ask the laundryman to make a special

delivery on Shabbath, unless a duly qualified halachic authority advises that it is permissible in the circumstances of the case.

12. *a.* One may ask the deliveryman of a diaper (nappy) service, who calls on fixed days of the week, to call on Shabbath too, provided *diaper service*
   1) the service is owned and operated by non-Jews,
   2) the diapers are not brought through an area which fits the definition of a *r^eshuth ha-rabbim* and
   3) the baby needs them.
   b. Regarding payment, see paragraph 11 above.
   c. Regarding the return of soiled diapers, see paragraph 13 below.

13. *a.* It is forbidden to give dirty washing even to a non-Jewish laundryman on Shabbath or Yom Tov, regardless of whether or not it will be washed the same day. *collection of laundry*
   b. By way of exception, one may return soiled diapers to a diaper service on Shabbath or Yom Tov, if the deliveryman refuses to leave clean diapers without receiving an equal number of dirty ones. (See paragraph 12 above.)

14. *a.* 1) It has been seen, in Chapter 15, paragraph 25, that one may not remove dust from a garment which one is normally particular to keep clean, whether one does so by shaking the garment or by any other method. *cleaning clothes*
   2) Nevertheless, one may have the dust removed by a non-Jew, especially when wearing the garment while it is dirty bothers one.
   b. 1) As appears from Chapter 15, paragraph 28, it is also forbidden to remove mud or any similar substance which has dried onto a garment, as this would be an infringement of the prohibition against "Grinding."
   c. Nevertheless, one may have it removed by a non-

Jew, because it would be unpleasant to wear the garment while it is dirty.

carbon
copies

15. *a.* A Jew must not ask a non-Jew, even before Shabbath, to make him a carbon copy of something he (the non-Jew) will be writing for himself on Shabbath.

b. What the Jew may do is

1) tell the non-Jew, before Shabbath, that he should make an extra copy for himself, and

2) promise to buy it from him for a small sum after Shabbath.

c. In these latter circumstances, the non-Jew is regarded as acting for his own benefit.

buying

16. *a.* One may give a non-Jew money shortly before Shabbath commences and ask him to buy something, without being concerned that he may buy it on Shabbath, but

1) one must not tell him to buy it for one specifically on Shabbath and

2) the non-Jew must be acting for his own gain, in other words with the object of receiving a reward. (Compare Chapter 30, paragraph 25.)

b. On the other hand, it is forbidden to tell a non-Jew, even before Shabbath, to buy something for one on Shabbath, notwithstanding that one gives him the money only after Shabbath, that is to say one refunds to him the money he has already laid out.

c. Where

1) one gives the money to the non-Jew on Thursday, or even on Friday if enough time remains to buy the desired items before Shabbath begins, **and**

2) one does not tell him to buy on Shabbath,

one may ask him to make the purchase even if he is not acting in his own interest, to obtain a reward.

d. 1) One may tell a non-Jew to buy something for himself on Shabbath.

2) One may, prior to Shabbath, even just before its

commencement, also
    a) lend him money for the purpose and
    b) promise him that, after Shabbath, one will buy from him what he has bought and reward him for his trouble.
  3) In these circumstances, the non-Jew is regarded as acting in his own interests.

17. *a.* One may give a non-Jew merchandise shortly before *selling* Shabbath commences and ask him to sell it, without being concerned that he may sell it on Shabbath, but
  1) one must not tell him to sell it specifically on Shabbath and
  2) the non-Jew must be acting for his own gain, in other words with the object of receiving a reward.
  b. On the other hand, it is forbidden to tell a non-Jew, even before Shabbath, to sell something for one on Shabbath.
  c. Where
  1) one gives the merchandise to the non-Jew on Thursday, or even on Friday if enough time remains to sell it before Shabbath begins, and
  2) one does not tell him to sell on Shabbath,
one may ask him to sell even if he is not acting in order to obtain a reward.

18. A fully qualified halachic expert should be consulted *rent, loan* on all matters concerning such subjects as rental *and* agreements with non-Jews, borrowing from a non-Jew, *partnership* lending to a non-Jew and partnerships with non-Jews.

19. *a.* For the switching on of electric fans and air con- *cooling and* ditioning by a non-Jew, and their use on Shabbath *heating* and Yom Tov, see Chapter 13, paragraphs 34 and 35, and Chapter 30, paragraph 11.
  b. For the switching on of heating by a non-Jew, and its use on Shabbath and Yom Tov, see Chapter 23, paragraph 24.

MAIL AND COMMUNICATIONS ON SHABBATH AND YOM TOV

sending
letters and
telegrams

20. *a.* One may mail a letter on Friday (in a place where the post office employees are not Jewish), even though it is clear that it will reach its destination on Shabbath.

b. 1) One must not, however, mail an express-delivery letter or send a telegram just before Shabbath is due to start.

2) In these cases, since one is making a point of having the letter or telegram delivered on the following day, one is, to all intents and purposes, specifying to the non-Jews involved that they should perform the required prohibited activities on Shabbath.

c. Nevertheless, in a case of great need or for the purpose of a mitzva, there is room for permitting an express-delivery letter or a telegram to be sent off shortly before the beginning of Shabbath.

delivery of
letters

21. *a.* One is allowed to ask a non-Jewish mailman who brings a letter on Shabbath to put it down on the table, but one should not accept it from his hand.

b. It is none of one's concern if the mailman notes in his book that he has delivered the letter.

c. Mail left in a mailbox in the lobby of an apartment building may be brought to one's apartment, provided one is indeed permitted to carry articles about inside the building (as to which it is important to see Chapter 17, paragraph 11).

d. If it is necessary to sign for the receipt of a letter, one should inform the non-Jewish mailman that one is not permitted to sign that day and let the mailman sign instead, of his own accord. (See Chapter 30, paragraph 2c.)

opening
and reading
letters

22. *a.* 1) One is permitted to say to a non-Jew on Shabbath that one is not allowed to open a letter, so that the non-Jew himself understands that he is to open it.

2) All one has done is to tell the non-Jew of the situation which gives rise to the need for him to perform a forbidden activity, as explained in Chapter 30, paragraph 2c.

b. Concerning the reading of letters on Shabbath and the handling of papers of a commercial nature, see Chapter 29, paragraph 45.

23. a. One may use on Shabbath the contents of a parcel delivered that day by a non-Jewish mailman.

parcels delivered on Shabbath

b. This is so provided that the sender was not particular that the parcel should be delivered on Shabbath.

c. It makes no difference if the parcel was brought from beyond the limit to which one is permitted to walk or through an area where there is no *eiruv*.

d. The cases mentioned in Chapter 30, paragraph 60, should be distinguished:

1) there, if the Jew were allowed to use food delivered, he might come to tell the non-Jew to deliver it on Shabbath;

2) here, in the case of a postal delivery, such a fear is not relevant.

24. a. 1) A subscriber to a daily newspaper which is also printed (by non-Jews) on Shabbath is not allowed to read it on Shabbath, if most of its regular readers are Jewish.

newspapers printed on Shabbath

2) On the termination of Shabbath, too, he may not read the newspaper until sufficient time has elapsed for it to have been printed.

b. If most of the regular readers are not Jewish, one may, strictly speaking, read such items as news reports, but not those dealing with business matters (as mentioned in Chapter 29, paragraph 46).

c. However, as stated in Chapter 29, paragraph 46, it is desirable not to read newspapers at all on Shabbath.

d. 1) a) When a non-Jew has brought a newspaper to a Jew on Shabbath through an area where there

is no *eiruv* and carrying items about is
forbidden, there are no grounds for permitting
the Jew to read it on Shabbath.

b) Since the essence of a daily newspaper is same-
day delivery every day, including Shabbath,
ordering the newspaper is equivalent to
requiring delivery every single day, including
Shabbath. (Compare paragraphs 20 and 23
above.)

2) Yet, the Jew may read the newspaper as soon as
Shabbath ends.

e. It is as well, when ordering a newspaper, to tell the
non-Jewish paperboy not to deliver it on Shabbath,
and if he nevertheless proceeds to do so, that is his own
business.

publication on Shabbath

25. *a.* One is forbidden to insert any advertisement or article
in a newspaper which is to appear on Shabbath.

b. It is also forbidden to make a recording for broad-
casting on Shabbath.

telephone

26. *a.* A Jew who is in a country where Shabbath has not
yet commenced may talk to a non-Jew who has
telephoned him from a country where it is already
Shabbath.

b. Likewise, a Jew who is in a country where Shabbath
has already ended may talk to a non-Jew who has
telephoned him from a country where it is still
Shabbath.

c. What is more, a Jew may telephone from a place where
it is not yet, or is no longer, Shabbath to a non-Jew in a
place where it is Shabbath.

d. By way of contrast, an observant Jew who is in a place
where it is not Shabbath may not hold a conversation
with a non-observant Jew who has telephoned him
from a place where it is Shabbath.

YOM TOV SHEINI SHEL GALUYOTH

27. *a.* Jews who live outside Eretz Yisrael* are obliged to observe, as additional days of Yom Tov,
    1) the second and an eighth day of Pesach,
    2) a second day of Shavuoth,
    3) the second day of Sukkoth and
    4) the day after Sh^emini Atzereth, on which they celebrate Simchath Torah. *(status of yom tov sheini shel galuyoth)*

b. This observance of what is known as *yom tov sheini shel galuyoth* has its origin in the doubt which existed in distant places as to when exactly the first day of the month had been proclaimed in Jerusalem.

c. Even before the time of the compilation of the Talmud, the doubt had ceased to be relevant, as the exact time when the new month began could be calculated, but the Rabbis decreed that Jews living outside Eretz Yisrael should maintain the custom handed down to them by previous generations and continue to observe *yom tov sheini shel galuyoth.*

d. Ever since, there has been no practical difference (with a few exceptions mentioned below) between the observance of *yom tov sheini shel galuyoth* and the observance of the day of Yom Tov which precedes it.

e. Similarly, there is no practical difference today (except as mentioned below) between the observance of the first and the second day of Rosh Hashana.

28. *a.* 1) By way of exception to what has been stated in the preceding paragraph, one may, on *yom tov sheini shel galuyoth* (but not on the second day of Rosh Hashana), perform an act which *(medical treatment)*
    a) is intended for a medical purpose **and**
    b) is forbidden on Yom Tov only by virtue of a Rabbinical (and not a Torah) prohibition.

---

*See glossary.

[497]

2) One must consult a competent halachic authority as to which acts are forbidden by the Torah and which are the subject of a Rabbinical prohibition.

b. 1) For example, one may take medicines on *yom tov sheini shel galuyoth*, even if one is only suffering from a minor ailment, despite the fact that there is a Rabbinical prohibition forbidding this on Yom Tov. (See Chapter 34, paragraph 3.)

2) One may also put wet compresses on a sprain on *yom tov sheini shel galuyoth*, but

    a) the cloths used for the purpose should be clean **and**

    b) the cloths used must not be squeezed out, as this would involve a Torah prohibition.

(See also Chapter 33, paragraph 19, on the application of compresses on Shabbath or Yom Tov in general.)

burial   29. a. The Rabbis went still further in making another exception to the rule in the case of the burial of the dead.

b. In this instance, they permitted the performance, both on *yom tov sheini shel galuyoth* and on the second day of Rosh Hashana, even of activities which are forbidden by a Torah prohibition.

c. A competent rabbinical authority must be consulted to ascertain the detailed application of the Halacha in such a case.

ascertaining whether to observe yom tov sheini shel galuyoth   30. a. There are many detailed laws governing whether or not *yom tov sheini shel galuyoth* should be observed by

1) a Jew who is in Eretz Yisrael but does not live there,

2) a Jew who lives in Eretz Yisrael but is elsewhere and

3) a Jew who has two homes, one in Eretz Yisrael and one outside Eretz Yisrael, and divides his time between the two.

b. A qualified halachic authority who is versed in these laws should be consulted whenever the problem arises.

31. One should also consult a competent halachic authority as to whether one may permit workmen to work on *yom tov sheini shel galuyoth*

factory owned abroad

   a. in a factory which is outside Eretz Yisrael, but which is owned by a Jew living in Eretz Yisrael, or

   b. in a factory which is inside Eretz Yisrael, but is owned by a Jew living outside Eretz Yisrael.

32. *a.* Many questions arise in connection with such matters as

participation of Jew from Eretz Yisrael in prayers

   1) whether a Jew living in Eretz Yisrael can be called up to the reading of the Torah at a service held on *yom tov sheini shel galuyoth* by Jews living outside Eretz Yisrael, and

   2) whether, at such a service, he can be counted towards the quorum required for reciting certain prayers or for reading the Torah.

   b. In each case, these questions should be put to a competent rabbi who is well versed in these laws and is qualified to give an authoritative ruling.

33. *a.* A person who lives outside Eretz Yisrael, and is obliged to observe *yom tov sheini shel galuyoth*, should not, even when in Eretz Yisrael, ask his friend who lives there to perform a forbidden activity for him.

assistance of Jews living in Eretz Yisrael: general rule

   b. Furthermore, the friend ought not to perform such an activity for him of his own volition.

   c. It is also as well for a Jew from outside Eretz Yisrael not to travel on *yom tov sheini shel galuyoth* as a passenger in a car driven by a Jew who lives in Eretz Yisrael.

34. A person who lives outside Eretz Yisrael, and is obliged to observe *yom tov sheini shel galuyoth*, may also cook on that day for a Jew from Eretz Yisrael, in spite of the fact that, for the latter, it is an ordinary day of the week.

cooking for Jew from Eretz Yisrael

necessity
for eiruv
tavshilin in
Eretz
Yisrael

35. *a.* 1) a) Since a person who lives outside Eretz Yisrael is obliged to observe *yom tov sheini shel galuyoth* even if he is in Eretz Yisrael,

  b) he has a duty to make an *eiruv tavshilin* (reciting the appropriate blessing) when *yom tov sheini shel galuyoth* falls on a Friday.

  2) The *eiruv tavshilin* should be made on the preceding Wednesday, before Yom Tov begins.

b. 1) It is otherwise if he is the guest of a Jew living in Eretz Yisrael who cooks his guest's food together with his own and attends to all his other Shabbath preparations for him.

  2) Nonetheless, if he wishes to light his own Shabbath candles, he would do well to make an *eiruv tavshilin* (but without reciting the usual blessing).

forgetting
to make
eiruv
tavshilin

36. *a.* If Jews who are obliged to observe *yom tov sheini shel galuyoth* forget to make an *eiruv tavshilin*, as required by the rule set out in paragraph 35 above, they may not cook on that Friday (*yom tov sheini shel galuyoth*) for the purposes of Shabbath.

b. Moreover, in such an event, a Jew who is not obliged to observe *yom tov sheini shel galuyoth* should not cook their food for them, even if he does the cooking inside his own house.

c. However, they may ask him to add food for them to whatever he is cooking for himself and his household for Shabbath.

Jew from
Eretz
Yisrael
abroad:
general
rules

37. A resident of Eretz Yisrael who happens to be abroad should behave in the following manner on *yom tov sheini shel galuyoth:*

a. He should not perform, even in private, an act which is forbidden to the local residents on *yom tov sheini shel galuyoth.*

b. He should wear his Yom Tov clothes.

c. He should put on *t^efillin* in the house (unless it is

Shabbath), recite the *Sh*ᵉ*ma* while wearing them and say the prayers appropriate to a day which is not Yom Tov.

d. He should then go to the synagogue so that he can hear the *kaddish* and *k*ᵉ*dusha* prayers.

38. A resident of Eretz Yisrael who happens to be abroad may cook for Shabbath on *yom tov sheini shel galuyoth* which falls on a Friday, and he does not make an *eiruv tavshilin.*

when eiruv tavshlin unnecessary

39. A resident of Eretz Yisrael who happens to be abroad must not make preparations on *chol ha-mo'ed* for *yom tov sheini shel galuyoth.*

preparations on chol ha-mo'ed

40. A person who happens to be in Eretz Yisrael, but lives elsewhere, should not eat in the *sukka* on Sh*ᵉ*mini Atzereth, even though he is obliged to observe *yom tov sheini shel galuyoth.*

*Sh*ᵉ*mini Atzereth*

SEPARATING CHALLA OUTSIDE ERETZ YISRAEL

41. *a.* Even at the time when the Temple stood and the whole of the Jewish people lived in Eretz Yisrael, the obligation to separate *challa* from dough kneaded outside Eretz Yisrael was only a Rabbinical one.

what to do if one has forgotten to take challa

b. 1) As a result, the Rabbis took a more lenient attitude to the separation of *challa* outside Eretz Yisrael.

2) They permitted bread or cake to be eaten even though *challa* had not yet been taken, so long as one had the intention of taking it later from the bread or cake remaining.

c. Consequently, if one has forgotten, outside Eretz Yisrael, to separate *challa* from bread or cake before Shabbath or Yom Tov, and the quantity is such that one is obliged to take *challa*, then one should

1) leave over a piece of bread or cake **and**

>   2) separate the *challa** from that piece at the end of
>   Shabbath or Yom Tov,
>   since to separate the *challa* on Shabbath or Yom Tov
>   is prohibited. (See Chapter 11, paragraph 16.)
>
> d. 1) Eating first and then separating *challa* after
>   Shabbath or Yom Tov is permissible only outside
>   Eretz Yisrael.
>   2) For the position in Eretz Yisrael, see Chapter 11,
>   paragraphs 16 to 28, and in particular paragraph
>   28.

---

*This course of action is allowed only where *challa* has to be
removed, but not where one has to separate *t^erumoth* and *ma'asroth*
from food which comes from Eretz Yisrael; so one should be
especially careful to remove *t^erumoth* and *ma'asroth* before the
commencement of Shabbath or Yom Tov.

Chapter 32

Laws Relating to the Saving of Human Life

THE OBLIGATION TO VIOLATE SHABBATH
IN ORDER TO SAVE HUMAN LIFE

1. *a.* 1) It is permitted to violate the Shabbath in order to *the supreme* save human life; indeed there is a positive ob- *importance* ligation to do so whenever there is danger, or a *of saving* possibility of danger, to life. *life*
   2) What is more, in a situation of this kind, the more diligent and speedy one is in violating the Shabbath, the more praiseworthy are one's actions.

   b. Maimonides (*Mishneh Torah, Hilchoth Shabbath* 2:3) put it this way: "When doing these things [violating the Shabbath for the purposes of a Jew who is suffering from a dangerous, or possibly dangerous, illness], one should not act through the agency of non-Jews, nor of minors..., but through the agency of the great and wise men of Israel [unless this course be less expedient]. One must not delay in profaning Shabbath for a person who is seriously ill, or in any other case of danger to life, as shown by the reference [in Leviticus 18:5] to [the commandments] 'which a person shall perform and by which he shall live,' and not by which he shall die. So you may deduce that the laws of the Torah are not vindictive to the world, but [bring] compassion, kindness and peace to the world, and of those heretics who say [where there is danger to life], 'It is a violation of Shabbath and prohibited,' the Prophet [Ezekiel 20:25] says, 'I too have given them

[503]

statutes which are not good and laws by which they shall not live.'"*

prolonging life

2. One should violate the Shabbath to save human life, even if what one does cannot be effective to prolong life for more than a brief time.

lives of adults and children

3. One should violate the Shabbath to save human life, regardless of whether the person to be saved is an adult or a child.

violation by the person in danger or someone else

4. When Shabbath is violated in order to save human life, it makes no difference whether the violation is carried out by the person who is in danger himself or by other people who are trying to help him.

where person in danger objects to violation of Shabbath

5. *a.* If the person who is in danger refuses to violate the Shabbath in order to save his life, or does not want to let others save him in this way, one should convince him that the violation of Shabbath for the purposes of saving life is a mitzva.

   b. If he remains unconvinced, one compels him to take the necessary action or violates Shabbath for him, notwithstanding his protests.

violation by observant Jew preferable

6. *a.* When it becomes necessary to violate the Shabbath to save a human life, one should not act through the agency of a non-Jew (unless this be more expedient) but should try to do whatever is needed oneself, violating the Shabbath as required.

   b. One should take special care not to bring about a situation in which the required violation is performed by a Jew who is not particular about Shabbath observance.

---

*That is to say, the very laws, as perverted by them, shall bring about their death.

7. When one has violated the Shabbath for the purpose of saving a life and it subsequently transpires that there was no need to do so, because, for example,

   a. the condition of the patient has already improved,

   b. the patient has died or

   c. someone else has already done what was necessary, one has, nonetheless, performed a mitzva and will receive a worthy reward from the Almighty for one's good intentions.

violation which proves to have been unnecessary

SITUATIONS IN WHICH LIFE IS CONSIDERED
TO BE ENDANGERED

8. In the following cases, the opinion of a doctor justifies (and indeed makes obligatory) the violation of the Shabbath for the patient's sake:

   a. where the doctor says that the patient's life is in danger;

   b. where the doctor fears that the patient's life may be in danger;

   c. where the patient's condition is not dangerous for the moment, but the doctor fears that it may worsen and endanger his life if he is not provided with a particular treatment that day.

dangerous condition diagnosed or suspected by doctor

9. *a.* If the patient himself feels that his condition is serious and that his life is in danger, he comes within the definition of a dangerously ill person, and one violates the Shabbath for him.

   b. This is so even if the doctor's opinion differs from that of the patient.

opinion of patient as to his condition

10. In a place where there is no doctor, one relies upon whoever claims that he has a sufficient acquaintance with the condition in question to be able to say that it is, or may be, or may develop into, a dangerous one, as long as

   a. the person expressing the opinion is God-fearing and

opinion of laymen as to patient's condition

has an appreciation for the sanctity of the Shabbath, or

b. one can tell, from what he says, that he is speaking in earnest.

conditions considered dangerous even without medical opinion

11. In the following cases, one should act as if the patient's life were in danger, even when this has not yet been established by a medical opinion:

a. where the patient has a temperature considerably above the normal, for which no cause has yet been determined, and feels ill;

b. where the patient has an above-normal temperature resulting from a disorder of the lungs or other internal organs, in circumstances which usually give rise to a suspicion that an element of danger may be present;

c. 1) where there is a wound within the body (including the mouth from the gums and inwards);

   2) in the case of an internal hemorrhage;

   3) in the event of a strong, internal pain, whose cause is unknown and which arouses a suspicion of a serious complaint;

d. if an artery or a vein hemorrhages, but not if blood is merely oozing slowly from a vein and ceases within a reasonable time (see Chapter 35, paragraph 13);

e. when the patient has, or is suspected to have,

   1) a compound fracture,

   2) a fracture of a long bone, involving a displacement of the broken ends,

   3) a fractured skull,

   4) a fractured spine or

   5) any other fracture within the trunk of the body;

f. in the case of an injury on the back of the hand or on the instep, where damage to blood vessels is feared;

g. where the patient has sustained

   1) a deep cut or a deep wound caused by a knife or other metal instrument,

   2) a heavy blow from a metal object,

   3) a cut caused by something dirty, or

4) a wound which has been contaminated with earth or anything else that can cause an infection, and which, if not properly treated, could endanger the patient's life;

h. in the case of an infected wound
1) which is swollen **or**
2) which has caused an inflammation of the lymphatic glands behind the ear, in the armpit, in the groin or down the neck;

i. where a wound has a red line coming from it and there is a suspicion of blood poisoning;

j. in the case of
1) a large furuncle, or even a small one if it is on the lips, or
2) an ailment of one of the organs of the body, if there are grounds for fearing that a danger to the whole body is liable to develop;

k. where a thorn or splinter has penetrated beneath a fingernail;

l. in the event of
1) heatstroke or sunstroke or
2) serious and extensive burns (see Chapter 35, paragraph 37);

m. when a wasp, bee or other insect has stung a person who is particularly sensitive to that kind of sting;

n. where the patient has been bitten by a rabid dog, a snake, a scorpion (including a black scorpion) or any other creature, such as a horse or a donkey, whose bite could be dangerous, or where he has been scratched by a cat;

o. where a person has swallowed
1) poison (for instance in the form of kerosene, detergent, fruit coated with insecticide, a poisonous plant, naphthalene balls, rat poison, or an overdose of sleeping tablets) or
2) a needle or any other sharp object;

p. in the case of
1) loss of consciousness, or

2) shock or suspected shock (resulting, for example, from the falling of a heavy weight on a person or from an extremely severe pain).

childbirth **12.** *a.* A woman who gives birth to a baby is treated as being in danger of her life

    1) during the birth,

    2) for the next three days,

    3) from the fourth to the seventh day inclusive, as far as necessary in the circumstances set out in Chapter 36, paragraph 14, and even

    4) after the seventh day

       a) where she has developed an above-normal temperature as a result of the birth or

       b) where a complication of some kind has come to light and one fears that it may involve danger to life.

b. These days are counted from the time of the birth, each succeeding period of twenty-four hours being reckoned as a day.

c. The halachic rules relating to childbirth are explained in Chapter 36 below.

preventing **13.** *a.* One may violate the Shabbath in an attempt to protect
spread of   a healthy person from the risk of contracting a
dangerous   contagious disease which is liable to endanger his life.
disease

b. Consequently, one may transport a person suffering from a contagious disease to the hospital in a motor vehicle, even if he himself is now out of danger, where

    1) it is not possible to keep him in isolation otherwise until after Shabbath **and**

    2) there is a fear that he will infect his family, potentially endangering their lives.

c. One may violate the Shabbath in these circumstances, even if one cannot be at all sure that one's action will indeed help to avert the danger. (Compare paragraph 18 below.)

d. See also paragraph 62 below.

14. If there exists the slightest chance that people may be *fallen* buried beneath fallen debris, one violates the Shabbath *debris* in order to save them, even when it is doubtful whether they are still alive.

15. *a.* The following situations are dangerous for a small *trapped or* child, and one should violate the Shabbath to the *lost* extent necessary to rescue him from them: *children*
    1) where he is trapped behind a locked door;
    2) where he has fallen into a hole;
    3) where he is missing;
    4) where he is found wandering about, in a distraught state, and cannot be quieted without being restored to his family.
    b. See also Chapter 41, paragraph 28.

16. *a.* One should violate the Shabbath, in the hope of saving *disasters* human life, whenever a disaster or an accident occurs, *and* or if a dangerous situation arises. *accidents*
    b. This can happen, for instance,
    1) when a fire breaks out,
    2) when flooding takes place,
    3) when a severe electric shock has been sustained, or
    4) when electric wiring is exposed and there is a risk that someone will touch it, thus endangering his life.
    c. See further Chapter 41, paragraphs 20 to 22.

17. *a.* Sometimes, considerations of security during a state *state of* of emergency justify, or demand, a violation of the *emergency* Shabbath.
    b. The rules applicable are too numerous to detail here, and no two situations are alike, so that one cannot draw parallels between them in deciding what to do.
    c. See further Chapter 41, paragraphs 30 to 40.

PRINCIPLES APPLICABLE

general rule **18.** A person whose life is regarded as being in danger should be given any treatment required for his recovery, or to prevent a worsening of his condition,
   a. even if there is no more than a risk that his condition will worsen,
   b. even if the treatment involves the violation of Shabbath by transgressing a Torah (and not merely a Rabbinical) prohibition, and
   c. even if it is by no means certain that the action undertaken will indeed help to remove or minimize the danger.

doubtful **19.** *a.* Even when the patient's condition is such that it is
cases of doubtful whether his life is in danger at all, one should
danger violate the Shabbath, if necessary, to protect him against whatever risk there may be.
   b. The rules applicable are the same as those applying where one is sure the patient's life is in danger.

resusci- **20.** Shabbath should be violated in the use of instruments to
tation effect resuscitation, even if the prospects of success are of the faintest.

compliance **21.** *a.* One should follow a doctor's instructions in doing
with anything
doctor's   1) which he says needs to be done
opinion as   a) to bring about the recovery of a patient whose
to urgent   life is, or is suspected to be, in danger or
needs   b) to prevent a worsening of his condition, **and**
      2) which he says cannot be put off until after Shabbath.
   b. The instructions should be followed, even if
      1) the prohibitions infringed are Torah prohibitions **and**
      2) the doctor is not Shabbath observant or is a non-Jew.

c. Illustrations appear in the following paragraphs, for
example in paragraphs 48, 52, 57 and 62 below.

22. *a.* One may do on Shabbath anything which, although *providing*
not specifically connected with curing the dangerous- *relief or*
ly ill patient, is pressingly needed *reinvigora-*
1) to alleviate his suffering or *tion*
2) to make him feel stronger or refreshed.
b. This may be done,
1) even if it involves the infringement of Torah
prohibitions **and**
2) even if it is clear that withholding the attention in
question from the dangerously ill patient will not
result in an increase of the danger with which he is
threatened.
c. Illustrations appear in the following paragraphs, for
example in paragraphs 52, 57, 72 and 81 below.

23. *a.* There are activities of such a nature that, *essential*
1) on the one hand, if they are not performed at all, the *activities*
life of the patient will be, or could possibly be, *which can*
endangered, whereas, *be left until*
2) on the other hand, there is plainly no need for them *after*
to be done specifically before Shabbath ends. *Shabbath*
b. This situation can arise where, for instance, it is close
to the termination of Shabbath and one can put the
matter off until afterwards.
c. Where this is the case, then,
1) if the activity involves the transgression of a Torah
prohibition, it should not be carried out on
Shabbath, whereas,
2) if it involves the transgression only of a Rabbinical prohibition,*
a) it may be done on Shabbath, although,

---

*One should consult an authorized halachic expert in order to ascer-
tain what is prohibited by the Torah and what by Rabbinical
injunction.

b) when possible, one should not do it in the normal manner, but in a different way from that which one would adopt on an ordinary day of the week.

d. For some illustrations, see Chapter 40, paragraphs 28, 38 and 39.

inessential needs of dangerously ill patient

24. *a.* One may violate Shabbath, but only to the extent of infringing Rabbinical prohibitions,* in order to do an act

   1) which is in some way needed for a dangerously ill person, **but**

   2) failure to perform which would not bring about an aggravation of his condition or reduce his prospects of recovery.

b. It makes no difference whether the act relates to the patient's medical, nutritional or other needs.

c. Here too, when possible, one should not do the act in the normal manner, but in a different way from that which one would adopt on an ordinary day of the week.

d. For some illustrations, see paragraphs 56 and 61 below and Chapter 38, paragraph 3.

complying with requests of dangerously ill patient

25. *a.* It may happen that a dangerously ill person requests something which is unconnected with his medical treatment, but which would set his mind at rest or soothe him.

b. One may not violate Shabbath by the infringement of a Torah prohibition in order to comply with such a request (except in the circumstances outlined in paragraph 26 below), but

c. one may infringe a Rabbinical prohibition,** although

d. here too, when possible, one should not perform the activity in the normal manner, but in a different way

---

*See note to preceding paragraph.
**See note to paragraph 23 above.

from that which one would adopt on an ordinary day of the week.

e. An illustration may be seen in Chapter 38, paragraph 3.

26. a. There are dangerously ill patients whose prospects of overcoming their illness and recovering their health depend on their mental state.

b. In such cases, one should be lenient and perform even acts prohibited on Shabbath by the Torah, if their omission might possibly result in a disturbance of the patient's mental equilibrium.

c. One should beware that the patient does not fall into a state of depression out of fear that he is not being properly taken care of.

d. One may violate Shabbath in cases of this kind, even when one has not been requested to do so by the patient.

e. Illustrations may be found in paragraphs 73 and 80*b*2 below and in Chapter 40, paragraphs 17 and 70.

allowing for patient's mental state

27. a. One violates Shabbath in order to save human life only if there is no other equally effective way of achieving the object without violating Shabbath.

b. If, however, such a way does exist, it is prohibited to violate Shabbath, unless there are grounds for fearing that adoption of the alternative permissible method may result in a delay which is liable to endanger the life of the patient.

c. If treatment in the manner which violates Shabbath is more effective than the alternative method, one should act in the forbidden manner and violate Shabbath.

d. Some illustrations may be found in paragraphs 38, 65 and 83 below and in Chapter 38, paragraph 2.

alternative courses of action avoiding violation of Shabbath

28. a. When violating Shabbath in order to save human life, one should (where the patient will not be adversely affected)

minimizing number and degree of violations

[513]

1) reduce to a minimum the number of violations perpetrated **and**

2) mitigate, as far as possible, the severity of the prohibitions infringed.

b. Thus, if the life can be saved by the infringement of a Rabbinical prohibition, it is forbidden to infringe a Torah prohibition.

1) A prohibited act which can be performed in a manner which differs from the way in which it would be done on an ordinary day of the week should be performed in that different manner.

2) A prohibited act which is normally done by a single person alone should be performed by two people together.

3) If it cannot be performed by two people together, and it is normally done with one hand, one should do it with both hands at the same time.

c. Some illustrations may be found in paragraphs 40, 49, 53, 58, 60, 64, 76, 81, 84 and 86 below.

d. 1) Whenever there is the slightest fear that the above restrictions

a) could result in a detrimental delay in the treatment of a dangerously ill patient, or

b) could bring about a weakening in his condition, they should be ignored.

2) In such circumstances, one should do everything as one would on an ordinary day of the week for the good of the patient, in order to save his life.

minimizing effect of Shabbath violation **29.** a. The effect achieved by the forbidden activity should also (insofar as possible) be limited to what is essential for the person who is dangerously ill.

b. One should not bring about a more extensive effect, even if this could be accomplished without the performance of any additional act.

c. The rule can be more readily understood by reference to the illustrations which appear below in paragraphs 66, 67, 68 and 75.

30. *a.* Where it is permitted to do something for a person who *incidental* is dangerously ill, one may do it even if the inevitable *violation of* result will be the performance of a forbidden act *Shabbath*

1) which, in itself, is of no use in saving the patient's life, **but**

2) without which there is no possibility of doing what is required to help the patient.

b. It is as well that one should not intend this incidental, albeit inevitable, violation.

c. It is forbidden to cause an unnecessary violation of the Shabbath, side by side with the activity one has to perform for the sick person, unless the essential activity itself would otherwise be retarded and the patient placed in jeopardy.

d. Some illustrations may be found in paragraphs 43 and 71 below and in Chapter 40, paragraphs 21, 54, 55, 60 and 73.

31. *a.* Shabbath should be violated only to save human life. *saving*

b. It is absolutely forbidden to perform any act which is *property* prohibited on Shabbath in order to save property.

c. Even the infringement of only a Rabbinical prohibition is forbidden in this latter case (with certain specific exceptions in defined circumstances discussed in Chapter 41, paragraphs 13, 14, and 15).

d. For some examples, see Chapter 41, paragraphs 3 and 25.

32. *a.* While one may violate Shabbath when human life is in *irrelevance* danger, one must remember that there is a difference *of popular* between *conception*

1) something which has to be done to save human life *of what is* and *essential*

2) something which is popularly regarded as being "essential."

b. 1) To save human life, one is not only permitted but is obliged to violate Shabbath, whereas

2) one is not allowed to violate Shabbath for some-

thing which is "essential" only because it is popularly regarded as so.

c. 1) An instance of something which fits the popular idea of "essential" to survival is bread.

2) It is an "essential" constituent of a human being's nourishment.

3) Nevertheless, it is forbidden to violate Shabbath

a) in order to prepare bread for a person who can survive on other food for one day without endangering his life, or even

b) in order to prepare any food for a person who has none at all but who can fast for one day without endangering his life.

avoiding non-urgent surgery from Wednesday onwards

33. a. From Wednesday onwards, it is prohibited to do something as a result of which a situation will be created involving risk to human life and so necessitating the violation of Shabbath.

b. 1) Consequently, someone who has to undergo an operation which is not urgent, such as the removal of tonsils, should, if the possibility exists, arrange it for the beginning of the week.

2). This should be done to avoid the need for violating Shabbath in the course of post-operative treatment.

3) Nevertheless, if, contrary to the requirements of the Halacha, a person has undergone the operation at the end of the week, one may violate Shabbath to do whatever is necessary for him, now that he is in the category of a patient whose life is in danger.

making prior preparations to avoid violation of Shabbath

34. a. 1) a) A person is obliged to prepare, before the commencement of Shabbath, everything he will need on Shabbath for the dangerously ill patient, and

b) he must not rely on the fact that he will be allowed to violate Shabbath if he did not make adequate preparations before Shabbath.

2) a) It may happen that, before Shabbath, there is no dangerously ill patient, but a situation in which one has to save human life is liable to arise on Shabbath.

b) This is sometimes the case in a doctor's house or a hospital.

c) In these circumstances it is not obligatory to make preparations in advance, but

d) one would do well to prepare what one can before Shabbath, so as to reduce the necessity which will arise for violating Shabbath, should a dangerously ill patient arrive or the condition of an existing patient worsen.

3) For some illustrations, see paragraphs 63 and 71 below and Chapter 40, paragraphs 22 and 26.

b. 1) By contrast, in some situations,

a) the necessity may arise to violate Shabbath in saving life, but

b) action could be taken to render the violation unnecessary; yet,

c) the Halacha, strictly speaking, imposes no obligation to take such action.

2) These are cases in which taking the action required would involve a great deal of bother.

3) Illustrations may be found in paragraph 74 below and in Chapter 40, paragraphs 13 and 72.

35. The application of the above principles is explained in the paragraphs which follow. *application of principles*

SUMMONING THE DOCTOR

36. *a.* One may violate Shabbath, transgressing even Torah prohibitions, to summon a doctor for a person whose life is in danger (as defined in paragraphs 8 to 16 above), or for a person who feels unwell and may possibly be dangerously ill, if *general rule*

[517]

    1) one cannot summon the doctor without violating Shabbath or

    2) time is of the essence and summoning the doctor in a permitted manner will delay his arrival.

  b. In order to summon the doctor to visit the patient, or to obtain from him instructions for treatment, one may, by way of example,

    1) telephone him or

    2) travel to him by car.

  c. One may do these things even if it is not certain that one will indeed find the doctor at home.

leaving the patient alone

37. *a.* Sometimes, if one leaves the house to summon a doctor, the patient will remain by himself and is liable to be afraid.

  b. In such a case, too, one is permitted to call the doctor, or to ask him for instructions, by telephone.

choice between doctor who is near and doctor who is far away

38. *a.* 1) In the absence of the considerations mentioned below, where there is a choice of doctors, one should call a doctor who lives nearby.

    2) There will, thus, be no need for the doctor to violate Shabbath in coming to see the patient.

  b. However, in the following cases, one may call a doctor who lives far away, despite the fact that this will inevitably involve violation of the Shabbath:

    1) if the doctor who lives far away is more competent;

    2) if the doctor who lives far away has been treating the patient regularly and knows his medical history;

    3) if the patient demands that one call his own private doctor (believing that he will give him more devoted attention).

  c. It is forbidden to call the doctor who lives a long way off if one's motives are purely financial, as where

    1) the doctor is a relative and will not make any charge for the visit, or

    2) the doctor works for a sick-fund (medical insurance

scheme) to which the patient belongs, so that there will be no need to pay him for the visit.

39. Even when a doctor has already been brought to the patient, one may call a second doctor, notwithstanding that this may unavoidably involve violation of the Shabbath, if
   a. there is a need to call in a greater specialist **or**
   b. one wishes to obtain a second opinion.

additional doctors

40. *a.* When one has to telephone a doctor to come, or for instructions as to treatment, one should, where possible, remove the receiver in a manner which differs from that which one would use on an ordinary day of the week.
   b. For instance, one should displace the receiver with one's elbow or wrist, or
   c. in the event that this is not possible, one should lift it off its rest together with another person, or
   d. if nobody else is there, one should take it off with both hands at the same time.

lifting the telephone receiver off its rest

41. *a.* When speaking on the telephone for the purposes of a dangerously ill patient, one is not obliged to be sparing in words, weighing each word to see whether it is required, but
   b. one should say everything that has to be said concerning the patient.
   c. One may even end the conversation with some such phrase as, "Good-bye," or, "Thank you very much."
   d. However, one should certainly not talk about matters which have no connection with the patient or his treatment.

speaking on the telephone

42. *a.* At the end of the conversation, one should not replace the receiver on its rest, except in the following circumstances, when it *must* be replaced:
   1) if one may need to take an incoming call that

replacing the telephone receiver

Shabbath on the same instrument or line for the purpose of saving a human life;

   2) if there is reason to suppose the number one has called may be needed again that Shabbath in connection with saving human life.

b. Thus, if one has telephoned a doctor or a hospital, one *must* replace the receiver on its rest after the conversation, because, until one does,

   1) the doctor or hospital will not be able to receive another incoming call on that line,

   2) nor will they be able to use it to contact anybody else (in case of need).

c. At all events, even when it is permissible to put the receiver back on its rest, one should do so

   1) with one's elbows or wrists, or,

   2) if this is not possible, together with another person, or

   3) if one is alone, with both hands at the same time. (Compare paragraph 40 above.)

use of a public telephone

43. a. One may use a telephone token or a coin (even though they are *muktzeh*) to make a call from a public telephone for the purpose of saving a human life, if there is no other telephone as readily available in the vicinity.

b. 1) Likewise, if one has no other telephone equally available, one may, even at night, use a public telephone booth in which a light is automatically turned on when one enters, but

   2) one should not have the intention, when entering the phone booth, to read by the light which comes on something that has no connection with saving the person who is in danger.

c. As far as leaving the phone booth is concerned, one may do so, in spite of the fact that this will cause the light to go off, if there is a possibility that one may be needed for the purposes of the person whose life is in danger.

d. If one is not needed for the person who is in danger, what one can do with regard to leaving the phone booth depends on the circumstances.

1) a) Where the light is operated by pressure on the floor of the phone booth, one may be able to avoid its being turned off by bringing in some heavy object whose weight will maintain the pressure when one leaves.

   b) When nothing else is available, one may even use a heavy stone, despite the fact that it is *muktzeh*.

   c) Use of a heavy object in this way is possible only in a place where one is permitted to carry it into the phone booth, for example, where there is an *eiruv*.

2) One may be able to ask a friend to stand in the booth in one's place, taking turns with him to stand there throughout the Shabbath.

3) a) One can tell a non-Jew to stand in the booth in one's place.

   b) One need not be concerned that the non-Jew may leave the phone booth afterwards, thereby causing the light to go off.

4) Should none of the above possibilities present themselves, as where no obliging friend or non-Jew is at hand and there is no *eiruv*, or where there is no one about who can pass one the required heavy object into the phone booth, then

   a) if it is close to the end of Shabbath, one ought to stay where one is and not leave, but,

   b) if there is still a long time to go to the end of Shabbath and one experiences great difficulty in remaining in the phone booth, there is room for being less strict and leaving, notwithstanding the fact that the electric light will be extinguished as a result.

returning
44. Someone who is sent to summon a doctor to a person *with doctor*

whose life is in danger may accompany the doctor back in a car

a. to show the doctor the way,

b. to ensure that the doctor comes to the patient's house as fast as he can,

c. if there is a possibility that he may be required to run another errand for the patient, or

d. if there is a possibility that the patient may need him or is afraid to be without him.

45. a. All other things being equal, it is preferable to turn to a doctor who observes Shabbath. (See paragraph 6 above.)

doctors who do not observe Shabbath

b. One may turn to a non-Jewish doctor, or to a Jewish doctor who does not observe Shabbath, even where there is a Shabbath-observant doctor at hand, if the latter is not as competent.

c. One may, in the interests of expediency, turn to a non-observant doctor even when one knows he will violate Shabbath without there being any necessity at all to do so, as by

1) driving to the patient's house, notwithstanding that it is close by, or

2) lighting a cigarette on the way.

paying the doctor

46. a. The rules relating to payment of a doctor for treating a patient whose life is in danger are analogous to those contained in paragraph 55 below.

traveling to and from the patient.

b. For detailed rules in connection with traveling to and from the patient's house, see Chapter 40, paragraphs 50 to 73.

doctor answering the telephone

47. a. If the telephone rings in a doctor's house, he may pick up the receiver, if there is a possibility that someone is trying to contact him about a person whose life is in danger.

b. He would do well to pick up and replace the receiver in

a manner different from that which he uses during the rest of the week. (See paragraphs 40 and 42 above.)

WRITING

48. *a.* 1) One may write anything which has to be written on Shabbath for a person whose life is in danger. *what may be written*
   2) This could include, by way of example,
   a) urgent prescriptions for medicines,
   b) an urgent letter referring a patient to a hospital, and
   c) important medical particulars which are liable to be forgotten, or confused with those of another patient, if left unrecorded.
b. 1) However, it is forbidden to write down something which does not directly affect the patient's treatment (for instance, that he belongs to a medical insurance plan).
   2) Moreover, one must limit oneself to writing the absolute minimum without which one would be unable to do what is necessary to save the patient.
   3) One must not add one letter more, nor even a period (full stop) at the end of the sentence.

49. *a.* One should try to write whatever is essential in a manner different from that which one would adopt on another day of the week, for example by using one's left hand. *manner of writing*
b. Of course, where speed is vital and writing in a different manner is liable to result in delay, one should write in one's usual way.

50. *a.* Sometimes, a doctor summoned to a patient whose life is in danger, or is suspected to be in danger, concludes that one must await developments in the patient's condition before deciding *documents which may be required later*
   1) whether he requires a particular medicine or
   2) whether he should be taken to a hospital.

[523]

   b. Except in the situations mentioned below, the doctor should not write out
    1) the prescription for the medicine or
    2) the letter referring the patient to the hospital
    before it becomes clear that they are indeed necessary.

   c. This applies even where, to obtain them afterwards, one will have to violate Shabbath, for instance by traveling to the doctor or by telephoning him.

   d. Yet, the doctor may write out the prescription or the letter on the spot, if there is a risk
    1) that it will be difficult to find the doctor again when it subsequently transpires that the prescription or the letter are needed or
    2) that, later, waiting for the letter or prescription to be written might endanger the patient's life.

doctors who write more than necessary

51. *a.* 1) If a doctor asks for a pen to write out something which is essential for saving the patient's life, one may pick it up and hand it to him.
    2) This is so even where one has reason to suspect that the doctor will, in addition to what is essential, write things which are not vital and which one is forbidden to write on Shabbath.

   b. When the doctor wants the pen to write out only things which are not immediately necessary for saving a life, such as a prescription for drugs to be purchased after Shabbath, then,
    1) if he is a Jew, one may not assist him, but
    2) if he is a non-Jew who, for some reason, is unable to take the pen himself, one may pick it up and give it to him even in this case.

MEDICINES

violating Shabbath to obtain essential medicines

52. *a.* One is allowed, indeed it is a mitzva, to violate Shabbath in order to prepare or bring medicines for a person whose life is in danger, if, in the doctor's opinion, they are required

1) for his recovery,
2) to prevent an aggravation of his condition or
3) to alleviate his suffering (as in paragraph 22 above).

b. The same applies with regard to medicines which the dangerously ill person himself demands (despite the fact that Shabbath is dear to him and he would be afraid to violate it without justification), provided that

1) he believes and feels, in the light of his experience, that they can be of some use in his treatment (even though the doctor, in spite of the patient's insistence, thinks otherwise),
2) the medicines have some reasonable connection with the malady from which the patient is suffering **and**
3) the doctor does not think the medicines are liable to harm the patient.

c. One does not violate Shabbath to satisfy the patient's demands if

1) there is no reasonable connection between the medicines and the patient's malady, **or**
2) the doctor says the medicines are liable to harm the patient, **or**
3) a) the doctor who knows the patient's illness contends that these medicines cannot help him **and**
   b) the patient himself is not too insistent in his demands.

53. a. If one has to travel to bring medicines for someone whose life is in danger, it is preferable to use public transport rather than operate a special motor vehicle (provided the delay caused will not have an adverse effect on the patient's condition). *traveling to bring medicines*

b. 1) Whenever possible, one should (where the delay caused will not have an adverse effect on the patient's condition) use a means of transport which

does not involve the transgression of Torah prohibitions.

2) For instance, where one does not have to pass
through an actual *r^eshuth ha-rabbim* (as defined in
Chapter 17, paragraph 3), no Torah prohibition
need be infringed if one
   a) rides a bicycle or
   b) travels in a horse-drawn cart.

carrying **54.** *a.* If one is in a place where there is no *eiruv* — so that
medicines carrying articles about is forbidden — and has to carry
medicines through *r^eshuth ha-rabbim*, one should try,
as much as possible, to carry them in a different
manner for that which one would adopt during the rest
of the week.

b. By way of example, one could put them
   1) on one's head, under one's hat,
   2) inside one's shoes or
   3) between the clothes one is wearing.

c. One should not keep them in one's hand or inside one's
pocket, unless the adopting of an alternative method
might result in a delay which could further endanger
the life of the patient.

paying the **55.** *a.* 1) Where the pharmacist requires payment on Shab-
pharmacist bath in return for medicines he is supplying for a
dangerously ill patient, it is best to put him off until
after Shabbath, giving him, if necessary, some
object by way of security.

2) One need not be concerned if the pharmacist notes
down one's name when taking a security, although,

3) if he is Jewish, one should try to prevent this by
giving him something which already bears one's
name and address.

b. 1) In the event that one has nothing to give as
security, or if the pharmacist is not willing to

accept a security, one may pay him, but

2) one must not accept change from him on Shabbath, since this does not benefit the patient in any way, and

3) one should pay in cash and not write a check, unless there is no alternative. (In connection with writing, see paragraph 48*b* above.)

56. *a.* It is permitted for a dangerously ill patient to take even medicines which are not essential for saving his life. (See paragraph 24 above.)

b. For instance, he may take a pill to ease a toothache.

c. One must, however, be careful in such cases not to violate Shabbath by the infringement of Torah prohibitions.

d. Thus, one must not

1) write out a prescription for such medicines, nor

2) drive a car to bring them.

(See also Chapter 33, paragraph 4, since, insofar as taking inessential medicines is concerned, the dangerously ill patient is on the same footing as a patient whose life is not in danger.)

inessential medicines for dangerously ill patient

INJECTIONS

57. *a.* One is allowed to violate Shabbath in order to administer an injection to a person whose life is in danger, if, in the doctor's opinion, it has to be done on Shabbath

1) to bring about the patient's recovery,

2) to prevent an aggravation of his condition or

3) to alleviate his suffering (as in paragraph 22 above).

b. Moreover, one may violate Shabbath in order to inject the patient with vitamins, or to give him pain-killing injections, if, in the doctor's opinion, they are urgently needed

essential injections for dangerously ill patient

1) to save the patient's life or
2) to make him feel stronger or refreshed.

different kinds of injections
58. a. The administration of a subcutaneous or intra-muscular injection does not in itself comprise a violation of a Torah prohibition.
   b. On the other hand, according to some authorities, the administration of an intravenous injection does involve the transgression of a Torah prohibition.
   c. Consequently, one should not give a patient an intravenous injection when it is possible to give him a subcutaneous or an intramuscular one, unless the intravenous
      1) is more effective **or**
      2) takes effect more quickly and time is important.

swabbing
59. a. The skin around the area where the injection is given may be cleaned by pouring a little liquid onto it and wiping it dry with absorbent cotton (cotton wool) or a paper pad.
   b. Iodine may be used for this purpose.
   c. One may also dip a brush with synthetic bristles into iodine and clean the skin with that.
   d. One should refrain, as much as possible, from using absorbent cotton soaked in liquid.

sterilization
60. a. When one can, one should prepare a sufficient supply of disinfected or sterilized medical instruments before Shabbath begins.
   b. Where one has not managed to do so, or one's stock has run out, one may boil up water for the purpose of sterilizing those instruments one must have, but
      1) one should preferably use water which has already been boiled once, before Shabbath, and is still not completely cold;
      2) if one has no such water, but has water which was boiled before Shabbath and is now altogether cold, one should, as much as possible, use that, since

many authorities hold that boiling it up again infringes only a Rabbinical prohibition;

3) failing this, one may of course use any water, as the instruments are required to save a human life.

c. If

1) one does not use the instruments immediately after sterilization, and

2) they are lying in a jumbled pile, one should not sort them into their different kinds for putting into their individual allotted places, but should leave them mixed together as they are.

61. a. 1) It may happen that a person whose life is in danger will not be adversely affected if a particular injection is postponed until after Shabbath.

injections which could be postponed until after Shabbath

2) He may nevertheless be given that injection on Shabbath, but only if Shabbath is not violated by the infringement of a Torah prohibition.

b. Therefore,

1) the doctor should not write out a prescription for injections of this kind,

2) one should not drive in one's car to collect the injections,

3) one should not boil water for any sterilization which is required and

4) these injections should not be given intravenously.

62. a. One may give a healthy person a prophylactic (immunizing) injection when there are grounds to fear that he may contract an illness which can endanger his life.

prophylactic injections

b. If, in the opinion of the doctor, the matter is urgent, even Torah prohibitions may be infringed for this purpose, for example

1) by writing out a prescription or

2) by driving to the pharmacy to buy the injection.

TURNING LIGHTS ON AND OFF

when
necessary
for patient
whose life
is in danger

63. *a.* When there is a sick person in the house, one should turn on a light before Shabbath (preferably just outside his room), so that one will be able to see well enough to attend to his needs during the night hours.* (See paragraph 34 above.)

b. One may turn on the light on Shabbath for a person whose life is in danger,

1) whenever the dark or the poor light hinder one in doing what is required to save him, **or**
2) so that he should not be afraid of the dark, **or**
3) to make him feel that he is being taken care of and to avoid his having the impression that he is being neglected or not receiving proper attention, an impression which is liable to have a detrimental effect on his state of health.

how to turn
the light on

64. *a.* Where possible, if one has to turn on the light for a dangerously ill person, one should do so in a different manner from that which one would adopt on an ordinary day of the week.

b. For example, one should switch on the electric light with one's elbow, and not with one's hand.

bringing
light

65. *a.* If there is a need for a light in the room of a dangerously ill person, and there is a lamp burning in another room, one should bring in that lamp (while it is still burning), rather than put on another light.

b. This is because one should, to whatever extent possible, minimize the degree to which one violates the Shabbath, and transferring the lamp from one room to another is an infringement only of the Rabbinical prohibition against moving a *muktzeh* object.

---

*One ought not to leave a kerosene lamp or a kerosene stove burning in the room of a person who is ill or of small children, as they are liable to be harmed by the fumes and lack of oxygen.

c. One should, of course, turn on another light, and not bring the lamp from the other room, if
1) the light emitted by the lamp is not sufficient for one's purposes **or**
2) time is pressing and any delay is liable to endanger the patient.

d. 1) Where necessary, one may turn a light on for a dangerously ill patient even when there is a lamp already burning in a neighbor's house, if making the lamp available to the patient will cause the neighbor considerable hardship and inconvenience.
2) An example of this occurs when the neighbor is asleep and one would have to wake him.

66. *a.* As explained in paragraph 29 above, the effect achieved by any forbidden activity which has to be performed should be limited (as much as possible) to what is essential for the person who is dangerously ill. *minimizing the number of lights turned on*

b. Consequently, if
1) one switch will turn on only one bulb, whereas another will turn on two, and
2) all that is required is the light of only one bulb, then one should operate the switch that turns on only one bulb.

c. 1) Likewise, if one
a) has to turn on the electricity by means of the main switch and yet
b) only needs the light urgently in one room, one should first turn off the switches in the other rooms and only afterwards turn on the main switch.
2) a) Alternatively, where the bulbs are of the type which screw into their sockets, one can prevent unnecessary bulbs from being lit by screwing them out a little before turning on the main switch, but
b) this is only permitted with bulbs which are

from time to time taken out of their sockets. (See Chapter 13, paragraph 29.)

d. 1) Insofar as one can, one should not handle the bulbs in the normal manner, because they are *muktzeh*.

2) One should move them with one's elbow or wrists, or in some other way which differs from that which one would normally employ.

choice between larger and smaller bulb

67. a. When

1) there are two bulbs, one large and one small, that one could turn on for the purposes of a dangerously ill person, but

2) either one of them, by itself, would suffice to serve the patient's needs,

it is better to turn on the smaller bulb.

b. The reason for this is that by turning on the larger bulb one would be igniting a larger filament than necessary.

choice between two kerosene lamps

68. a. 1) If one has to turn on a light for a patient whose life is in danger, and has available two kerosene lamps,

a) one of which contains just enough kerosene to last as long as is essential for the patient's needs, while

b) the other is so full of kerosene that it will burn for many hours longer than is required for the patient,

one should light the lamp containing the correct amount.

2) If one wishes to use a lamp containing more than enough kerosene, one should pour off the excess before the lamp is lit.

choice between long and short candles

b. If one has two candles, one which is long and one which is short but sufficient to meet the needs of the person whose life is in danger, one should kindle the short candle and not the long one.

69. *a.* A light which was turned on on Shabbath for a person *using a* whose life is in danger may also be used by other *light turned* people. *on for a*

b. Since a light which is sufficient for one person is *sick person* equally sufficient for any number of people, there is no reason to fear that permitting other people to use the light will lead to the turning on of additional lights.

c. 1) Other people may even use a light turned on by means of a main switch which turned on all the lights in the house at the same time that it turned on the sick person's light.

2) This situation could occur when there is no possibility of first shutting off the switches in the rest of the house, as required by the rules set out in paragraph 66 above.

turning off
70. *a.* One may turn off the light on Shabbath to enable a *the light* dangerously ill person, for whom sleep is beneficial, to go to sleep, but one may do so only if there is no possibility

1) of moving the patient, without difficulty, to another room,

2) of moving the still-burning light out of the room,

3) of covering the burning light or

4) of resetting a timer (which has been operating since before Shabbath) to turn off the light after a short interval.

b. If possible, when one has to turn off the light, one should do so in a way which one would not use on another day of the week, for instance by switching off the electricity with one's elbow rather than with one's hand.

c. See also Chapter 38, paragraph 2.

PREPARING AND COOKING FOOD

71. *a.* 1) Before Shabbath, one should disconnect, or *refrigera-* remove, the internal light of a refrigerator one is *tors* going to use on Shabbath, so as to prevent its being automatically turned on by the opening of the door.

2) Nevertheless, even if one has not done so, one may open the refrigerator on Shabbath to remove whatever one needs for a patient whose life is in danger, despite the fact that this will cause the light inside to come on.

3) While the door is open, one may also make use of the opportunity to take out food for other people (who are not dangerously ill).

b. 1) One should not close the door of a refrigerator whose internal light will thereby be extinguished,* unless this is essential for the purposes of a patient whose life is in danger.

2) a) Subject to the fulfillment of the four conditions enumerated below, one may, and indeed must, close the door.

   b) However, if one may have to open the refrigerator for the patient again that Shabbath, one should, before closing the door, disconnect or remove the internal bulb (and, if possible, one should do so in a manner one would not normally adopt).

   c) This will prevent its being turned on and off again every time one has to open and close the door.

3) The conditions referred to are that

   a) there are still things in the refrigerator which are, or may possibly be, required that Shabbath, or even after Shabbath, for a person whose life is in danger;

   b) the items one has in the refrigerator for the patient will spoil if the door is not closed;

   c) one will not be able to obtain other such items in their place;

   d) there is no other place where these items could

---

*But see Chapter 31, paragraph 1.

be kept, for example in a neighbor's refrigerator.

72. *a.* One may cook on Shabbath for a dangerously ill person who needs hot food to strengthen and refresh him, if
   1) there is no suitable hot food at hand or
   2) the hot food which is available is not fresh enough for the patient.
   b. Similarly, if there is no hot water at hand, one may boil up hot water on Shabbath for a dangerously ill patient who needs a hot drink.

cooking permitted where no other suitable food available

73. One may cook on Shabbath for a dangerously ill patient who (despite the fact that Shabbath is dear to him and he would not violate it unjustifiably) demands fresh, hot food, claiming that the food prepared before Shabbath is liable to harm him, provided
   a. the patient gives a reason for what he is saying and
   b. one can tell that his fears are sincere.

patient's claim that food prepared is unsuitable

74. *a.* One may cook on Shabbath for a person whose life is in danger and who needs hot food or drink, as described in paragraphs 72 and 73 above,
   1) notwithstanding that one's neighbor has hot food and drink available,
   2) if putting them at the patient's disposal would cause the neighbor considerable hardship and inconvenience, as where
      a) the neighbor is asleep and it would be necessary to wake him or
      b) the neighbor would himself be left without hot food and drink for Shabbath.
   b. Moreover, neither the neighbors nor anyone else is obliged, by the strict letter of the law, to avert the necessity of cooking on Shabbath by giving up his own food if, as a result, he himself will be left without hot food for Shabbath.

availability of neighbor's food

32:75 *Shᵉmirath Shabbath Kᵉhilchathah*

quantity to be cooked

75. *a.* 1) Except in the circumstances mentioned below, one should cook only the quantity of food required for the dangerously ill patient, and no more.

2) It is forbidden to add anything over and above the required amount, even if
   a) one puts it into the same pot that one is using to cook for the person who is ill and
   b) one adds it before turning on the stove.

b. 1) Nonetheless, if time is pressing, there is no need to be particular about the quantity, and one should put into the pot a generous estimate of the amount the dangerously ill patient will require.

2) Similarly, one may put into the pot, and cook, more than the patient requires, when
   a) the only pot available is a large one, and
   b) to cook in it only the amount the patient requires will spoil the pot, leaving him without the hot food.

minimizing violation of Shabbath

76. When heating water or cooking food for a dangerously ill person, one should reduce the violation of Shabbath to the minimum necessary, and, therefore,

a. if the gas is already burning, one should not ignite another flame;

b. if there is a candle burning, one should not light the gas with a match (which itself has to be lit), but should touch the burning candle to the gas to light it.

c. if one has a choice between using an electric stove and a gas stove, one should preferably use the electric stove, since
   1) turning on the gas stove requires two acts of ignition, the striking of the match and the kindling of the gas flame (unless there is a pilot light or a candle burning), whereas
   2) turning on the electric stove requires the performance of only one such action;

d. if possible, one should change one's normal method of turning on the stove, for example, by rotating the knob with one's elbow, or with the backs of one's hands, rather than with one's fingers;

e. if one uses a stove powered by bottled gas and the circumstances are that

1) of two cylinders connected to the stove, the one in use is full of gas, while the reserve cylinder is empty,

2) one is not pressed for time, and

3) it is possible to transfer a sufficient quantity of gas for cooking the patient's food from the full cylinder to the empty cylinder, subsequently shutting off the full cylinder,

then one should indeed transfer the amount of gas needed for use, and not light the stove until one has cut off the flow of gas from the full cylinder;

f. 1) a) one may not purposely light only a small flame, to be turned higher afterwards (unless one has to do so in the process of cooking), since this involves two acts of ignition, but

b) what one should do is to turn the gas tap on to the extent required and only then light the flame;

2) a) however, when using a gas stove, one may light either a large or a small burner, according to one's choice;

b) this is because the same gas is being ignited in each eventuality;*

c) the difference in the rate at which it burns is not a decisive consideration.

77. a. When one has finished cooking, one may neither extinguish nor reduce the power of the burner.

extinguishing or lowering flame

---

*Contrast with

a. paragraph 67 above, where one is igniting more filament than necessary, and

b. paragraph 68 above, where the superfluous kerosene or length of candle will cause the flame to burn on Shabbath for longer than necessary.

b. This applies whether the stove is powered by gas, kerosene or electricity.

eating food cooked on Shabbath for a dangerously ill person 78. a. 1) There are no grounds for permitting even another person who is ill, if he is not dangerously ill, to eat on Shabbath the remains of food or water which one cooked or boiled for a dangerously ill person on Shabbath.

2) This was prohibited by the Rabbis because one might come to cook more than is required for the dangerously ill patient, in order to take into account also the needs of the healthy, or healthier, person.

b. One may, however, taste food that one is cooking for a dangerously ill patient to find out if it is good for him.

c. Moreover,

1) the food left over may be eaten by a healthy person immediately after Shabbath, and

2) there is no reason to question the use of the utensils in which one cooked the food (as one might do if food were unjustifiably cooked on Shabbath).

when the food cooked is muktzeh 79. a. If the situation contains the following two elements, food cooked on Shabbath for a person whose life is in danger is *muktzeh*, and should not be moved, except for the needs of the patient:

1) the patient fell ill only on that day **and**

2) the food was prepared from materials which would not have been fit for consumption without cooking.

b. Examples of materials of this kind are raw meat, fish and potatoes.

c. Nevertheless, the remains of the food may be removed, or even put into the refrigerator, if it would otherwise be liable to attract flies and insects.

d. If the patient has been ill since before Shabbath, the food may be moved, even if this is not being done for the purposes of the patient.

80. *a.* When a person who is dangerously ill must eat meat to *slaughter-* give him the strength to overcome his illness, and *ing* there is no suitable meat available, one should slaughter an animal or a fowl for him on Shabbath.
  b. This could occur, for instance, where
    1) the meat which is available is not fresh enough or
    2) the only meat one can obtain is halachically unfit for consumption by Jews, and one is apprehensive lest it be so repulsive to the patient that he refuses to eat and further endangers himself.
  c. After slaughter, one should also salt the meat, in accordance with the requirements of the Halacha, before cooking.
  d. 1) It makes no difference, from the point of view of the Halacha, whether one slaughters a small chicken, for a person whose life is in danger, or a large ox.
    2) This is because the essence of the act of slaughter is the taking of a creature's life, and no distinction can be made between the life of a large creature and that of a small one.
  e. 1) If
      a) the animal one slaughters is of a variety whose blood the Halacha requires one to cover after slaughter, or if
      b) one slaughters a fowl (all varieties of which are required to have their blood covered),
      one should, nonetheless, not cover the blood on Shabbath, even when one has ready in the house, since before Shabbath, loose earth with which to cover it.
    2) However, should any blood remain visible after Shabbath, one should cover it then.

HEATING WATER TO WASH THE PATIENT

81. *a.* 1) One may heat water on Shabbath to wash a *when* dangerously ill patient, provided that *permissible* a) this will refresh and invigorate his body and *and to what* *degree*

have a favorable effect on his state of health,
b) there is no non-Jew at hand to heat the water*
   and
c) one does not have any readily available water
   which can be used for the purpose with equal
   effect.

2) One may do so even if failure to wash him with
   warm water will not increase the danger which
   threatens him.

b. If possible, one should take care not to heat the water
   on Shabbath to a temperature of 45 degrees centigrade
   (113 degrees Fahrenheit) or more.

c. It is preferable
   1) to heat a large quantity of water to the temperature
      required for washing the patient, which will be less
      than 45 degrees centigrade,
   rather than
   2) to heat a small quantity to 45 degrees or more, for
      mixing with cold water.

operating
water
heaters

82. a. In order to warm water for a dangerously ill person (in
       the circumstances set out in the previous paragraph),
       one may switch on an electric boiler, even though it
       heats up a larger quantity of water than is essential to
       wash the patient.

b. It is also permitted to extract the hot water from the
   electric boiler for the purposes of the person whose life
   is in danger, despite the fact that cold water
   1) will flow in to replace it and
   2) will be heated by the electricity which continues to
      activate the boiler or by the hot water which is
      already there.

c. 1) On the other hand, it is forbidden to turn off the hot-

---

*In spite of what is stated in paragraph 6 above, one should, when
practicable, use the services of a non-Jew, as there is no immediate
urgency about heating the water.

water tap, unless there is a chance that one may need more hot water for the dangerously ill patient and leaving the tap running will prevent it from being available.

2) The reason for the prohibition is that turning off the tap also stops the inflow of cold water to the boiler, and this, in turn, accelerates the heating up of the cold water which has already flowed in.

d. 1) When one does have to turn off the hot-water tap (due to the patient's needs), it is as well not to do so with the intention of deriving a personal benefit from the water which will now (on Shabbath) be heated.

2) This would include making use of the still hot water for one's own purposes after Shabbath.

e. 1) Where available, one should preferably use an electric boiler which can be adjusted to prevent cold water from flowing in to replace the hot water flowing out.

2) Use of a boiler adjusted in this way will also enable one to turn off the hot-water tap even when this is not required for the patient's needs.

HEATING AND COOLING A ROOM CONTAINING A DANGEROUSLY ILL PATIENT

83. a. Since the cold is liable to harm a person who is dangerously ill, one may, if the patient is cold, turn on a heater for him, provided that _when heating may be turned on_

1) there is no non-Jew at hand who could do it* **and**

2) the heater warms the patient more satisfactorily than one could warm him by giving him additional blankets.

---

*In spite of what is stated in paragraph 6 above, one should, when practicable, use the services of a non-Jew, as there is no immediate urgency about turning on the heater.

[541]

b. When possible, one should vary one's normal method of turning on the heater. (Compare paragraph 86 below.)

how to turn on a heater   84. a. If one has to turn on an electric heater containing a number of heating elements, each of which can be operated by its own separate switch, one should
   1) first adjust the separate switches so that only the required elements will come on, and
   2) afterwards insert the plug into the electricity socket.

b. In this way, one will have avoided performing more than one act of ignition.

when heating may be turned off   85. a. If the heat from a heater burning in the room of a dangerously ill patient is oppressive and burdensome to him, and there is no possibility of either
   1) taking the heater out of the room **or**
   2) transferring the patient to another room without disturbing him excessively,
   then one is allowed to lower the heat or, should this be insufficient, to turn the heater off altogether.

b. When possible, one should vary one's normal method of lowering the heat or turning off the heater. (Compare paragraph 86 below.)

operating fans and air conditioners   86. a. On a hot summer's day, when
   1) the heat is oppressive and burdensome to a dangerously ill patient and
   2) there is no non-Jew at hand,*
   one may activate cooling equipment, such as a fan or an air conditioner.

b. Where equipment of this kind is producing chill air which disturbs the patient and is liable to harm him, one may turn it off, provided there is no other manner of achieving the same object, such as

---

*See note to paragraph 83 above, referring to an analogous case.

      1) by swivelling the fan to face in a different direction
       or

      2) by transferring the patient elsewhere.

c. 1) When possible, one should vary the method of turning the fan or air conditioner on and off from that which one would adopt during the rest of the week.

      2) By way of example,

         a) one should use one's elbows or wrists, instead of one's hands, or,

         b) if the situation permits, one can reset a timer (which has been operating since before Shabbath) to perform the required activity after a delay, however short.

Chapter 33

Laws Relating to Persons Who Are Ill, But Whose Lives Are Not in Danger

DEFINITION OF A PERSON WHO IS ILL BUT WHOSE LIFE IS NOT IN DANGER

categories covered by definition

1. The following are considered by the Halacha to be persons who are ill but without danger to their lives (unless, of course, they come within the categories described in Chapter 32, paragraphs 8 to 16, in which case their lives are considered to be in danger, and one must act as set out in that chapter):

a. a person who is confined to bed on account of his illness;

b. somebody who, although not confined to bed, is suffering from what for him is an above-normal temperature, if the same complaint would, as a rule, inhibit a person from leaving the house (compare Chapter 32, paragraphs 11*a*, 11*b* and 12*a*);

c. an individual who, although not confined to bed, is suffering from pain to such an extent that his whole body feels weakened, as in the case of a migraine attack;

d. someone who walks about like a healthy person but is liable to become confined to bed if he does not receive treatment in time, as where he suffers from

1) asthma,

2) diabetes,

3) rheumatic fever or

4) a heart disease which does not endanger life;

e. 1) a person who is in danger of losing the normal use*

---

*This includes not only the risk of a total loss of use of the limb or organ in question, but even a risk that it will no longer function in the same way as the corresponding limb or organ of a normal person, as where a limp may develop.

of one of his limbs or organs, provided the facts are such that

  a) the danger to the limb or organ will clearly not develop into a danger to the patient's life and,

  b) in the doctor's view, there is no fear that delaying treatment until the evening will bring about a deterioration in the patient's condition to a state where his life will be in danger;

  2) this could occur, for example, in the case of a simple fracture, with no displacement of the broken ends of the bone (see Chapter 32, paragraph 11e);

f. someone who is suffering from an eye inflammation (the treatment of which is discussed in Chapter 34, paragraph 8);

g. a woman who has given birth to a baby, from the eighth day after the birth until the expiry of thirty days after the birth, as explained in Chapter 36, paragraph 15;

h. a small child, as discussed in detail in Chapter 37.

WHAT MAY AND WHAT MAY NOT BE DONE ON SHABBATH
AND YOM TOV FOR A PERSON WHO IS ILL BUT
WHOSE LIFE IS NOT IN DANGER

2. *a.* 1) Whenever possible, the medical needs of a person *general rule* who is ill, but not dangerously so, should be attended to without infringing any prohibitions.

  2) Where this is not possible, one may attend to all of the patient's needs through the agency of a non-Jew.

    a) The non-Jew's services should be used only to do things which are required for the patient on Shabbath, and not things which are required for after Shabbath.

    b) When the use of his services is permitted, the non-Jew may be employed even to perform an act which is the subject of a Torah prohibition.

    c) The rules regarding the use of a non-Jew in

these cases are discussed in Chapter 38, paragraphs 4 to 12.

b. 1) A Jew must not violate Shabbath by committing an act forbidden by the Torah, even if the patient is in danger of losing the use of a limb or organ, so long as it is clear that no danger to his life will develop as a result.

2) If the act does involve a Torah prohibition, then,

a) according to one view, even varying its method of performance from that normally adopted does not make it permissible, whereas

b) other great halachic authorities hold that the medical needs of a person who is ill, albeit not in danger of his life, justify the performance of such an act, provided the variation is introduced.

c. As to the infringement of Rabbinical* prohibitions** for a person who is ill, but not dangerously so, the situation is as follows:

1) In a case where there is a risk that the patient will lose the normal use of a limb or organ (as in paragraph 1e above),

a) one may, for the purpose of attending to his medical needs, perform an act which is the subject of a Rabbinical prohibition, and

b) one need not even introduce a variation into the

---

*Since it is not always easy to distinguish in practice between a Torah prohibition and a Rabbinical prohibition, one ought to consult the opinion of an expert in the Halacha, in order to establish how best to proceed.

** a. This chapter deals only with the infringement of prohibitions involving a violation of Shabbath.

b. As to other prohibitions, a distinction must be made between

1) the consumption of forbidden food or drink and

2) other breaches of the Halacha.

c. 1) A person who is ill, but not dangerously so, may consume forbidden food or drink only if

a) it is unpleasant to the palate (for instance where the

manner one would adopt on an ordinary day of the week.

2) In a case (such as those described in paragraph 1a-d above) where there is no such risk to a limb or organ,

   a) one may, for the purpose of attending to the patient's medical needs, perform an act which is the subject of a Rabbinical prohibition but should introduce a variation into the way in which one would perform it on an ordinary day of the week;

   b) if it is impossible to introduce a variation, one should have the act performed through the agency of a non-Jew;

   c) only if there is no non-Jew available may the act be performed by a Jew without variation.

3. Owing to the fact that one may not transgress a Torah prohibition for a patient who is ill but whose life is not in danger, one is not allowed, on Shabbath, to do the following for him: *telephones, cars, lights, X-rays and plaster casts*

   a. telephone the doctor;

   b. drive in one's car to buy medicines;

   c. turn the light on or off;

   d. take X-ray photographs;

   e. put on a plaster cast.

---

   forbidden ingredient of a tablet is bitter) **and**

   b) it assists his recovery.

2) Consequently, one should watch out for medicines containing such items as

   a) ingredients from which *t^erumoth* and *ma'asroth* still have to be separated,

   b) *chametz* on Pesach or

   c) animal products which a Jew is forbidden to eat.

3) See further Chapter 40, paragraphs 74 to 80, 85, 86 and 88.

d. The patient may undergo treatment involving other breaches of the Halacha if the infringement is of a Rabbinical, and not of a Torah, prohibition.

medicines required for treatment

4. *a.* A person who is ill may take medicine,* such as pills, syrups and drops, even though his life is not in danger.

b. If one does not have the requisite medicines in the house, and one cannot obtain them from a neighbor, one may go into a pharmacy to acquire them, but
   1) a Jewish doctor must on no account write out a prescription for them,
   2) one is not permitted to bring the medicines or anything else through a *r^eshuth ha-rabbim* and,
   3) as far as payment for the medicines is concerned, one should proceed as set out in Chapter 32, paragraph 55, except that one *may not* write a check.

c. One may tear the wrapping around a pill but should make every effort to tear it only in a place where there is no lettering.

d. One may cut a pill or a suppository in half (even if one is particular to cut it into two equal halves), with the object of using only one half, or one half at a time.

e. 1) One may crumble a pill and dissolve it in water;
   2) however, one should not mix the crumbled pill (or any other powder) with only a small quantity of water, but should make a thinner solution.

f. Hydrogen peroxide may be mixed with water for gargling.

taking medicine for minor ailment forbidden

5. *a.* Although, as explained in paragraph 4 above, a person who is ill but whose life is not in danger may take medicine, he is not permitted to take a medicine which he needs in order to treat some minor ailment that he also happens to have.

---

*a. As a rule, every medicine is *muktzeh* on Shabbath or Yom Tov, even if its taste is not bitter (so that it would be palatable to eat in the normal way), and one should not handle it except for the purposes of the patient.

b. However, if the patient has been ill since before Shabbath or Yom Tov commenced, one has in mind to use his medicines, so they do not become *muktzeh* and may be handled.

b. Thus, someone who is suffering from a severe bout of influenza may not take a pill to assuage a slight toothache.

6. *a.* 1) A person who is ill but whose life is not in danger may handle and eat something which is *muktzeh*, if nothing else is available.

2) Examples of such items are
   a) food cooked by a non-Jew on Shabbath,
   b) milk milked on Shabbath with a milking machine, in a permissible manner, or by a non-Jew, or
   c) fruit which dropped off the tree on Shabbath.

3) a) Even another person, who is not ill, may handle items of this nature for the purposes of the patient.
   b) One should not, however, handle *muktzeh* items more than is essential for the patient.

b. 1) One may move a lamp (including an electric light), in order to see, with its aid, what the patient needs.

2) Nonetheless (as mentioned in paragraph 3 above), it is forbidden to turn on a light on Shabbath for a person who is not dangerously ill.

3) If one has to move a kerosene lamp, one must be careful to do so very slowly, so that, in the process, one does not cause kerosene to move closer to, or farther away from, the wick.

c. In all of the above cases, one should try to vary the manner in which one moves the *muktzeh* item from that used on an ordinary weekday.

eating and handling items which are muktzeh

7. *a.* 1) One is allowed to give a patient who is ill, but not seriously so, a subcutaneous or intramuscular injection.

2) One should not give him an intravenous injection.

b. 1) It is forbidden to ask a Jewish doctor for a prescription for any of these injections on Shab-

injections one is allowed to administer

[549]

bath or Yom Tov (when the patient is not dangerously ill).

2) It is also forbidden to drive in one's car to bring
them.

3) With regard to cleaning the skin around the area
where the injection is given, see paragraph 10
below.

alerting the **8.** *a.* In the event that it is going to be necessary to give the
nurse　　　　　　patient an injection on Shabbath, one should, when-
before　　　　　　ever possible, notify the nurse (if she is Jewish) in
Shabbath　　　　advance, so that she can prepare the syringe and the
to prepare　　　 needles before Shabbath begins.
for
injections　　　*b.* If the nurse has not made the necessary preparations,
　　　　　　　　　 there is room for being lenient and allowing her

1) to transfer boiling water from an urn standing on
the fire into an empty saucepan,

2) to place the syringe and needles in the saucepan
and

3) to stand it on the (covered) fire.

(See Chapter 1, paragraphs 16, 18 to 20 and 46.)

inserting　　**9.** *a.* Whenever possible, the nurse should insert the needle
needle in　　　　 into the syringe before Shabbath commences, pro-
syringe　　　　　 vided it can be kept sterile.

b. When this is not practicable, there is room for being
lenient and allowing her to insert the needle into the
syringe even on Shabbath.

cleaning　　**10.** *a.* One should not clean the skin around the area where
skin where　　　　the injection is given with alcohol-soaked absorbent
injection　　　　　cotton (cotton wool), because of the prohibition
given　　　　　　 against squeezing the alcohol out of the cotton.

b. One may use a non-absorbent, synthetic material
(such as a plastic bag) for the purpose.

c. Another method is to pour a little alcohol onto the skin
and wipe it dry with absorbent cotton.

d. One may also wipe the area clean with a specially

prepared, alcohol-impregnated paper pad. (Compare Chapter 14, paragraph 33.)

e. Iodine can be used in the same way as alcohol ·to prevent infection.

f. One is allowed to dip a brush with bristles made of synthetic fibers into iodine (or alcohol) and to disinfect the skin with that.

11. a. One is permitted to insert ready-made suppositories into the patient's body, but   *supposi-tories*

b. one may not shape material into the form of a suppository.

12. a. A person suffering from severe diarrhea or indigestion may take medication.   *diarrhea*

b. 1) One may give him an enema made from salt water or tea.

2) One may also

a) prepare the salt water on Shabbath or

b) pour tea essence into water on Shabbath for this purpose, or water onto tea essence, and this is not an infringement of the prohibition against coloring on Shabbath.

c. A child who is suffering from severe diarrhea is to be treated as a person whose life is in danger, and a doctor should be consulted immediately.

13. a. Someone who is ill, although not dangerously so, may rub liquid camphor on his skin to soothe pain.   *camphor*

b. He may do this by hand or with the aid of some non-absorbent material.

c. He is not allowed to rub himself with ointment.

14. a. 1) A dressing on which ointment was spread before the beginning of Shabbath* may be applied to the   *ointment*

---

*It is recommended that when preparing a dressing with ointment before Shabbath one should, for practical and medical reasons,

[551]

body of a person who is ill, even though his life is not in danger.

2) Thus, it may be applied to a wound which causes the patient so much pain that his whole body is weakened. (For the treatment of superficial wounds see Chapter 35.)

b. If one has not prepared a dressing, one may
1) squeeze ointment out of a tube or
2) take it out of its container with a stick,
and put it onto the patient's body, for instance onto a wound, or onto the gauze of a dressing.

c. 1) When engaging in the above activities, one should be extremely careful not to smear the ointment onto the body or onto the gauze.

2) Nevertheless, one may apply a dressing to the skin and need not be concerned if ointment underneath is thereby spread over the dressing and the skin.

d. For the use of adhesive bandages and other dressings, see Chapter 35, paragraphs 20 to 29.

hot-water bottles   15. a. 1) One may use a hot-water bottle to assuage the pain from a bad stomachache (after consulting a doctor) or from a severe earache, but

2) one should take care that the inside of the bottle is perfectly dry before it is filled.

b. 1) One may also fill the bottle with ice and use it to bring down a fever.

2) Furthermore, lumps of ice may be made smaller, so that they will go into the bottle.

sleeping pills   16. A person who suffers greatly from lack of sleep may take sleeping pills.

---

1) use a piece of cloth, and not gauze, and
2) keep the ointment-spread dressing clean
a) by covering it with another piece of cloth, or
b) by folding it over, with the ointment on the inside.

17. *a.* 1) A bone which has become dislocated from its joint *dislocated* may be put back in its place, because the *bones* dislocation endangers the limb.

     2) Sometimes, there may even be a risk to the patient's life.

  b. When there is a need to anesthetize the patient, then,

     1) if, in the doctor's opinion, there is no danger to life, but only to a limb, the anesthetic should be administered in such a way that only Rabbinical prohibitions are transgressed, but,

     2) if there is the slightest fear of a possible risk to life, the anesthetic may be administered even when it involves the infringement of a Torah prohibition.

18. *a.* One may put a dressing on a broken bone, to hold it *fractured* firmly in position, even if the fracture is clearly not a *bones* danger to the whole body.

  b. One may also tie a dressing or a sling, to keep the fracture in a raised position.

  c. However, one should not tie it with a double knot, unless the practice is to change it every day.

  d. One may also secure a dressing or a sling with a safety-pin. (See Chapter 15, paragraph 70.)

  e. See also Chapter 35, paragraph 22.

19. *a.* In certain cases where one is suffering from a severe *compresses* pain to such an extent that one's whole body feels weak, one may make a compress, but one should do so in accordance with the instructions set out below.

  b. This may be necessary where a pain of such severity results, for example, from

     1) a sprain,

     2) having caught one's finger in a door or

     3) superficial phlebitis, or some other inflammation.

  c. When making a compress, one should take care not to squeeze it out, except in the limited circumstances specified in *h* below.

  d. Where possible, compresses should be made from

pieces of cloth which were made wet before Shabbath
began.

e. If one has no such cloths, one may put dry cloths into
colored liquid to wet them (but one should not color
water on Shabbath for this purpose).

f. If one has no colored liquid either, one should apply
the dry cloths to the appropriate part of the patient's
body and wet them there, but the cloths must be
absolutely clean.

g. If it is impossible to do this, there is room for taking a
lenient attitude and permitting the wetting of the
cloths before they are applied to the patient's body,
even with clean water, but only if the cloths are
absolutely clean.

h. The only circumstances in which one may squeeze out
the cloths are when all of the following factors are
present:

1) the cloths are too wet for use as a compress;
2) the liquid which has been used to wet the cloths is
colored;
3) one squeezes the cloths out into a sink, or onto the
floor, but not into a clean receptacle.

urine tests   20. a. One may test a patient's urine with special dipsticks,
by means of which one can tell whether the urine
contains traces of blood, sugar and so forth.

b. One should not, however, make such a test with the aid
of tablets specially intended for that purpose if they
contain a substance which makes the urine boil.

c. Moreover, there are those who question the propriety
of making urine tests even with dipsticks, unless the
tests are done to prevent a danger, or even a possible
danger, to life.

diabetes   21. A person suffering from diabetes, who receives an
injection before each meal to reduce the quantity of sugar
in his blood, may be given that injection on Shabbath
too. (See paragraphs 7 to 10 above.)

22. *a.* A person suffering from asthma may operate a *asthma* "spinhaler" (and, if there is a danger to life, even an electrically powered apparatus) containing a medicinal substance to alleviate his breathing difficulties.

b. He may use it even on Yom Kippur.

c. He may also use capsules which are punctured by needles inside the apparatus, to release the powder they contain.

23. Where there is no *eiruv*, a person ordered by the doctor *need to* not to leave the house unless he takes with him specified *carry* medicines, for use in case of need, should conduct himself *medicines* as set out in Chapter 40, paragraph 7. *with one*

ATTENDING ON YOM TOV TO THE NEEDS OF A PERSON WHO IS ILL
BUT WHOSE LIFE IS NOT IN DANGER

24. *a.* Subject to one exception, there is no distinction *general rule* between Shabbath and Yom Tov with regard to what may be done for a person who is ill but whose life is not in danger.

b. 1) The exception concerns those activities which are forbidden on Shabbath but may be permitted on Yom Tov in the course of preparing food [such as cooking (see Chapter 2) and crushing (see Chapter 7)].

2) An activity of this kind may be permitted on Yom Tov for the purposes of a person who is ill but not dangerously so, even when one is not preparing food, provided that

   a) it is required for Yom Tov **and**

   b) the type of benefit to be derived is commonly indulged in by most ordinary people.

3) Consequently, if the only benefit to be derived is medical, the activity is forbidden, as most ordinary people do not commonly take medication (not usually being ill).

preparing and bringing medicines

25. *a.* When a patient's life is not in danger, it is prohibited, on Yom Tov,

    1) to cook him a preparation to be used for medicinal purposes or

    2) to bring him a medicine from *r^eshuth ha-rabbim* to *r^eshuth ha-yachid* (or vice versa), where there is no *eiruv*,

unless the remedy in question is one which it is also usual for a healthy person to eat or drink.

  b. 1) What one could do is

    a) put a pot containing medicine on the stove,

    b) stand at its side a pot containing food one needs for Yom Tov and then

    c) light the fire (from a fire which is already burning as described in Chapter 13, paragraph 3), so that the one flame will heat both pots together.

    2) There is, however, a view which hesitates to permit such a course.

  c. If one has to bring medicine to the patient's home through *r^eshuth ha-rabbim*, one can put it into the same receptacle as other items one requires for Yom Tov, and bring them all together. (Compare Chapter 19, paragraph 6.)

hot-water bottles

26. When heating water on Yom Tov in order to fill a hot-water bottle for the patient (as to which, see paragraph 15 above), one should proceed as follows:

  a. One should heat the water by adding it to water one is about to heat for drinking purposes, for washing dishes and so forth.

  b. One should

    1) put all the water on the stove at once, and

    2) not add the water for the patient's hot-water bottle to a pot already standing on the stove.

sterilizing syringe and needles

27. *a.* If there is a need to boil up water on Yom Tov for sterilizing a syringe and needles, one should proceed

as specified in paragraph 26 above.

b. One may also place on the fire a pot containing only the water for sterilization on condition that one intends to use the hot water afterwards, on Yom Tov, for a purpose which is common to most ordinary people (who are not ill), such as washing the hands.

Chapter 34

Slight Indispositions, Minor Ailments and Disabilities

examples of minor complaints

1. *a.* Included in this chapter are the laws relating to minor complaints, such as
1) a toothache,
2) a sore throat,
3) a headache
4) colds and
5) coughs.

b. As far as these laws are concerned, there is no difference between Shabbath and Yom Tov.

c. For the specific case of *yom tov sheini shel galuyoth,* however, see Chapter 31, paragraph 28.

grades of pain

2. *a.* One must distinguish between
1) slight pains and
2) more severe pains, as a result of which one
   a) has to go to bed or
   b) feels weak all over.

b. Whether a pain is classified as slight or severe depends on the reaction of the person who is suffering.

taking medication: general rule

3. *a.* 1) A person who is suffering merely from a slight pain is forbidden to take any medication* (except as mentioned in paragraphs 4 and 5 below).
2) For example, he may not
   a) take pills,
   b) have drops administered or
   c) gargle.

b. 1) A person who is suffering from a more severe pain,

---

*Any medicine which one is forbidden to take is *muktzeh* and should not be handled, even if it does not have a bitter taste (and would thus be palatable to eat in the normal way).

as a result of which he has to go to bed or feels weak all over, is placed in the category of persons who are ill but whose lives are not in danger, and he may take medication. (See Chapter 33, paragraph 4.)

2) This could occur in the case of a severe headache. (See paragraphs 6 and 16 below.)

4. *a.* Although, as stated in the preceding paragraph, a person who is suffering merely from a slight pain is forbidden to take any medication, he is permitted to eat food which healthy people eat and which is likely to cure him. *taking normal food as a remedy*

b. Consequently,

1) someone who has a sore throat may
   a) eat honey,
   b) drink a solution of milk and honey,
   c) suck ordinary candies (sweets) (but not medicated lozenges),
   d) eat lemon,
   e) squeeze lemon onto sugar* and eat that, or even
   f) suck a lemon;

2) someone who is hoarse may eat a raw egg;

3) someone who is suffering from heartburn
   a) may eat food which is likely to have a soothing effect, such as butter, milk or an egg, but
   b) should not take bicarbonate of soda, although,
   c) in case of pressing need, such a person may rely on the view of those authorities who permit one to drink bicarbonate of soda, provided it was prepared before Shabbath. (It is advisable to cover it until use, to prevent it from losing its efficacy.)

5. *a.* Furthermore, the prohibition set out in paragraph 3 above relates only to the taking of medication in the normal manner. *taking medication in an un- usual way*

---

*See Chapter 5, paragraphs 3 and 5.

  b. One is, accordingly, allowed to drink water, or some other liquid, containing medicine in the form of drops or dissolved tablets, as long as

   1) the drops or tablets are mixed or dissolved in the water or other liquid before the beginning of Shabbath,

   2) it is not usual to take these drops or tablets in this form **and**

   3) other people cannot tell that one is drinking the mixture for medicinal reasons.

  c. It is not permitted to mix or dissolve the drops or tablets in the liquid on Shabbath itself.

  d. If it is usual to take medicinal drops on an ordinary weekday by mixing them in water, one is not allowed to drink such a mixture on Shabbath, even if one prepared it before Shabbath commenced.

headaches **6.** *a.* A person who has a headache, but

   1) summons up his strength and walks about like a healthy individual **and**

   2) does not have what for him is an above-normal temperature,

  may not take any medication.

  b. If, however,

   1) he feels that he cannot stand on his feet, **or**

   2) he has what for him is an above-normal temperature,

  he is treated as a person who is ill but whose life is not in danger, and he may take medication, as explained in Chapter 33, paragraph 4.

  c. See also paragraph 16 below.

toothaches **7.** *a.* 1) Somebody who has a slight toothache should not take a pill to assuage the pain.

   2) What he may do is have a strong drink, of a kind which healthy people are accustomed to drink, such as brandy or whisky, but he should take care to swallow it straight down and not

    a) rinse his mouth out with it and then spit it out, nor even

    b) retain it in his mouth for longer than usual before swallowing.

  b. Somebody who has such a violent toothache that he feels weak all over

    1) may take medication to assuage the pain and,

    2) in case of need, may ask a non-Jew to extract the tooth.

  c. Whenever there is any fear of danger to life, for example due to the presence of a large amount of pus, a doctor should be consulted immediately as to the proper course of action to be adopted.

8. *a.* A person who is suffering from a slight pain in the eye should not receive any medical treatment.   *eye ailments*

  b. In the case of a more severe pain in the eye, or if the eye is inflamed, one is permitted

    1) to put drops in the eye,

    2) to apply ointment to the eye (directly out of the tube or by means of a stick) and

    3) to clean the eye with borax, while complying with the following directions:

      a) The boracic crystals may be dissolved in boiled water, even if it is still hot, but

      b) it is preferable to avoid pouring water from a *kᵉli rishon* onto the crystals and

      c) one should instead put the crystals into water which is already in a *kᵉli sheini*.

      d) One should not apply the boracic solution with absorbent cotton (cotton wool), because of the prohibition against squeezing the liquid out, even if one holds the absorbent cotton with tweezers, and not in one's fingers.

      e) One may bathe the eye with the assistance of an eyecup.

      f) There is also room for permitting the end of a cloth (provided it is absolutely clean) to be

soaked in a boracic solution and applied to the
eye, but it is forbidden to squeeze out the cloth.

c. On the subject of prolonged treatment of the eyes, see
paragraph 17 below.

d. Serious eye ailments can endanger life, and the
considerations set out in Chapter 32 apply.

earaches   9. a. The insertion of absorbent cotton into an aching ear is
not considered to be a medical treatment and is,
accordingly, permitted (subject to what is stated
below), even if the pain is only slight.

b. One may not roll up the cotton into a ball on Shabbath
and insert it into the ear, but there is nothing wrong
with pressing an unshaped piece of cotton into the ear.

c. The halachic principles applicable in the treatment of
an earache correspond, as far as is relevant, to those
mentioned in paragraph 8 above.

d. One is allowed to go out into *r^eshuth ha-rabbim* with
absorbent cotton in an aching ear.

e. 1) Whenever there is any fear of danger to life, the
doctor may examine the ear even with an
electrically operated instrument.

2) Where possible, the instrument should be switched
on before Shabbath and left on.

3) If one is unable, or has forgotten, to switch it on
before Shabbath,

a) one may do so on Shabbath, in order to examine
a patient whose life is, or may be, in danger,
but,

b) where possible, one should then switch it on in
a manner which differs from that which one
would adopt on another day of the week.

4) A properly qualified halachic authority should be
consulted as to the special considerations relevant
in the case of battery-operated instruments.

colds and
coughs   10. a. 1) Someone who is suffering from a mere cold or

cough is not allowed to receive any remedial treatment.

2) The prohibition extends also to treatment which provides only temporary relief, for instance
   a) the application of nasal drops,
   b) the breathing in of vapors (where one can tell that it is being done for remedial purposes), or
   c) the use of an inhaler.

b. If, however, the cough or cold is so severe that the patient feels weak all over, or is forced to lie down, he may receive treatment, whether it affords temporary relief, or has a more lasting effect. (See Chapter 33, paragraph 4.)

11. *a.* 1) A person who is suffering from an ordinary stomachache may (after consultation with a doctor) apply to his stomach *stomach-aches*
   a) a receptacle which previously contained hot water and is still hot, or
   b) a dry towel which has been warmed up (even on Shabbath) in front of the fire.

2) He is not allowed
   a) to alleviate the pain by the use of a hot-water bottle which has hot water inside it (except in the circumstances described below),
   b) to take castor oil, Epsom salts or some other laxative,
   c) to take charcoal tablets, or
   d) to be given an enema of soapy water or of water containing some medicinal substance.

3) a) Despite the above, a person who is accustomed to warming his bed with a hot-water bottle even when he is well may also use it when he has a stomachache.
   b) He may not only place it in his bed, but even on his stomach, since it is not generally apparent that his intention is the alleviation of pain.
   c) What is more, in a place where people are

accustomed to using a hot-water bottle when they are well, a person who himself does not normally use a hot-water bottle may use it too, even when he is ill.

b. A person who is suffering from a more severe stomachache, as a result of which he is forced to lie down or feels weak all over, may do any of the things mentioned in *a* above.

c. If someone has very severe stomach pains, giving rise to fears that he may be dangerously ill, one may violate Shabbath for him, as set out in Chapter 32, for example, in order to call a doctor or take the patient to the hospital. (See Chapter 32, paragraph 11c.)

d. For the use of an electric cushion or blanket see Chapter 38, paragraph 7.

e. For the heating of water for a hot-water bottle on Yom Tov, see Chapter 33, paragraph 26.

skin irritations

12. a. 1) Somebody suffering from a slight skin irritation (for instance on the hands or feet) may smear oil on his skin, but not ointment.

2) However, if the skin is peeling because of the irritation,

a) one is not allowed to rub even oil into the skin, but

b) one may pour oil onto a part of the body which is not peeling, so that the oil should run from there onto that part of the body which is peeling.

sweating

b. 1) Somebody who sweats excessively may sprinkle ordinary talcum powder (that is to say, without formalin or any other therapeutic additive) on those parts of his body which exude the perspiration.

2) This is because the talc operates to absorb the perspiration and not to cure it.

dry lips or skin

13. a. If one is suffering from dry or cracked lips, one should

neither
1) smear them with lipstick or any other material, nor
2) oil them.
b. The same applies in the case of dry or chapped hands.

14. A person suffering from rheumatism is not permitted to bathe in a therapeutic hot spring on Shabbath or Yom Tov.* *therapeutic baths*

15. One may wear copper necklaces and bracelets (which are reputed to be effective in relieving rheumatic pains) on Shabbath and may go out into r^eshuth ha-rabbim wearing them, even in a place where there is no eiruv. *therapeutic necklaces and bracelets*

16. a. As explained in paragraph 3 above, a person who is suffering merely from a slight pain is forbidden to take any medication. *risk that slight pain will worsen*
b. If, however, there is a fear that failure to take medication will lead to an aggravation of the pain and to the classification of the sufferer as a person who is ill, although not in danger of his life, he is allowed to take medication to avoid this happening.
c. An example would be the case of a person who is suffering from a headache and has a tendency to migraine. (See Chapter 33, paragraph 1c.)

17. a. In a case where someone is ordered by the doctor to take medication for several consecutive days, Shabbath included, there are authorities who take a lenient approach and permit the taking of the medicine on Shabbath too (even if failure to do so would not lead to the situation referred to in the previous paragraph). *remedies prescribed for a number of consecutive days*
b. A person who has been ill (even though not dangerously so) may continue taking medication after he has recovered, to avoid having a relapse.

---

*For laws relating to bathing in general on Shabbath and Yom Tov, see Chapter 14, paragraphs 1 to 26.

immuniza-
tion

18. *a.* Except as mentioned below, one may not take any immunizing preparation on Shabbath as a protection against pains or a minor ailment.
b. Some authorities take a more lenient view when the preparation has to be taken for several consecutive days, Shabbath included.
c. All authorities agree that one may take the preparation if there is a risk that failure to take it may result in actual illness, even without danger to life.

enabling or
inhibiting
conception

19. *a.* A woman who has to take medication for several consecutive days in order to enable her to become pregnant need not interrupt her prescribed course on Shabbath.
b. The same applies when a woman has to take contraceptive drugs for several consecutive days. (The use of such drugs is generally forbidden but may be sanctioned in specific cases by a duly qualified rabbi, after considering all of the circumstances which the Halacha regards as relevant.)

vitamins

20. *a.* 1) One should not take vitamins or fish oil (such as cod-liver oil) on Shabbath, unless one is ill (even if not dangerously so).
2) This is the case even when one is used to taking them daily.
b. 1) However, there are authorities who adopt a lenient view and permit the taking of vitamins on Shabbath, in countries where they are commonly taken at every meal.
2) Nevertheless, other authorities adopt a stricter approach and forbid the taking of vitamins, except when they are taken as a substitute for a particular food.
c. 1) Regarding pregnant women see Chapter 36, paragraph 1.
2) Regarding children see Chapter 37, paragraph 4.

21. *a.* One is not allowed to treat a person for drunkenness by giving him an infusion.   *drunken-ness*
b. Nor may he take an emetic to make him throw up the liquor he has consumed.
c. What he may do is drink strong, black coffee (without sugar). (Regarding the preparation of the coffee see Chapter 1, paragraphs 49 and 55.)
d. He may also insert his finger into his throat to induce vomiting.

22. *a.* One may not do strenuous physical exercises on Shabbath.   *physical exercises*
b. Nor may one engage in muscle-building exercises with the aid of spring-fitted, physical-training apparatus.
c. One may do simple exercises with one's hand, even if one's purpose in so doing is to relieve or alleviate pains.

23. *a.* It is not permitted to engage in physiotherapy or in occupational therapy on Shabbath.   *physio-therapy and occupa-tional therapy*
b. For someone who comes within the category of persons who are ill but whose lives are not in danger, it may be allowed, depending on the prohibitions involved in the particular kind of treatment. (See Chapter 33, paragraph 2.)

24. *a.* Inflatable, rubber cushions may be blown up on Shabbath.   *inflatable rubber cushions*
b. One may even blow them up with a special pump designed for the purpose.
c. Nonetheless, one should not blow them up if they have never been used before.

25. *a.* Taking snuff is permissible, even if one's reasons for doing so are medicinal.   *taking snuff and chewing tobacco*
b. One may likewise chew tobacco.

26. With regard to carrying a cane (walking-stick) in a place where there is no *eiruv*, see Chapter 18, paragraph 13.   *canes*

wheelchairs **27.** *a.* Whether or not an invalid who is unable to walk by his own unaided efforts may be transported in a wheelchair depends on the type of place through which he has to be taken.

1) In a place where there is an *eiruv*,
   a) it is permissible to wheel the invalid about in his chair, and,
   b) of course, the invalid too may wheel himself about, but
   c) one must on no account activate any motor by which the chair is propelled.

2) In a place where there is no *eiruv*, but which is not actually *r*ᵉ*shuth ha-rabbim* (as defined in Chapter 17, paragraph 3), the invalid may travel in the wheelchair on Shabbath only to the synagogue, or for the purpose of another mitzva, and then only if
   a) the chair is pushed by a non-Jew or
   b) the invalid turns the wheels himself.

3) In a place which fits the definition of a *r*ᵉ*shuth ha-rabbim* (set out in Chapter 17, paragraph 3), the invalid may travel in the wheelchair only for a mitzva (as above), and then only if
   a) the invalid is capable of turning the wheels by himself **and**
   b) the chair is in fact propelled jointly by a non-Jew pushing from behind and the Jew in the chair turning the wheels at the same time.

b. A Jew should not push a wheelchair on Shabbath in a place where there is no *eiruv* and carrying articles about is forbidden, even if the place is not actually a *r*ᵉ*shuth ha-rabbim*.

c. Whenever it is permitted for a non-Jew or the invalid himself to propel a wheelchair through a place where there is no *eiruv* and carrying articles about is forbidden,

1) everything which is not necessary to enable the invalid to sit in the chair should be removed from it, and

2) tho invalid ohould not koop anything in his pockets, but

3) the cushion on which the invalid sits is treated as if it were an article of clothing which he is wearing, and may be wheeled about with him.

d. On Yom Tov, one may push the invalid in his wheelchair even in a place where there is no *eiruv*, and even in an actual r^eshuth ha-$rabbim$.

28. *a.* 1) A person who is hard of hearing may use an electric hearing aid on Shabbath, on condition that it was switched on before Shabbath. *hearing aids*

2) The volume may be adjusted on Shabbath, provided that

a) increasing the current does not make a wire glow red and

b) decreasing it does not cause the red glow of a wire to fade away.

3) It is recommended that a person wishing to use a hearing aid should consult an expert before Shabbath to ascertain the facts as to his particular device.

b. 1) a) One may not go out in a place where there is no *eiruv* wearing a hearing aid if part of it (such as the battery) is in one's pocket.

b) The part in one's pocket is not being worn, and one is consequently regarded as carrying it in the normal way.

2) Some authorities permit one to go out in a place where there is no *eiruv* wearing a hearing aid which is entirely contained in the frame of a pair of glasses (spectacles), whereas others forbid it.

29. *a.* A person who wears a dental brace for straightening his teeth may put it in on Shabbath. *dental braces*

b. He may also go out into r^eshuth ha-$rabbim$ wearing it.

orthopedic
30. *a.* A person who wears an orthopedic brace for the *braces*

[*569*]

correction of a deformity may put it on on Shabbath.

b. He may also go out into *r^eshuth ha-rabbim* wearing it.

c. The brace may be fastened on by means of "velcro" strips (special strips of material which have tiny "teeth" that cling tightly to each other when brought into contact).

preventing sleep

31. a. One may not take medicines on Shabbath to prevent oneself from falling asleep.

b. On the subject of sleeping pills see Chapter 33, paragraph 16.

Chapter 35

Treatment of Wounds on Shabbath and Yom Tov

TREATMENT OF WOUNDS WHICH CAN ENDANGER THE LIFE OF THE PATIENT

1. *a.* The following are examples of dangerous wounds, as explained in Chapter 32, paragraph 11*f* and *g*: *examples of dangerous wounds*
   1) a deep cut, a deep wound or a heavy blow which have been occasioned by a knife or any other metal instrument;
   2) a cut caused by something which is not clean;
   3) a wound which has come into contact with earth or dirt;
   4) an injury on the back of the hand or on the instep.
   b. A danger to the whole body can develop if these injuries are not properly treated.
   c. Therefore, one may do anything necessary to avert the danger.
   d. Instances of the steps one may have to take appear in the succeeding paragraphs.

2. *a.* Where possible, an infected wound should be cleaned *cleaning the wound*
   1) with a scrap of non-absorbent, synthetic material or
   2) by pouring the cleansing liquid onto the wound. (See also Chapter 32, paragraph 59.)
   b. Failing this, one should not hesitate to use absorbent cotton (cotton wool) soaked in liquid.

3. *a.* One may cut away the hair around the wound, if there is a fear that the hair may be a cause of infection. *cutting hair around a wound*
   b. However, one should be careful to cut only hair which it is essential to remove.

cutting the
edges of a
wound and
stitching

4. *a.* One is allowed to snip off the edges of an infected wound in order to prevent it from becoming inflamed.

    b. 1) The wound should not be stitched until after Shabbath if it can be left that long without risk of aggravating the patient's condition.

       2) This is because there is a need, when stitching, to tie the surgical thread with a permanent knot, of the kind one is forbidden to make on Shabbath.

    c. See also paragraph 24 below and Chapter 40, paragraph 40.

X-rays and
plaster
casts

5. *a.* One takes an X-ray in the event of a fractured bone or even in the event of a suspected fracture.

    b. Yet, the application of a plaster cast should be postponed until after Shabbath or Yom Tov, provided it is clear from the X-ray that the patient's condition will not be at all aggravated as a result of the delay.

    c. See also Chapter 33, paragraph 18.

catching
dog to check
for rabies

6. *a.* One may catch a dog which has bitten someone, in order to check whether it is healthy or is infected with rabies.

    b. 1) This is essential for deciding how properly to treat the person bitten.

       2) Incorrect treatment could endanger the patient's life.

TREATMENT OF WOUNDS WHICH ARE EXTREMELY PAINFUL
OR ENDANGER A LIMB, BUT DO NOT ENDANGER THE LIFE
OF THE PATIENT

general rule

7. *a.* A person suffering from wounds which are not dangerous, but which

    1) cause a pain so severe that it affects his whole body, or

    2) give rise to a fear that the normal use of the injured limb or organ may be at risk,

is considered to be within the category of persons who are ill but whose lives are not in danger.

b. 1) One may attend to his needs through the agency of a non-Jew.

2) This includes the performance of acts which are the subject of a Torah prohibition.

3) The non-Jew's services should only be used for things which the patient actually needs on Shabbath.

c. 1) A Jew may violate only Rabbinical prohibitions in attending to the patient's needs.

2) What is more, if there is no danger to the normal use of a limb or organ, the Jew must vary his normal manner of performing the prohibited act.

d. A more detailed exposition of the rules in question can be found in Chapter 33, paragraphs 1e, 2, 14 and 19.

e. Their application is illustrated below.

8. a. If one has a wound which, while not a danger to life, is extremely painful, as mentioned in the previous paragraph, one may apply ointment, but without spreading it. *applying ointment*

b. That is to say, one may, on Shabbath, apply to the wound a strip of material on which ointment was smeared before Shabbath (and which has all the time been covered, to prevent contamination).

c. In a case where
1) it has not been possible to prepare a dressing of this kind before Shabbath, or
2) one has forgotten to prepare it, or
3) the injury occurred on Shabbath,
one may squeeze ointment directly from a tube onto the wound (or, where this is difficult, onto the dressing), but without smearing it on.

d. If the ointment is in a receptacle, it may be taken out with a stick and applied to the wound or to the dressing (without smearing).

e. Putting a dressing on an ointment-covered wound is

permissible and is not in itself an infringement of the prohibition against spreading the ointment.

f. With regard to cutting the dressing, see paragraph 23 below.

bathing a wound

9. *a.* 1) If one is suffering from an extremely painful wound (as mentioned in paragraph 7 above), one may bathe it in soapy water, so that it becomes soft and the pus comes out.

2) Concerning the preparation of soapy water see Chapter 14, paragraphs 5 and 16.

b. The treatment of dislocated or fractured bones is discussed in Chapter 33, paragraphs 17 and 18.

TREATMENT OF SUPERFICIAL WOUNDS

examples of superficial wounds

10. The following are examples of superficial wounds, covered by the rules set out in Chapter 34:

a. everyday cuts and abrasions;

b. cuts between the toes caused by "athlete's foot" (see also Chapter 34, paragraph 12);

c. light burns;

d. ordinary sunburn;

e. slow bleeding;

f. penetration of a thorn beneath the skin (but not under a fingernail);

g. sprains;

h. non-dangerous stings.

cleaning a wound

11. *a.* One may wash a wound with water or hydrogen peroxide.

b. If one wishes to wipe it clean, one should do so with a synthetic material which is non-absorbent and to which the prohibition against squeezing out does not apply.

c. Should one not have such material available, one should

1) **first** pour the water or hydrogen peroxide onto the wound (with the aid of a dropper, if one wishes), and

2) **only then** wipe it clean with absorbent cotton (cotton wool) or a paper pad. (See also paragraph 19 below.)

d. 1) One should not take absorbent cotton or a paper pad and dip them into water or hydrogen peroxide.

2) This is forbidden even if one does not touch the cotton or paper pad with one's fingers, but holds them in a pair of tweezers.

3) The reason is that, in the course of cleaning the wound, one is bound to squeeze out some of the absorbed liquid.

12. a. One is allowed to sprinkle styptic, surgical dusting powder (such as "Dermatol") onto a wound in order to stop the bleeding.

b. One may also apply tincture of iodine, brilliant-green, gentian violet or some other antiseptic solution in order to cleanse the wound and prevent infection.

c. 1) These antiseptic solutions can be applied in the same way as hydrogen peroxide in the preceding paragraph.

2) Apart from using a dropper, one could also apply them with the aid of such instruments as a glass rod or a brush whose bristles are made of a non-absorbent, synthetic fiber.

arresting bleeding and applying iodine

13. a. 1) One should not violate Shabbath in the case of slow bleeding from a vein (unless it does not stop within a reasonable time).

2) The bleeding can generally be stopped by applying direct pressure to the wound* or by raising the injured limb.

hemor-rhages

---

*But see paragraph 15a below.

b. 1) A more serious hemorrhage can present a danger to life (as mentioned in Chapter 32, paragraph 11*d*), and one should have no hesitation in taking whatever steps are necessary to stop it.

2) Thus, one may tie an artery from which blood is gushing.

sucking
blood

14. *a.* It is prohibited to suck the blood of a wound on Shabbath or Yom Tov (and this includes blood from the gums).

b. Blood which has previously come out of the wound must not be swallowed, even on a weekday.

nosebleeds

15. *a.* One should preferably not try to staunch a bleeding nose with a handkerchief or cloth. (According to medical opinion, one should not thrust absorbent cotton into the nostril even during the week, since the fibers are liable to adhere to the skin and start the bleeding again when the cotton is removed.)

b. If one has no alternative, or if the blood will not stop flowing, one may staunch it in this way.

c. It is permissible to stop the bleeding by the application of pressure to the side of the nose.

abscesses

16. *a.* One may puncture an abscess, either with one's hand or with a needle, in order to extract the pus.

b. One may also use a knife or scissors.

c. The abscess may be punctured despite the fact that a little blood is liable to be exuded with the pus.

d. 1) When a needle or other instrument is used, one must not previously sterilize it by heating it till it glows.

2) What one may do is to pass it back and forth through the flame.

3) The preferable course, however, where the possibility exists, is to sterilize instruments by dipping them in a disinfectant, such as alcohol.

e. One should not press an abscess after the pus has

come out, since fresh blood will be squeezed out of the surrounding flesh.

f. It is also forbidden to cut skin away from the abscess or to pull it off.

g. Where there is a non-Jew available, it is better for the Jew not to treat the abscess, but to have the pus removed by the non-Jew.

h. 1) One is not allowed to open a wound and insert a drain.

2) Nevertheless, one is permitted to insert a drain into an already open wound, to make sure that it stays open, but

3) one must be careful that one does not enlarge the opening.

i. It is forbidden on Shabbath to bathe a wound (which is not extremely painful) in soapy water with the object of softening it and extracting the pus, since one does not normally bathe in this way except in the process of healing a wound.

j. A large furuncle, or even a small one if it is on the lips, is dangerous and should be treated in whatever way is necessary. (See Chapter 32, paragraph 11j.)

17. a. 1) A thorn or splinter which has penetrated the skin *thorns and* may be extracted with the fingers, with tweezers or *splinters* with a needle.

2) One need not be concerned if a little blood unavoidably comes out with the thorn.

3) Yet, in this case too one must be careful not to extract blood unnecessarily.

b. 1) If the thorn or splinter is under a fingernail, there may be danger to life. (See Chapter 32, paragraph 11k.)

2) One should accordingly do anything necessary in the circumstances, including cutting the fingernail open with a pair of scissors.

18. a. If one has to dress a bloody wound with material *bloody* *wounds*

which is not intended for that purpose, one ought to wash the blood off first.

b. However, if that is not practicable, or if the wound continues to bleed, one may apply the dressing to the unwashed wound.

c. Gauze, a bandage, a paper pad or any other dressing specifically intended for the purpose may be applied to a bloody wound in any case.

use of
absorbent
cotton

19. a. 1) One should not make cotton swabs.
2) They should be prepared before Shabbath.
b. 1) It is desirable to refrain from tearing cotton on Shabbath.
2) It is advisable to prepare a sufficient quantity of cotton tufts before Shabbath begins.

dressing to
be applied
without
ointment

20. a. 1) One may put a dressing on a superficial wound to prevent it from becoming contaminated, but
2) one should not put ointment of any kind on it.
b. 1) Likewise, one may change a dressing, and
2) the fresh dressing should not have any ointment on it either.
(See also paragraph 27 below.)
c. A wound on which it is forbidden to put ointment may not have foodstuffs, such as butter or oil, put on it either.
d. One is allowed to tear the paper wrapping around a dressing, provided one takes care not to tear it in a place where there is lettering.
e. If the pain from a wound is so severe that it affects one's whole body, one may apply ointment but may not spread it. (See paragraph 8 above.)

cutting a
bandage

21. a. 1) It is prohibited to cut a bandage which is too long.
2) Instead, one should wind the whole bandage around the wound.
b. It is also forbidden to cut a bandage along the middle of its length, to produce two ends which can be tied.

c. One should be careful not to pull threads out of a bandage.

22. *a.* A bandage may be secured   *securing a*
    1) with a bow, that is to say a loop, or a pair of loops,   *bandage*
       over a single knot,
    2) with a safety pin or
    3) with special bandage clips.
    b. 1) One should not tie it with a double knot, except in
       the circumstances described in Chapter 15,
       paragraph 52.
    2) Thus, one may tie a bandage with a loose, double
       knot, if it is changed every day, and the knot is
       untied for that purpose.

23. One must not cut or tear adhesive plaster — including   *cutting*
    "Salvaplast," "Elastoplast" and "Band-Aid" — to size.   *plaster*

24. One may bring the edges of a wound together and stick a   *closing*
    specially shaped plaster over it to hold it closed.   *wound with*
                                                           a plaster

25. *a.* One is not allowed to stick adhesive plaster onto a   *securing a*
    bandage or dressing in order to secure it.   *bandage*
    b. This is forbidden whether the plaster   *with a plaste*
    1) attaches one part of the bandage to another or
    2) attaches the dressing itself directly to the patient's
       skin.

26. *a.* While the use of adhesive plasters to dress a wound is   *preparing*
    permitted, one is not allowed, on Shabbath,   *plasters*
    1) to cut plaster into strips of the required size (as   *before*
       mentioned in paragraph 23 above) or   *Shabbath*
    2) to peel off the paper, plastic or gauze covering
       which protects the surface that is applied to the
       skin.
    b. Therefore, plasters should be prepared before Shab-
    bath by

1) cutting them to the appropriate size and
2) removing the protective covering.*

replacing a dressing

27. *a.* 1) One may remove a dressing in order to put it back again more firmly.
2) One can rely on the view that the dressing may be replaced even if there is ointment smeared on it (from before Shabbath).

b. One may also put back a dressing which has come off (and is still clean), as long as it has not fallen onto the ground.

removing a plaster from a dressing

28. *a.* It is forbidden on Shabbath to remove an adhesive plaster from a dressing which it secures.

b. Nonetheless, when the presence of the dressing bothers one, it may be cut apart, in a way which spoils it, even if a pair of scissors has to be used for the purpose.

removing a plaster from hairy skin

29. *a.* It is better not to pull an adhesive plaster off a hairy part of the body, since some hairs are bound to stick to the plaster and be torn out.

b. What one can do, if one has had benzene ready for the purpose since before Shabbath, is to pour some onto the plaster, so that it comes away without the hair.

wiping ointment off the skin

30. *a.* One may wipe away ointment remaining on the skin.

b. 1) Dry absorbent cotton may be used for this purpose.
2) It is forbidden to use cotton steeped in alcohol or water.

removal of scabs

31. One may remove a scab from a wound with one's hand, unless one knows that this will cause fresh bleeding.

---

*To keep the plasters clean, one can cover them afresh, and one will be allowed to peel the covers off again on Shabbath before use.

32. *a.* Warts or dry skin may be neither cut away nor removed with the hand on Shabbath. *removal of warts or skin*
   b. Furthermore, small pieces of skin which are peeling off around a fingernail, or on any other part of the body, but which are still connected, may not be pulled off or cut off with an instrument, by hand or even with the teeth.

33. One must not scratch parts of the body which are tender if one knows that scratching will cause bleeding. *scratching tender skin*

34. *a.* One is allowed to press a knife or a similar instrument against the skin, where a blow has been received, to prevent or minimize swelling. *swellings*
   b. Likewise, one is allowed to wash a swollen limb with water.
   c. One is not allowed to apply a compress, unless the pain is so severe that the whole body is affected. (See Chapter 33, paragraph 19 for details of the laws applicable.)

35. *a.* 1) When someone has suffered a sprain, one may bring the sprained limb into a comfortable position and secure it there. *sprains*
   2) For instance, one may
      a) tie a sprained arm (subject to the limitations mentioned in paragraph 22 above) to keep it raised or
      b) bind it with an elastic bandage.
   b. If the patient is not experiencing severe pain, one may not
      1) smear the sprain with oil or camphor (even liquid),
      2) massage the sprain or
      3) apply a compress to the sprained limb.
   c. If the patient is experiencing pain so severe that he feels weak all over, one may treat the sprain in any of the above ways; however,
      1) one should not use camphorated ointment, but

thin, camphorated oil, and

2) the instructions contained in Chapter 33, paragraph 19 should be followed in preparing and applying compresses.

chapped lips **36.** Regarding the treatment of a person suffering from dry
or hands or chapped lips or hands see Chapter 34, paragraph 13.

burns, **37.** *a.* 1) A person who

    a) has sustained light burns **and**

    b) does not have severe pain

    should not be given any medical treatment.

2) This applies whether the burn was caused by fire, by the sun or in any other way.

b. In the case of more serious burns, which cause severe pain, the situation is as follows*:

1) One may pour oil onto the affected parts and cover them with gauze.

2) One may sprinkle them with a powder, such as "Dermatol."

3) One may squeeze ointment onto the burns from a tube (as in Chapter 33, paragraph 14), but one must not smear the ointment on.

4) One may take medicine to ease the pain.

c. In the event of severe burns, which cover an extensive area of the skin, one should immediately consult a doctor, as a danger to life could be involved. (See Chapter 32, paragraph 11*l*.)

stings **38.** *a.* 1) If one has been stung by a wasp or a bee, one may wash the affected part with diluted vinegar, lemon juice or ice water to prevent irritation.

2) However, one should not soak the affected part in any of these, since it would be obvious that one was doing so in order to heal the wound.

---

*The possibilities listed are of course subject to their being medically advisable.

3) If the sting itself is still in the wound, one may take it out.

4) Where the person stung is particularly sensitive to that kind of sting, a danger to his life may be involved, and one should immediately consult a doctor as to the appropriate treatment. (See Chapter 32, paragraph 11*m*.)

b. A person who has been stung by a scorpion, even a black scorpion, is considered to be in danger of his life and should be treated accordingly. (See Chapter 32, paragraph 11*n*.)

Regarding the treatment of bedsores, see Chapter 40, paragraph 5.   *bedsores*

a. If   *immunization*

1) in the doctor's opinion, an injured person requires   *against*
an injection against tetanus and   *tetanus*

2) it is close to the termination of Shabbath,
one should, when possible, wait and not violate Shabbath by administering the injection, but,

b. when, in the doctor's opinion, one cannot wait until after Shabbath one must administer the injection without delay, even if one has to travel in order to obtain the antitoxin. (See further Chapter 32, paragraph 59.)

Chapter 36

Laws Relating to Pregnancy, Childbirth and Breast-Feeding on Shabbath and Yom Tov

PREGNANCY

taking medicines

1. *a.* A pregnant woman may take all necessary medicines or vitamins on Shabbath to avoid any risk of injury to her health or that of her baby.

b. 1) Nevertheless, this does not permit her to take any other remedy which she may require in order to treat some other, minor ailment that she happens to have.

2) For example, if she is suffering from a slight toothache, she may not take a pill to relieve the pain.

saving the baby: general rule

2. *a.* One violates Shabbath to save the life of a fetus.

b. This is so even in a case where the length of the pregnancy is less than forty days.

saving the baby: operating on the mother

3. When a doctor has determined

a. that there are fears for the life of the fetus **and**

b. that, in order to save the fetus, one must operate on the mother,

the operation may, if necessary, be performed on Shabbath.

CHILDBIRTH

compared with dangerous illness

4. *a.* 1) A woman who gives birth to a baby is treated like a patient whose life is in danger. (See Chapter 32, paragraph 12.)

2) One is allowed (and indeed is obliged) to violate Shabbath and Yom Tov for her, as described in Chapter 32.

b. 1) However, since the pain and danger of childbirth are a natural and accepted phenomenon, the Rabbis have adopted a somewhat more restrictive attitude towards it than in the case of other dangerous conditions.

2) a) Thus, when one performs forbidden acts for the woman giving birth, one should be especially careful, where possible, to vary the manner of their execution from that which one would adopt on another day of the week.

b) No such variation should, of course, be made where it could result in a detrimental delay in doing what is necessary.

a. The rules governing the violation of Shabbath are the same for a woman who is unfortunate enough to have a stillbirth as for a woman whose baby is born alive.

b. The rules affecting a woman who gives birth are also applied to a woman who has an abortion or a miscarriage more than forty days after the commencement of her pregnancy.

stillbirths and miscarriages

a. It is proper, in order to reduce the violation of Shabbath to a minimum, for a woman who reaches the ninth month of pregnancy to prepare before Shabbath everything she will need in the event that the birth takes place on Shabbath.

b. Thus, she should leave a light burning in case she needs to look for something before going to the hospital during the night.

c. Similarly, she should write her name and personal details on two slips of paper, so that she can hand

1) one to the ambulance driver — if indeed she has to go to the hospital on Shabbath by ambulance — to save him from writing and

preparing for a Shabbath birth

2) one to the hospital reception clerk to avoid his having to register her on Shabbath.

d. Of course, if she has failed to make suitable preparations, she may, nonetheless,
1) ride to the hospital and
2) be admitted to the hospital on Shabbath, even though the clerk will note down her registration particulars on Shabbath.

e. The principles governing payment of the ambulance driver's charge are analogous to those set out in Chapter 32, paragraph 55.

avoiding travel on Shabbath

7. a. An expectant mother is not obliged to stay within the vicinity of the hospital, in order to avoid the necessity for traveling on Shabbath, if this presents a difficulty or occasions inconvenience.

b. Intelligent anticipation will not, however, come amiss, and, if she begins to feel labor pains before Shabbath, she should not wait until the pains become worse but should proceed immediately to the hospital.

c. See further paragraph 10 below.

phoning for an ambulance and traveling to the hospital

8. a. From the moment a woman feels the time has come for her to give birth,
1) one may telephone for an ambulance and
2) she may travel to the hospital.

b. That moment is considered to have arrived when she feels regular labor pains, even if it is doubtful whether the birth is immediately imminent.

c. She may travel to the hospital at which she has been registered, even where there is another hospital nearer, if
1) she is afraid she will not be admitted to the nearer hospital or
2) she fears there may be delays in admitting her there or
3) she thinks she will not receive the necessary attention there or

4) she believes there are more proficient personnel at the hospital where she has registered.

d. She may not travel to the more distant hospital for purely financial reasons.

e. She may be accompanied to the hospital, as explained in paragraph 11 below.

f. Even if the route is not included within an *eiruv*, she may take with her anything which is essential for her on Shabbath and which she will not be able to obtain at the hospital.

g. The laws relating to traveling are dealt with in detail in Chapter 40, paragraphs 50 to 73.

9. *a.* Notwithstanding the above, activities which can be delayed should not be performed in violation of the Shabbath until the moment when

1) the womb opens to an extent which indicates that the birth is imminent or

2) the waters break or

3) the bleeding which precedes the birth starts or

4) the patient is no longer able to walk.

postponement of inessential activities

b. Consequently, until that moment arrives, one may only take those essential steps which are connected with the birth (such as transporting the patient to the hospital), but may not, by way of example,

1) boil up water to make the patient a cup of tea,

2) activate an air conditioner or similar apparatus or

3) turn on a light so that the patient can see. (In this connection, see paragraph 6*a* and *b* above.)

10. *a.* It sometimes transpires that a woman who has arrived at a hospital to give birth has come too early, with the result that she is discharged or refused admission.

returning from hospital after arriving too soon

b. If this happens, she is not allowed to return home in a vehicle driven by a Jew.

c. There is room for permitting her to return in a vehicle driven by a non-Jew, if

1) there is nowhere in the vicinity of the hospital for her to stay till after Shabbath,
2) it is a hardship for her to wait in the street **and**
3) her home is within the distance that she is allowed to walk on Shabbath.

accompany-
ing an
expectant
mother to
hospital

11. A relative, or any other person in whom the expectant mother has confidence, may travel with her to the hospital to keep her company, as explained in Chapter 40, paragraph 70.

violating
Shabbath
for the
newborn
baby

12. *a.* One violates Shabbath to serve all the physical needs of the newborn baby, so long as there is hope that it will live, or that its life can be prolonged, for however short a time.

b. 1) a) On the other hand, there are no grounds for permitting a Jew to write the mother's name on a strip of material on Shabbath and tie it to the baby's hand (as is done in various hospitals).

b) This is not done for medical reasons but for the purpose of identification and to prevent babies being exchanged.

2) The recommended practice is
a) to write the mother's name on the strip when she first registers for admission (before Shabbath), or
b) to prepare identically numbered strips for mother and baby.

3) It is better to prepare strips which can be fastened with bandage clips, or by similar means,* so as to avoid tying a double knot on Shabbath.

4) If identification strips of this kind were not prepared before Shabbath, one may on Shabbath request a non-Jew to write out the required data.

---

*A plastic strip that can readily be fastened and re-opened by hand by means of a plastic button may also be used.

13. *a.* For the first three days (or, to be more exact, seventy-two hours) after the end of the birth, the mother is regarded by the Halacha as a patient whose life is in danger.

violating Shabbath during the first three days after birth

b. 1) One may violate Shabbath to do whatever anyone who has some acquaintance with medical matters sees as being necessary for her.

   2) This is so

    a) even if there is no doctor or midwife at hand and the person whose opinion is being relied upon is just a friend with a little medical knowledge **and**

    b) even if the mother herself says that she does not need what is being done for her.

c. 1) All the more so should one violate Shabbath at the mother's request.

   2) In such a case, one should do everything for her which she demands for the sake of her health or to make her feel better, even if the doctor says that she has no need of it.

   3) See, in this regard, Chapter 32, paragraphs 52 and 73.

d. By way of illustration,

   1) one may heat water for her if she needs hot water and none is available (see Chapter 32, paragraphs 72 to 80 for the detailed rules applicable);

   2) if she is suffering from the cold, one may turn a heater on for her, even if it is the middle of summer. (See further Chapter 32, paragraphs 83 to 85 and also paragraph 27 there.)

e. In both of the cases illustrated, if there is a non-Jew available, it is preferable for him to do what is required, as explained in the note to Chapter 32, paragraph 83.

f. The manner in which one performs the forbidden acts should, as much as possible, be varied from that which one would adopt on an ordinary day of the week, as explained in paragraph 4 above.

g. One does not violate Shabbath when
   1) the mother herself says there is no need **and**
   2) the doctor and the midwife agree with her.

violating
Shabbath
4 to 7 days
after birth

14. *a.* 1) For the next four days (or, to be more exact, ninety-six hours), the Halacha continues to regard the mother as a patient whose life is in danger, but
   2) a distinction is, nevertheless, made between the first three days and the subsequent four.

b. During this latter period of four days,
   1) one should not violate Shabbath for anything which the mother says she does not need, so long as the doctor or the midwife do not say that the violation is necessary for her;
   2) the non-professional opinions of laymen, who claim that the act in question is required for the patient, have no weight against the woman's own assertions.

c. Only if
   1) the mother herself expresses no view **and**
   2) there is no contrary medical opinion of a doctor or midwife
   does one violate Shabbath in reliance upon the non-expert opinion of a layman (for instance, one of the mother's friends) who has a little medical knowledge.

d. If
   1) the mother herself requests it **and**
   2) a) she is God-fearing and would be afraid to profane the Shabbath for no good reason **or**
      b) one can tell that she is speaking sincerely and is not telling a lie,
   then one violates Shabbath for her, even when the doctor says there is no need to comply with her wishes.

violating
Shabbath
8 to 30 days
after birth

15. *a.* 1) From and including the eighth day (commencing one hundred and sixty-eight hours after the end of the birth) until the termination of the thirtieth day

after the birth, the mother is considered to be out of danger.

2) She is regarded by the Halacha as a person who is ill but whose life is not threatened, and she should consequently be treated as outlined in Chapter 33.

b. As stated in Chapter 33, paragraph 2*a*, one may do anything necessary for the mother's health through the agency of a non-Jew, even if the act in question is the subject of a Torah prohibition.

c. A Jew may perform an act required in the patient's medical treatment if it involves the breach of no more than a Rabbinical prohibition, but he should do it in a different way from that which he would adopt on another day of the week. (See Chapter 33, paragraph 2*c*.)

d. In any case of doubt, a rabbi who is competent in the Halacha should be consulted.

e. If any possibly dangerous complication arises in the mother's condition, even after the seventh day, she should be treated as a patient whose life is at risk.

16. a. Even a woman who has just given birth is obliged to light the Shabbath or Yom Tov candles. *lighting the Shabbath candles*

b. It is proper for her to light them at the table at which the Shabbath or Yom Tov meal is to be eaten.

c. If she cannot rise from her bed, her husband should light them in her stead.

d. While she is still in the hospital, she should light the candles where the meal is to be eaten or by her bed (and she should insist that the candles are not removed).

BREAST-FEEDING

17. a. Subject to what follows, a nursing mother may clean her nipples before feeding her baby. *cleaning the nipples*

b. The proper course is for her to use her hand, or a piece of non-absorbent, synthetic material, in order to apply the disinfectant (after consulting the doctor) or the water with which she washes the nipples.

c. 1) She should not use absorbent cotton (cotton wool) for this purpose, even if it is held in a pair of tweezers.

2) This is because she will not be able to avoid squeezing out some of the liquid.

d. See also Chapter 35, paragraph 11.

relieving pain during initial feedings

18. a. During the first few days, feeding is liable to be painful for the mother.

b. She may relieve this pain by dipping an absorbent-cotton swab in pitocin, or some similar substance, and holding it at the side of the nostril.

c. She must take great care not to squeeze out the absorbent cotton.

expressing milk to encourage baby to suck

19. a. While expressing milk is generally prohibited on Shabbath, if the baby will not begin sucking, the mother may express some of her milk into its mouth, to encourage it to take hold of the breast and suck.

b. She may not express the milk into a vessel.

expressing surplus milk

20. a. The Rabbis forbade the expressing of milk on Shabbath even where it goes to waste, but not when the object is to relieve the mother's pain or discomfort.

b. Thus, a nursing mother who is suffering discomfort because she has too much milk may dispose of the surplus by expressing it

1) into the sink or

2) onto a diaper (nappy) or some other cloth which one does not mind being wet.

c. A medically recommended method of expressing the milk in accordance with the rule set out in *a* above is to dip the breast into a basin of soapy water and squeeze the milk into that. (See Chapter 12, paragraph 6, for restrictions on making soapy water on Shabbath.)

d. 1) If the mother finds it difficult to express surplus

milk in this way, she may even use a special (non-electric) suction pump for the purpose.

2) Care should be taken, however, to empty out and throw away the accumulated milk at frequent intervals, in order to prevent more than a small quantity from collecting.

21. *a.* A mother may express milk from her breasts into a receptacle for her baby even on Shabbath, if, *expressing milk for*

    1) a) for some reason, the baby cannot suck from its mother's breasts or *baby who cannot suck*

       b) the baby is in the hospital and the mother has to bring it her fresh milk every day,

    and

    2) the main item of the baby's diet is mother's milk.

  b. The reason for this is that the baby is liable to be endangered if fed other milk.

22. *a.* A nursing mother whose nipples have become inflamed and will require attention on Shabbath should, before Shabbath commences, spread the necessary ointment on the dressings she will need (and keep them covered until use, to avoid contamination). *inflammation of the nipples*

  b. She will then be able to apply the dressings to her breasts on Shabbath.

  c. A nursing mother is permitted to take medicine and receive injections to avoid inflammation of the breasts.

Chapter 37

Laws Relating to Babies
and Small Children

preparing a
baby's food

1. *a.* A change of food is liable to upset the stomach of a baby who is used to mother's milk, or to any other kind of milk, or to any other specific food.

    b. Consequently, if its regular food was not prepared prior to Shabbath,

        1) one may violate Shabbath in order to prepare it and

        2) one should not experiment with other food.

    c. Of course, one should not rely on this but ought to avoid the situation by preparing the baby's food before Shabbath commences.

tending the
needs of a
small child:
general rule

2. *a.* A child up to the age of nine or ten — depending on the stage of his development — requires special treatment, on account of the sensitivity of his constitution.

    b. As a result, the Rabbis permitted one, when indeed the need arises, to do on Shabbath for a child of this age whatever one may do for a person who is ill but not dangerously so. (See Chapter 33.)

    c. This applies not only to the preparation of food, but also to tending other needs of the child which affect his health.

    d. In any case, each situation must be judged according to the prevailing circumstances, so that, if it is possible to satisfy the child's needs with something one has on hand, without having to violate the Shabbath, one is obviously forbidden

        1) to transgress even a Rabbinical prohibition or

        2) to perform a prohibited act even through the agency of a non-Jew.

milk
produced on
Shabbath

3. *a.* It follows that, when a small child needs milk and no other is available, one may give it milk which has been

1) extracted on Shabbath by means of a milking machine, in a permissible manner, or
2) milked by a non-Jew on Shabbath.
b. Such milk should not be handled, except for the purposes of the child, since it is *muktzeh.*
c. Milk which has been milked by a Jew, in violation of the Shabbath, must not be given to the child, as long as one has available milk produced on Shabbath in a permitted manner.
d. With regard to heating food for a baby or small child, see Chapter 1, paragraphs 13, 44 and 50, and Chapter 38, paragraph 11.

4. A child who, on the instructions of the doctor, has to be given daily vitamins or fish oil may be given them on Shabbath too. *vitamins and cod-liver oil*

5. a. If necessary, one may weigh or measure the amount of food which a child requires, but it is as well not to be exact in the weight or measurement. *weighing and measuring*
b. It is also permissible to weigh the child himself, when one has to ascertain how much weight, if any, he has gained after a meal.

6. a. 1) One may apply oil to a baby's body. *when oil may be applied*
2) As mentioned in Chapter 34, paragraph 13, oil may not be applied to an adult's cracked lips or chapped hands.
3) In the case of a baby, however, oil may be put even on those parts of the body where the skin has become chafed, for instance, from wet diapers (nappies).
b. 1) One may also apply oil to the scalp of a baby who is suffering irritation from scurf, if one would also do so on another day of the week.
2) In this case, only a little oil should be used.
c. 1) In none of the above cases should one smooth on a

[595]

thick mixture, such as zinc oil, but only a preparation which is liquid in consistency.

2) If the preparation one wishes to smooth on is of a thick consistency, one should thin it by the admixture of sufficiently large quantities of oil.

3) It goes without saying that the spreading of ointment is forbidden.*

how to apply oil

7. *a.* Oil may be applied

1) with one's hand or

2) by pouring it onto the baby's skin and gently wiping over it, even with absorbent cotton (cotton wool) which was torn off the wad and compressed before Shabbath.

(See also Chapter 14, paragraph 28.)

b. 1) One may not pour the oil onto the cotton and then smear it on the baby, even if the cotton was properly prepared before Shabbath.

2) This is because some of the oil will be squeezed out of the cotton, and that would be a violation of the Shabbath.

3) The prohibition applies to the use in this way of any absorbent material, even synthetic.

applying iodine

8. *a.* One may apply iodine or gentian violet to a child's wound, in order to prevent infection and assist the healing process.

b. The observations on the use of oil, set out in the preceding paragraph, apply in this case too.

c. Iodine (or gentian violet) may also be applied with a brush whose bristles are synthetic and are not close enough together to retain liquid between them.

d. One is not allowed to dip the absorbent cotton into the iodine, even if one holds the cotton in a pair of

---

*For ways in which ointment may be applied without spreading, see Chapter 33, paragraph 14.

tweezers, because, using the cotton in this way, one is bound to squeeze some of the iodine out of it.

9. *a.* It is permitted to give a child medication, including *medication*
   1) nose, ear or eye drops and
   2) any pills or syrups which he needs to make him well.
   b. One may even crumble a pill for him and dissolve it in water.
   c. See also Chapter 33, paragraph 4.

10. *a.* Subject to what is stated in *c* below, one is allowed, *cleaning* when treating a child, *and*
    1) to wash a wound, *treating a*
    2) to sprinkle "Dermatol" or some other styptic *wound* surgical dusting powder on a wound in order to stop it from bleeding,
    3) to dress a wound in order to avoid contamination and
    4) to remove a thorn which has penetrated the skin.
    b. One is not allowed to smear ointment onto a wound.
    c. 1) For details of the laws applicable, see Chapter 35.
    2) The contents of paragraph 2 above must, however, be borne in mind.

11. *a.* A baby or small child may be in danger, and one *stomach* should contact a doctor right away, if *trouble*
    1) it is suffering from acute diarrhea or
    2) it has severe stomach pains.
    b. With regard to squeezing out a pomegranate for a baby or small child suffering from slight diarrhea, see Chapter 5, paragraph 13.

12. *a.* If a baby's navel bleeds, it may be treated with *bleeding* "Dermatol" or another styptic powder to arrest the *navel* bleeding.
    b. One may also change the dressing. (See Chapter 35, paragraph 20.)

c. When necessary, one may even violate Shabbath, since the life of a baby in this condition is regarded by the Halacha as being in danger.

circumci-
sion

13. *a.* As a rule, when circumcision of a baby can take place on the eighth day (counting the day of birth as the first), its performance overrides the laws of Shabbath, subject to the reservations set out below.

b. All the dressings which will be required for use after the circumcision should be prepared prior to the beginning of Shabbath, coated with any necessary ointment and covered to keep them clean.

c. Likewise, where there is no *eiruv* and carrying articles about is forbidden, one must, before Shabbath, bring everything one needs for the circumcision to the place where it is to be performed.

d. 1) If

    a) one has not made the necessary preparations before Shabbath and

    b) one cannot, without violating the Shabbath, make up the deficiency (for example, by obtaining clean, albeit ointment-free, strips of material from someone living in the same house, for use in place of ointment-coated dressings),

then the circumcision may not be carried out at the proper time and must be postponed until the next day.

2) With such conditions, one is not permitted to perform the circumcision on Shabbath, in reliance upon the fact that the danger thereby caused to the baby will subsequently justify the violation of Shabbath, for instance

    a) in cutting dressings or

    b) in bringing items needed to treat the baby.

3) Nonetheless, in a case where the circumcision has taken place on Shabbath, one may, of course, do whatever is needed on Shabbath, regardless of

whether the decision to circumcise
a) arose from a mistaken assumption that all the necessary dressings (for example) were ready or
b) was taken in full knowledge that the dressings had not been prepared before Shabbath.

e. 1) a) Just as it is forbidden on Shabbath to bring things one needs for the circumcision through a place where there is no *eiruv*,
   b) so it is forbidden to bring the baby, through a place where one may not carry, to the synagogue for the circumcision.
   2) This is so, even if the *mohel* is unable to come to the house where the baby is and the circumcision will have to be postponed.

f. 1) One may request a non-Jew to bring things one needs for the circumcision to the house where it is to take place, through an area where carrying is forbidden, so long as that area does not fall within the strict definition of a *r^eshuth ha-rabbim*, as specified in Chapter 17, paragraph 3.
   2) Similarly, one may tell him to bring the baby to the synagogue for the circumcision.
   3) See also Chapter 30, paragraph 14.

g. One must remember that, subject to the above, no act which is a violation of the Shabbath (other than the circumcision itself) may be performed on Shabbath.
   1) whether the infringement is of a Torah prohibition or only of a Rabbinical prohibition and
   2) whether the act is done by a Jew or through the agency of a non-Jew.

14. a. When a baby is suffering from an earache, the doctor is allowed, if necessary, to switch on the light of the instrument he needs to make an examination, since the pain could be evidence of a dangerous condition. *examina-tion of ears*
    b. Furthermore, if there is a reasonable prospect that the doctor will be called upon to make a similar

[599]

examination on the same day, he may even switch off the light, to prevent the batteries from being used up.

breathing 15. There are various possible ways of treating a child
difficulties   suffering from breathing difficulties on Shabbath, subject to approval of the doctor in charge.

a. In light cases, where it is sufficient to spray the patient's room with an appropriate preparation, that is the course one should adopt.

b. 1) In more serious cases, the doctor is liable to require the evaporation of water containing eucalyptus drops.

2) In that event, a sufficient quantity should be placed on the fire before Shabbath.

3) Should the necessity arise, one may be permitted to add eucalyptus drops on Shabbath (if there is no non-Jew available who could do it).

c. 1) Where this is insufficient and the doctor requires the use of a vaporizer, one should

a) prepare boiling water before Shabbath,

b) leave it on the fire for refilling the vaporizer when necessary,

c) turn on the vaporizer before Shabbath starts and

d) leave the vaporizer on even after one has finished using it.

2) One may add boiled water, which is still at least partly warm, to the water in the vaporizer as and when necessary.

3) As models of vaporizers differ from each other, one would do well to obtain a halachic ruling as to the method of operating any particular model in such a way as to minimize Shabbath violation.

4) a) One may, of course, switch on and use the vaporizer on Shabbath if one neglected to switch it on and make the required preparations before Shabbath, or if the need for its use

arose on Shabbath itself and the doctor demands it.

b) Even so, one should, when possible, use only water which has been on the fire since before Shabbath.

5) Concerning the heating of water on Yom Tov for use in a vaporizer, see Chapter 33, paragraphs 26 and 27, and draw the appropriate analogy.

16. *a.* See Chapter 14 for laws regarding   *other*
 1) washing a baby or a child on Shabbath or Yom Tov,   *references*
 2) heating of water on Yom Tov for this purpose and
 3) combing and other attention to the hair.

b. See Chapter 15, paragraphs 4 to 8, regarding the treatment of soiled diapers (nappies), plastic pants and sheets.

c. See Chapter 40, paragraphs 2 and 3, with regard to taking a person's temperature.

d. See Chapter 38, paragraphs 24 to 28, regarding the performance of forbidden acts for the purposes of a baby or a child by means of a non-Jew.

Chapter 38

Caring for the Sick and for Small Children on Shabbath and Yom Tov with the Aid of a Non-Jew

PATIENTS WHOSE LIVES ARE CONSIDERED TO BE IN DANGER

Jew should attend to urgent needs

1. *a.* 1) It has already been explained in Chapter 32, paragraph 6, that whenever it becomes urgently necessary to violate Shabbath for a patient whose life is considered to be in danger, this should preferably not be done through the agency of a non-Jew.

2) The Jew himself should act as quickly as possible to save the patient's life.

b. Two reasons have been given for this:

1) The Jew will act with more urgency.

2) a) The mistaken impression could be created that one may violate Shabbath to save life only through the agency of a non-Jew.

b) Fatal results could ensue if, in a subsequent case, there were no non-Jew immediately at hand and one wasted valuable time looking for one while the danger to the patient grew.

c. Therefore, when, for example, it is necessary to travel in a vehicle in order to summon a doctor or purchase medicines,

1) the Jew should quickly go himself, or

2) the Jew should at least accompany the non-Jewish driver and not let him go alone.

needs which are not immediately vital

2. *a.* 1) Notwithstanding the above, the Rabbis said that, where possible, it is better for a non-Jew to attend to those needs of the dangerously ill patient which are vital but not immediately so (and which involve a violation of the Shabbath).

[602]

2) To be sure, if there is no non-Jew available, the Jew must of course attend to such needs of the dangerously ill patient, even when they involve the performance of acts which are prohibited by the Torah.

b. Therefore, on a cold day, when the dangerously ill patient requires the house to be heated,
   1) the heater should, if possible, be turned on by a non-Jew, but,
   2) if
      a) there is no non-Jew at hand **and**
      b) the heat given out by the heater is better for the patient than the warmth which could be provided by additional blankets,
      then the Jew should turn it on. (See further Chapter 32, paragraphs 83 and 84.)

c. 1) Similarly, where a dangerously ill patient, who would benefit from sleep, is disturbed by the light burning in his room, one should have it turned off by a non-Jew.
   2) A Jew should turn the light off only if
      a) there is no non-Jew at hand whose services can be enlisted,
      b) one cannot take the patient or the light out of the room **and**
      c) none of the other possibilities referred to in Chapter 32, paragraph 70a, exist.
   3) When a Jew turns off the light himself, he should, if he can, do so in a different way from that which he would normally adopt, for instance by nudging the switch with his elbow.

3. a. In the cases below, acts which would involve a violation of the Shabbath (whether the infringement is of a Rabbinical or a Torah prohibition) should be performed through the agency of a non-Jew:
   1) where something essential has to be done for a dangerously ill patient but can be left until after Shabbath (see Chapter 32, paragraph 23); *needs which can wait till after Shabbath or are inessential*

2) where
a) the thing needed to be done is in some way necessary for a dangerously ill patient, but
b) abstention from doing it will not bring about an aggravation of his condition
(see Chapter 32, paragraph 24);
3) where a dangerously ill patient requests something which
a) does not concern his actual medical treatment, but
b) would set his mind at rest or soothe him
(see Chapter 32, paragraph 25).

b. When there is no non-Jew available, a Jew may do what is required, but
1) he should transgress only Rabbinical prohibitions and
2) he should, if possible, introduce a variation into his usual method of performing the prohibited acts.

c. It follows from the above that
1) one may
a) have an operation performed,
b) have X-ray photographs taken or
c) have a plaster cast fitted
by a non-Jew for a dangerously ill patient, even though it is close to the termination of Shabbath and one could wait till then;
2) one may request a non-Jewish doctor to write a letter, on Shabbath, referring a dangerously ill patient for admission to a hospital on the following day;
3) one may request a non-Jew to cook food for a patient whose life is in danger, even though there is other food prepared and available for him, if for some reason the freshly cooked food is preferable (see further Chapter 32, paragraph 78, and paragraph 11 below);
4) a) if a dangerously ill patient asks for his relatives to be called to visit him, one may tell a non-Jew

to ride or to drive to where they live and alert
them;

b) alternatively, a Jew is allowed to walk there
even where it is beyond the distance normally
permitted, but he may not telephone or travel
by car.

(See also Chapter 32, paragraph 26.)

PATIENTS WHO ARE ILL BUT WHOSE LIVES
ARE NOT CONSIDERED TO BE IN DANGER

4. *a.* It has already been explained, in Chapter 33, para- *general rule*
graph 2, that one may request a non-Jew to attend to
the needs of a person who is ill although not dangerously so, even to the extent of his performing acts
which the Torah forbids on Shabbath, provided that

1) there is no possibility of a Jew's attending to the
patient's needs without infringing any prohibitions and

2) what the non-Jew does is required on Shabbath
(and not just for after Shabbath).

b. On the other hand, even where there is a non-Jew
available, a Jew may transgress a Rabbinical prohibition for the purpose of attending to the medical needs
of a patient who is not dangerously ill (as set out in
Chapter 33, paragraph 2), if either

1) a risk exists that the patient will lose the normal
use of a limb or organ **or**

2) the Jew introduces a variation into his normal
method of performing the prohibited act.

5. *a.* As a result,　　　　　　　　　　　　　　　　*lights*

1) one is allowed to tell a non-Jew to switch on the
light, so that one can see what the patient needs*
and

---

*Once the light is on, it may be used by others too. (See Chapter 30,
paragraphs 43 and 44.)

2) one is allowed to tell the non-Jew to switch the light off, so that the patient can sleep.

obtaining
medical
attention

b. One may also tell the non-Jew to do such things as
1) telephone a non-Jewish doctor,
2) purchase medicines for use on Shabbath and
3) drive the patient to the doctor.

dental
treatment

c. In the event of a very painful toothache, one may go to a non-Jewish dentist for the appropriate treatment, including extraction of the tooth causing the pain.

fractured
bones

6. In case of a fractured bone, even where it does not constitute a danger to the patient, one may ask a non-Jewish doctor to take an X-ray photograph or make a plaster cast.

stomach-
ache

7. a. Where the patient has a severe stomachache and the doctor's instructions are to warm the region of the stomach, then, even if the patient is not in danger, one may ask a non-Jew to switch on an electric cushion for application to the stomach.

b. One may also tell the non-Jew to increase or reduce the heat of the cushion.

c. 1) A Jew may move the electric cushion for the purpose of using it, but
2) he may not increase or reduce its heat.
3) It is a good idea to wind something around the electricity regulator as a reminder, so that one should not come to adjust the temperature.

heating

8. a. In countries with a cool climate, one may on Shabbath tell a non-Jew to turn on the heating if one is troubled by the cold.

b. This is because a person suffering from the cold is placed in the same category as someone who is ill.

c. If there are small children in the house, or a person who is ill, albeit not dangerously so, one may tell the non-Jew to turn on the heating even when the cold is not intense enough to bother adults or healthy people.

d. See also Chapter 23, paragraph 24, and Chapter 31, paragraph 6.

9. *a.* On a hot summer's day, one may request a non-Jew to switch on an electric fan or the air conditioning, *electric fans and air conditioning*
1) when one is suffering a great deal from the heat or
2) due to the presence of a person who is ill, albeit not dangerously so.

b. See also Chapter 13, paragraphs 34 and 35, and Chapter 30, paragraph 11.

10. One may ask a non-Jew to wind up a clock or a watch which has stopped going, if one needs it for the purposes of a person who is ill, for instance in order to know when he has to be given his medicine. *winding a watch or clock*

11. *a.* 1) It is permissible to tell a non-Jew to cook or to warm food or drink on Shabbath for a person who is ill, even though his life is not in danger. *cooking*
2) The prohibition which generally (but not always) forbids one to eat food cooked by a non-Jew does not apply to the person who is ill when he eats the food on Shabbath.

b. One may not do anything to assist in the cooking, as one would do on a weekday, and one may not even
1) put the food in the pot before it is placed on the fire,
2) cover the pot, so long as the food inside is not yet completely cooked, or
3) stir the food in the pot.

c. A healthy person may not eat this food on Shabbath, since
1) the non-Jew may have cooked, or may cook, more for the healthy person's benefit and, in addition,
2) the food itself may be *muktzeh*.

d. There is a difference of opinion among the authorities as to whether the prohibition against eating food cooked by a non-Jew applies to forbid a Jew (even the

patient himself) to eat the food after Shabbath has
ended.

e. There is also a dispute as to whether the vessels in
which the non-Jew cooked the food may be used again
without previous immersion in boiling water, in accordance with the rules applicable whenever one wishes
to render fit for use a vessel in which forbidden food
was cooked.

writing
prescrip-
tions

12. *a.* One is allowed to ask a non-Jewish doctor to write out
a prescription for a patient who is ill, even if his life is
not at risk.

b. If the doctor has no pen and, for some reason, cannot
take the Jew's pen, the Jew may himself pick it up and
hand it to him.

transport

13. *a.* If
  1) a Jewish doctor wishes to reach a Jewish patient
     who is ill, even though not in danger, and
  2) the patient's house is too far for the doctor to walk
     there,
  he may travel through the town by any means of
  transport operated by non-Jews.

b. He may return in the same way.

c. So much the better
  1) if he can arrange with the driver to pay him the fare
     after Shabbath or
  2) if he can request a non-Jew to pay the driver in his
     place.

d. Where
  1) the driver will not agree to wait for the fare until
     after Shabbath,
  2) there is no other non-Jew around who can pay the
     driver what he is owed, and
  3) there is an *eiruv* covering the area through which
     he has to travel,
  the Jewish doctor may take a pre-paid ticket with him.

e. Should this not be possible either, the doctor may even take money with him (where there is an *eiruv*) and pay the fare on Shabbath, but he should not accept change from the driver.

f. Notwithstanding the above, a doctor who finds himself in such a situation should consult a rabbi authorized to hand down halachic decisions, as onlookers are liable to conclude that the doctor is profaning the Shabbath without any justification.

SLIGHT INDISPOSITIONS AND MINOR AILMENTS

14. *a.* A distinction must be made between   *general rule*
    1) a person who feels slightly ill, that is to say,
        a) on the one hand, he is ill, but,
        b) on the other hand, he has no serious pain and his illness does not affect the whole body, and
    2) a person suffering from a minor ailment which does not cause him more than a minimal amount of pain.

  b. 1) For neither of them may one violate Shabbath,
        a) even by transgressing a purely Rabbinical prohibition and
        b) even if one does so in a manner one would not usually adopt.
    2) To neither of them may one give medicine on Shabbath.

  c. The difference between them is that,
    1) a) for a person who is slightly ill, one may request a non-Jew to do an act which involves no more than a Rabbinical* prohibition, and

---

*Whenever the violation of Shabbath through the agency of a non-Jew is restricted by Halacha to the performance of acts which are the subject only of a Rabbinical prohibition, one should consult a qualified rabbinical authority in order to ascertain what in effect is permitted and what forbidden.

    b) he may have medication administered to him by a non-Jew,

whereas

    2) a person who merely has a minor ailment may not be given any medical treatment, even through the agency of a non-Jew.

    d. Reference should be made to Chapter 34 for more precise details of the rules which apply in common to those who are slightly ill and those who merely have a minor ailment.

colds   **15.** *a.* It follows from the above that, in the event of a bad cold, one may have nasal drops or nasal ointment administered by a non-Jew.

    b. One may not have a vaporizer turned on by the non-Jew (since this could involve the infringement of a Torah prohibition), unless one is confined to bed or feels weak all over as a result of the cold.

diarrhea   **16.** In case of common diarrhea, one may ask a non-Jew to administer an enema, but not to heat water for this purpose (unless the diarrhea is severe).

toothache   **17.** In case of a slight toothache, one must not take any medical treatment, even from a non-Jew. (See also Chapter 34, paragraph 7.)

TREATMENT OF WOUNDS ON SHABBATH AND YOM TOV

classification of wounds   **18.** *a.* As explained in Chapter 35, the treatment of wounds depends on their classification in each individual case.

    1) Some wounds may be treated as on a normal weekday, because they can constitute a danger to the whole body.

    2) Someone suffering from a wound which is not so dangerous, but

    a) causes severe pains or

    b) endangers the normal use of the injured limb,

is treated in the same way as a person who is ill but whose life is not in danger.

3) No medical treatment may be given by a Jew in the case of a superficial wound, except insofar as necessary to prevent infection or arrest bleeding.

b. The following three paragraphs deal with the treatment of superficial wounds by non-Jews.

19. *a.* A Jew may tell a non-Jew to treat a superficial wound, as long as *superficial wounds*

1) the Jew is experiencing pain from the wound **and**

2) the Jew does not tell him to do an act which is the subject of a Torah prohibition. (See note to paragraph 14 above.)

b. Thus, one may let a non-Jew put a dressing that was spread with ointment since before Shabbath on a wound which is causing pain, but not on a wound which is not painful.

c. 1) One may not tell the non-Jew to spread the ointment over the dressing on Shabbath, but

2) one may tell him

    a) to squeeze ointment onto the wound from a tube or

    b) to take ointment out of a jar with a spatula and apply it to the affected part,

without asking him to spread it on the wound, and

3) one may tell him to put a dressing over the ointment.

d. 1) One may not request a non-Jew to cut a dressing which is too large, but

2) one may ask him to fasten a bandage with a double knot, if it is due to be untied at some time in the future.

e. Where the wound is sufficiently serious to place the patient in the category of persons who are ill although not dangerously so, one may tell the non-Jew to give whatever treatment is necessary, as explained in paragraph 4 above.

sprains　　20. *a.* 1) One may ask a non-Jew to put a compress on a sprain which is not causing severe pain, since this involves only a Rabbinical prohibition.

2) It is better if one tells the non-Jew to make the compress from a cloth which is absolutely clean.

b. One may also request a non-Jew to rub the painful area with oil or liquid camphor, but not with ointment.

c. Where the sprain is so painful that the patient is classified as a person who is ill although not dangerously so, one may tell the non-Jew to do whatever is necessary to heal the sprain and assuage the pain, as explained in paragraph 4 above.

opening　21. Although it is permissible for a Jew to open a wound in
wounds to　order to extract pus (as described in Chapter 35, para-
extract pus　graph 16), it is better to have it done by a non-Jew.

LAWS RELATING TO CHILDBIRTH

preference　22. *a.* As explained in Chapter 36, paragraph 4, one is
for using　allowed to violate Shabbath and Yom Tov for a woman
services of　who gives birth.
a non-Jew

b. However, since the process of childbirth is a natural and accepted phenomenon, the Rabbis have stated that, where possible, one should attend to the woman's needs through the agency of a non-Jew.

c. Of course, one should not use the services of a non-Jew where this could result in a detrimental delay in doing what is necessary for her.

eight to　23. *a.* From and including the eighth day (commencing one
thirty days　hundred and sixty-eight hours after the end of the
after the　birth) until the end of the thirtieth day after the birth,
birth　the Halacha regards the mother as a person who is ill

but whose life is not in danger. (See Chapter 36, paragraph 15.)

b. Subject to what is stated in paragraph 4 above, one may attend to all of her medical needs through the agency of a non-Jew, even if this involves performance of an act which infringes a Torah prohibition.

LAWS RELATING TO BABIES AND SMALL CHILDREN

24. *a.* From Chapter 37, paragraph 2, it can be seen that, due to the sensitivity of his constitution, a small child is treated by the Halacha in the same way as a person who is ill although not dangerously so. *general rule*

b. One may, consequently, tell a non-Jew to do whatever is essential for the child's health.

c. 1) One is, therefore, allowed to ask a non-Jew to cook or heat food for a baby who needs it.

2) If the food which he has cooked is *muktzeh*, the non-Jew should, when possible, also feed the baby.

3) See paragraph 11 above for further details.

25. One may ask a non-Jew to grate an apple for a baby who needs it. *grating apples*

26. *a.* One may request a non-Jew to turn on a light for a small child who is frightened or is liable to become frightened. *lights*

b. Others may also benefit from this light once it is on.

c. One may also tell a non-Jew to turn off the light so that the child should sleep.

27. Regarding the turning on of a heater for small children on a cold day, see paragraph 8 above, Chapter 23, paragraph 24, and Chapter 31, paragraph 6. *heating*

28. *a.* One may ask a non-Jew to take a sick child, even though not in danger, to the doctor *carrying or transporting a child*

      1) by carrying him through *r^eshuth ha-rabbim* or

      2) by driving him there.

  b. 1) A qualified rabbinical authority should be consulted if one wishes a non-Jew to push a baby carriage containing a healthy baby or child through a place

      a) where there is no *eiruv*, but

      b) which does not satisfy all the requirements for *r^eshuth ha-rabbim* set out in Chapter 17, paragraph 3.

      2) His decision on this particular matter should reflect the local practice.

      3) Where there is no fixed practice, there is room for a lenient decision, permitting one to tell the non-Jew to push the carriage.

Chapter 39

Laws Relating to Illness, Pregnancy, Childbirth and Breast-Feeding on Yom Kippur

ILLNESS

1. *a.* Just as it is permitted, and indeed there is a positive obligation, to violate the Shabbath in order to save human life in any case of danger or possible danger, so is it permitted, and indeed there is a positive obligation, *obligation to eat when life endangered*
   1) for a patient whose life is, or may be, endangered to eat on Yom Kippur and
   2) to violate the sanctity of the day in order to save his life.
   b. Even when
   1) there is no immediate danger to the patient, but
   2) there is a possibility that his life may be endangered if he does not eat,
   it is permissible, and indeed obligatory, for him to eat and for one to violate the sanctity of the day in order to save his life. (See paragraph 7 below.)

2. *a.* A person who, on account of his medical condition, needs to eat and does not do so takes upon himself the responsibility for his own death and will be answerable to his Maker for the loss of his life. *gravity of obligation to eat when life endangered*
   b. It is desirable for the greatest and most respected halachic experts to be present when a dangerously ill person is being fed, lest others are reckless with his life in the belief that he does not have to eat.

3. *a.* As elaborated in Chapter 32, paragraphs 8 to 10, when deciding whether it is necessary to violate Shabbath for someone who is ill, one relies, in varying degrees, *who judges how serious an illness is?*

upon the opinions of
1) doctors,
2) the patient himself and
3) other individuals who have some knowledge of the illness in question.

   b. Likewise, one relies upon them, in accordance with the rules set out in the following paragraphs, when they state that a patient needs to eat on Yom Kippur.

reliance on patient's opinion that he must eat

4. *a.* 1) The patient himself is relied upon when he says that he must eat,
     a) even if he did not say so until he was asked and
     b) even if the doctor thinks otherwise.
  2) It is, however, proper first to remind the patient that it is Yom Kippur, in case he has forgotten.

   b. Where the patient's condition is such that, in the doctor's opinion, eating is liable to harm him, one relies on the doctor, notwithstanding the patient's demands for food.

reliance on medical opinion that patient must eat

5. *a.* One relies on the doctor's opinion, whether he is Jewish or non-Jewish, when he says that the patient has to eat,
  1) even if the patient thinks otherwise and
  2) even if the patient is himself a doctor and a specialist.

   b. Where there is no doctor, one relies on the opinion of anyone else who has some medical knowledge and says that the patient must eat, even if the patient objects. (See Chapter 32, paragraph 10, which also applies here.)

quantity of food or drink permitted

6. *a.* Whenever one has to give a sick person to eat or drink on Yom Kippur, one should ask the doctor how much food or drink the patient requires.

   b. In the light of the doctor's opinion, one must consider
  1) a) whether it is sufficient for the patient to eat or drink in *shi'urim* (limited quantities, as speci-

fied in paragraphs 18, 20 and 22 below) or
   b) whether he has to be given to eat and drink as
      normal,
   and
2) a) whether he has to eat **and** drink or
   b) whether it is sufficient for him just to drink.
c. It is to be noted that, whether the patient eats or drinks
   in *shi'urim* or normally, he must not eat or drink more
   than is medically necessary.

7. a. 1) The lives of patients with certain illnesses or symp-
       toms which are not dangerous in themselves are
       liable to be threatened by the withholding of food or
       drink. *eating to avoid danger*
   2) This may be so in the case, for instance, of lung
      diseases or of high temperature.
   3) As far as concerns eating on Yom Kippur, patients
      with such illnesses or symptoms are treated by the
      Halacha as patients whose lives are in danger.
   b. 1) What is more, one sometimes relies on a doctor's
      opinion to permit a healthy person to eat.
   2) This occurs when there is a reasonable fear that
      abstinence from food could lead to weakness and
      susceptibility to a potentially dangerous illness.
   3) Such a fear may be justified in the case, for exam-
      ple, of a person prone to nervous disorders.
   c. All of the persons mentioned in this paragraph should,
      however, eat only in *shi'urim*, as explained below.

8. a. If a person who is ill, but whose life is not in danger, *taking medicines*
      must take pills or drops, it is better, where the pos-
      sibility exists, to ask the doctor instead for supposi-
      tories having the same medical effect.
   b. Failing this,
   1) he may swallow pills or drops which have a bitter
      taste, but
   2) he should not drink water to make them easier to
      swallow.

    c. 1) If the doctor requires them to be taken with water, he should mix something bitter into the water, to spoil its taste.

       2) Both a rabbi qualified to give halachic decisions and the doctor should be consulted regarding the amount of the bitter substance to be mixed into the water.

    d. Pills which do not taste bitter should be swallowed wrapped in thin paper.

    e. There are some who take a stricter attitude and require even bitter pills to be swallowed wrapped.

gargling   **9.** A person who is ill with a sore throat, albeit not dangerously so, is allowed to gargle on Yom Kippur, provided

    a. the gargle tastes bitter **and**

    b. he takes care not to swallow any of it.

PREGNANCY, CHILDBIRTH AND BREAST-FEEDING

who fasts,   **10.** The general rule is that pregnant women and nursing
as a rule?   mothers fast the whole day on Yom Kippur (but see paragraphs 11 to 15 and 17 below).

need for   **11.** *a.* If
food during   1) a woman during pregnancy is seized with a longing
pregnancy   for a certain food, **and**

       2) she demands to eat it,
one gives her the food to eat, in *shi'urim*, as explained below, until she becomes composed.

    b. 1) One should act similarly if one can tell by the appearance of a pregnant woman that she must eat to avert danger.

       2) In this case, one gives her to eat even if she does not demand it.

first three
days after   **12.** *a.* A woman who gives birth should not fast from the
birth   moment when the birth begins (in accordance with the

criteria listed in Chapter 36, paragraph 9) until seventy-two hours after it ends.

b. 1) In the following cases, she should eat as if it were not a fast day:
a) if she demands food;
b) if she does not mention food or says she does not know whether she needs to eat;
c) if her doctor says she needs to eat, even if she herself says she does not.

2) If she says she does not need to eat and is not contradicted by the doctor, she should eat only in shi'urim, as described below.

13. a. During the ensuing ninety-six hours also, the mother should be given food (except in the one case specified below). *four to seven days after birth*

b. 1) In the following cases, she should eat as if it were not a fast day:
a) if she says she needs food and is not contradicted by the doctor;
b) if her doctor says she needs to eat, even if she herself says she does not.

2) In the following cases, she should eat only in shi'urim, as described below:
a) if she demands food, but her doctor says she does not need to eat;
b) if she does not mention food or says she does not know whether she needs to eat, and there is nobody present who, on the basis of at least some medical knowledge, can state that she does need to eat.

3) If she says that she does not need to eat, then, in the absence of a contrary opinion based on at least some medical knowledge, she should fast.

14. a. From the termination of the seventh day (one hundred and sixty-eight hours) after the end of the birth, the mother is regarded by the Halacha as no more than a *more than seven days after birth*

[619]

person who is ill but whose life is not in danger, and she is obliged to fast.

b. It is otherwise, and she is indeed treated as a dangerously ill person, even during this period, if

1) a deterioration takes place in her condition as a result of a postnatal complication **and**

2) either she or the doctor says that she needs to eat.

beginning of fourth and eighth days after birth

15. *a.* The transition

1) from the laws applicable during the first three days after birth to those applicable during the ensuing four days and

2) from the laws applicable during the first seven days to those applicable to a person who is ill but not dangerously so,

can take place on Yom Kippur itself.

b. Thus,

1) if the birth occurred at ten o'clock on the morning of the seventh of Tishrei,

a) the laws applicable to the first three days will cease to have effect at ten o'clock on the morning of Yom Kippur, and

b) thereafter, until the end of the day, the laws referred to in paragraph 13 above will take effect,

while,

2) if the birth occurred at ten o'clock on the morning of the third of Tishrei, the woman will be obliged to fast from ten o'clock on the morning of Yom Kippur.

stillbirths and abortions

16. The above rules apply equally in the case of

a. a woman who has a live birth,

b. a woman who is unfortunate enough to have a stillbirth and

c. a woman who has an abortion or miscarriage more than forty days after the commencement of her pregnancy.

(Compare Chapter 36, paragraph 5, regarding the violation of Shabbath.)

17. *a.* A nursing mother may drink (but not eat) in *shi'urim*, *nursing* as explained below, in the event that *mothers*
  1) she would not otherwise have sufficient milk for her baby **and**
  2) the baby is entirely dependent on the mother's milk for its sustenance and would accordingly be endangered if she were to fast.
  b. She would do well to avoid this situation by drinking large quantities of liquid before Yom Kippur starts, so that she will have enough milk to feed the baby while she fasts.
  c. It is certainly forbidden for a nursing mother to go to the synagogue if there is any risk that this will reduce her to a condition in which she will have to drink. (See paragraph 28 below.)

EATING AND DRINKING IN SHI'URIM

18. *a.* Eating in *shi'urim* means eating not more than a pre- *quantity* scribed amount within a prescribed period of time. *one may*
  b. 1) The prescribed amount is defined in the halachic *eat* sources as being less than "a large date."
  2) In practice, the amount eaten may be equal in volume to two-thirds of an average egg in its shell (where we assume the average egg weighs 45 to 50 grams — or one and a half to one and three-quarter ounces).*

---

*a. One should not just estimate the quantity of food which makes up the prescribed amount but should make accurate measurements.
b. This can be done as follows:
  1) One takes a small cup, if possible before Yom Kippur, and weighs it empty.

[621]

c. 1) The prescribed period of time is nine minutes.

2) To ensure that one does not eat more than the prescribed amount within any period of nine minutes, one should, after eating the prescribed amount, allow nine minutes to elapse before starting to eat again.

3) One can then again eat not more than the prescribed amount, wait another nine minutes and so on, till one has eaten in total as much as (but not more than) one needs.

d. 1) If one cannot wait as long as nine minutes, one should wait as long as one can, depending on one's state of health.

2) At all events, one should try to wait for a period of at least two minutes.

e. 1) Food which is puffed up (like cake) should be measured only after it has been well compressed.

2) This is because the air content is not to be taken into account in measuring the volume.

when to measure   **19.** a. One is allowed to measure to ascertain the prescribed amount on Yom Kippur itself.

b. Yet it is better to do this before Yom Kippur begins.

quantity one may drink   **20.** a. 1) The prescribed amount, with respect to liquid, is less than half a mouthful.

---

2) One then fills it with water until it weighs 32 grams (approximately one and one-eighth ounces) more than when it was empty.

3) The level reached by the water should be marked (or remembered by an existing mark on the side of the cup if this is being done on Yom Kippur itself).

4) The quantity of food which, when compressed to expel the air, fills the cup up to the mark comprises the prescribed quantity for that particular kind of food.

5) It may be convenient, instead of an ordinary cup, to use a vessel marked with lines indicating how much it contains.

2) a) The quantity varies from person to person.

   b) Consequently, it is desirable for the person in question to measure the quantity in his own case, if possible before Yom Kippur.

   c) He can do this by filling one of his cheeks with liquid and ejecting it into a vessel where it can be measured.

   d) Each time he has to drink on Yom Kippur, he should drink a little less than the amount in the vessel.

   e) In the case of the average adult, the amount of water which can be held in just one side of the mouth is between 40 and 45 grams (roughly between one and two-fifths and one and a half ounces).

b. 1) After drinking the prescribed amount, one should wait for nine minutes, if one can, before drinking again.

   2) One can then again drink not more than the prescribed amount, wait another nine minutes and so on, till one has drunk as much as one needs.

   3) If one cannot wait as long as nine minutes, one ought to wait as long as one can, allowing a minimum of at least two minutes, as in the case of eating. (See paragraph 18*d* above.)

   4) Where it is not enough for one to drink in this way, one should, at all events,

   a) drink less than half a mouthful, wait just a little while, again drink less than half a mouthful, and so on, or

   b) drink slowly, a teaspoonful at a time.

21. *a.* As will be seen from paragraph 31 below, a person who has to eat or drink on Yom Kippur should recite the usual blessing before doing so. *reciting blessings*

b. Once he has done so, he should not, if eating in *shi'u-rim*, repeat it after every pause, each time he is about to eat or drink the prescribed amount, unless he has, in

the meantime, diverted his attention from the food or drink by, for example,
1) going out of the house or
2) deciding not to eat or drink any more.

c. The blessing normally recited after one has finished eating or drinking should not be said, since it is doubtful whether one can have eaten or drunk enough in a sufficiently short period to justify such a blessing.

persons who must both eat and drink

22. a. 1) When eating in *shi‘urim*, one may eat and drink the respective prescribed amounts of food and liquid quite independently of each other.
2) As a result, one need not pause between food and drink, but, immediately after eating the prescribed amount of food, may drink less than half a mouthful, and vice versa.

b. On the other hand,
1) in calculating how much one may eat, one must take into account all the different kinds of food one wishes to eat, and
2) in calculating how much one may drink, one must take into account all the different kinds of liquid one wishes to drink.

c. 1) A qualified halachic authority should be consulted whenever there is a doubt as to whether a substance is deemed to be food or drink.
2) The question could arise when one is dealing, for example, with loose porridge, cream or honey.

doubt whether shi‘urim suffice

23. a. One should not feed the sick person in *shi‘urim* unless it is clear that eating and drinking in this way is enough for him.

b. If there is any doubt about the matter,
1) he should start by eating as much as he needs, in the same way as he would on any other day of the year, and
2) only from the moment when he feels certain that he

no longer needs to eat normally should he eat in *shi'urim*.

24. Likewise, if the doctor says that it is not enough to eat or drink in *shi'urim*, the patient should eat or drink as much as he needs in the normal way. *doctor's opinion*

25. When the patient says that it is not enough for him to eat in *shi'urim*, the practice is to put food before him and say to him, "It is Yom Kippur today. If you are afraid that your life will be in danger if you do not eat more than the prescribed amount at one time, eat normally. If not, eat a little at a time, so that you do not eat more than the prescribed amount within the prescribed period." *when patient requests to eat normally*

26. A patient who has to eat in *shi'urim* must not eat or drink more than he needs that day in order to keep him out of danger. *eating more than needed forbidden*

27. It must be remembered that eating in *shi'urim* is permitted only in the limited circumstances set out in this chapter and that a person who is ill but not in danger must not eat or drink at all, even if confined to bed. *limited application of shi'urim*

MISCELLANEOUS

28. *a.* A person who is weak and finds it difficult to fast on Yom Kippur if he goes to the synagogue is nonetheless obliged to fast. *persons who are weak*

b. He should lie in bed and fast and should not go to the synagogue, so that he should not have to eat or drink, even in *shi'urim*.

29. *a.* Artificial feeding is permitted on Yom Kippur, but *artificial feeding:*

b. a needle should not be inserted into a vein on Yom Kippur if the patient is not dangerously ill. *when permitted?*

[625]

choice
between
normal and
artificial
feeding

30. *a.* A person who is dangerously ill, with the result that he is allowed to eat on Yom Kippur, should not inflict upon himself the ordeal of artificial feeding.

b. He should eat, as explained above, in the normal way or in *shi'urim*, depending on the circumstances.

blessings
before and
after food

31. *a.* A patient who has to eat on Yom Kippur is obliged to recite the usual blessing before doing so.

b. He should not, however, make *kiddush* (neither with wine nor with bread).

c. He is also free from the obligation to begin the meal with two whole loaves, even when Yom Kippur occurs on Shabbath.

d. He should, when necessary, wash his hands before the meal in the same way as he is obliged to do on any other day of the year, up to the wrist.

e. 1) If he eats a *ka-zayith** of food in four minutes or less, he should recite the blessing said after eating.

2) a) If he has eaten bread, he should recite *birkath ha-mazon.*

b) In *birkath ha-mazon,* he should add the *Ya'aleh Veyavo* prayer, with the insertion of the words, "בְּיוֹם הַכִּפֻּרִים הַזֶּה."

c) On Shabbath, the *Retzeh* prayer should also be added.

d) Nevertheless, if he finishes the blessing in which these prayers are always added and then realizes that he has forgotten either or both of them, there is no need to say *birkath ha-mazon* again.

f. 1) It is not clear whether three people who need to eat on Yom Kippur and who have eaten together are obliged to recite *birkath ha-zimun.*

2) To avoid being in this position of doubt, they should

---

*See Glossary.

see to it that they do not eat together on Yom Kippur.

g. A person who has to eat on Yom Kippur and eats, for example, cake or dates should insert the words, "וְזָכְרֵנוּ לְטוֹבָה בְּיוֹם הַכִּפֻּרִים הַזֶּה," in the *al ha-michya* or *al ha-peiroth* blessing which he says afterwards.

32. *a.* A person who is ill, even though not dangerously so, *patients* may, if it is indeed necessary for him, bathe himself or *who need to* wash parts of his body on Yom Kippur. (For details of *wash* the restrictions relating to washing on Shabbath, which also apply on Yom Kippur, see Chapter 14.)

b. A person suffering from an inflammation of the eyes *treatment* may put drops in them or bathe them in a boracic *of eye* solution. (See Chapter 34, paragraph 8.) *inflamma-*
tions

33. Despite the fact that applying oil to the body is *applying oil* prohibited on Yom Kippur, oil (but not ointment) may *to a* be spread, for medical reasons, on the skin of a person *patient's* who is ill, although his life is not in danger (subject to the *skin* limitations contained in Chapter 37, paragraphs 6 and 7).

34. The following may wear leather shoes on Yom Kippur: *persons*
a. a woman who has given birth during the previous *who may* thirty days; *wear shoes*
b. a person who is ill, even if his life is not endangered;
c. someone who is suffering from an injury to his foot and finds it hard to walk without leather shoes.

35. All of the rules relating to medical treatment which are *medical* followed on Shabbath are also followed on Yom Kippur *treatment* (and see paragraphs 8 and 9 above).

36. *a.* A person who, due to illness, has to eat on Yom Kippur *calling to* may be called up to the reading of the Torah in the *the Torah* morning. *persons*
who do not
b. This is so whether he is eating in *shi'urim*, as *fast*

[627]

explained in paragraph 18 above, or in the way in which he normally eats on any other day of the year.

c. If Yom Kippur occurs on Shabbath, he may also be called up to the reading of the Torah in the afternoon.

Chapter 40

A Medical Miscellany, Including Laws Relating to Doctors, Hospitals, Prayers, Traveling and Pesach

DIAGNOSIS, MEASURING TEMPERATURE, RECORDING INFORMATION,
TREATING BEDSORES, DISINFECTING CLOTHES AND CARRYING PILLS

1. *a.* The fundamental principle in relation to the saving of *immediate* life on Shabbath and Yom Tov is that, in the event of *action to* the slightest fear of immediate danger, *avoid*
    1) one must not stop to ask questions, but *danger to*
    2) one should forthwith do whatever is required to *life* save the patient.
  b. Our Sages put it bluntly: "Whoever asks at such a time is spilling blood." (See Chapter 32, paragraph 1.)
  c. 1) Even when it appears that there is no immediate danger to life, one should seek the advice of a doctor, since it is possible for a very small wound to be a source of danger.
    2) One should also consult a rabbi who is well versed in the Halacha on this subject in order to find out what one may or may not do, depending on the circumstances of the particular case.

2. *a.* It is permitted *measuring*
    1) to measure body temperature on Shabbath, *temperature,*
    2) to measure a patient's blood pressure and *blood*
    3) to take his pulse. *pressure*
  b. 1) When taking the temperature, one should not *and pulse* smear ointment on the thermometer.
    2) If necessary, one may dip the thermometer in oil.
    3) When no oil is available, one may, if essential, dip the thermometer into ointment, without smearing.
  c. 1) While one may clean the thermometer with alcohol

and may rub it and dry it with absorbent cotton (cotton wool),

2) one should not dip cotton into alcohol for this purpose, since one will inevitably squeeze some of it out.

(Compare Chapter 35, paragraph 11.)

d. One may shake down the mercury in a thermometer after use, if one intends to use it again that day.

e. Temperature may be measured not only in the case of suspected illness, but also to ascertain the days on which a woman is capable of becoming pregnant.

f. 1) Whether or not one may use a forehead thermometer (consisting of a strip of celluloid which changes color, according to the temperature, when held in contact with the forehead) depends on its type.

2) It may be used

a) if the temperature is read from a change of color alone, and no form of letter, digit or other symbol appears, or

b) if the temperature is read by means of letters, digits or other symbols which are visible before use, but change color or become more pronounced when the thermometer is placed in contact with the forehead.

3) If the letters, digits or other symbols by which the temperature is read are not visible before use, the thermometer may not be used.

recording temperature and weight with prepared symbols

3. *a.* One is allowed to record the temperature of a patient or the weight of a baby by slipping numbers (written down before Shabbath) into a frame on the patient's card, or by attaching them with a paper clip.

b. It is proper, before Shabbath, to prepare the different kinds of cards and auxiliary symbols one is likely to need, so as to minimize the problem of recording medical information on Shabbath.

c. See also paragraph 26 below.

4. *a.* If one needs to record the details of treatment in order to prevent confusion with those of another patient, and there is a non-Jew present, one should ask him to write them down.

recording information with the aid of a non-Jew

b. One may do this even in the case of a patient who is not dangerously ill.

c. One may ask the non-Jew to make a note also of matters which the patient will not need until the next day, such as tests requested by the doctor, if there is a fear that they will be forgotten.

5. *a.* 1) When a patient is bedridden over an extended period, it often becomes necessary to rub a suitable preparation into parts of his body daily to prevent bedsores.

treatment of bedsores

2) In that event, he should try to have a lotion, and not ointment, applied
   a) by hand or
   b) with some synthetic, non-absorbent material.
3) This is permitted even if the patient's life is not in danger.
4) He should try to avoid the use of ointment on Shabbath, since smearing it on is forbidden.

b. 1) It may be that a lotion cannot be used, because, for example,
   a) there is none or
   b) the ointment, and not the lotion, is medically effective.
2) In such a case, he should ask for the ointment to be applied once before Shabbath begins and again after it ends, thereby avoiding its use on Shabbath.

c. If the ointment has to be applied several times a day,
   1) it should be spread on a sufficient number of sterile gauze dressings before Shabbath,
   2) the ointment-coated gauze should be covered with other gauze, until use, to prevent contamination, and
   3) the dressings should be applied directly to the

affected parts on Shabbath, there being no further need then to spread the ointment.

d. When dressings have not been prepared, the ointment may be put on the gauze on Shabbath, without spreading.

e. Should the situation be such that
1) none of the above courses of action are possible **and**
2) there is a risk of danger to the patient from the bedsores,

the parts liable to be affected may be rubbed with ointment even on Shabbath.

f. 1) When Yom Tov occurs immediately before or after Shabbath, it is preferable, where the choice exists, to have the ointment rubbed into the skin on Yom Tov rather than on Shabbath.

2) This is because the performance of a forbidden activity is of a lesser gravity on Yom Tov than on Shabbath.

g. For the situation where the services of a non-Jew are available, see Chapter 38, paragraph 4, and compare paragraph 19 there.

disinfecting laundry 6. a. Although it is prohibited to soak laundry in water on Shabbath, one may soak the laundry of a patient suffering from a contagious or infectious disease in disinfectant, in order to prevent the illness from spreading. (See Chapter 15, paragraph 4.)

b. One must not, however, do anything else towards washing the laundry.

carrying pills and directions for treatment 7. a. 1) a) Sometimes a doctor will order a patient not to leave the house unless he takes with him a particular medicine for use in case of an emergency.

b) Likewise, a diabetic patient may always have to carry sugar with him.

2) If the patient needs to go out on Shabbath in a place where there is no *eiruv*, in order to perform a

mitzva, for example to go the synagogue or to study Torah, he may be lenient about taking the medicine or sugar with him, provided that

   a) he does not go through an actual r^eshuth ha-rabbim, as defined in Chapter 17, paragraph 3,

   b) he carries the medicine or sugar in an unusual way, as where he inserts it in his hat, and

   c) he does not carry with him more than he needs.

b. Similarly, a patient suffering from a dangerous condition may go out to perform a mitzva, wearing medical instructions on a chain around his neck, so that, in case of an emergency, one will know right away what treatment to give him.

c. 1) The patient in the above cases should try not to stand still while he is in the street.

   2) If the need to take the medicine or eat the sugar arises when the patient is in the street, he should, where possible, hurry into a nearby house, which is r^eshuth ha-yachid, and swallow the medicine or sugar there, before going back out into the street.

THE DOCTOR*

8. *a.* Subject to what follows, a person who is ill but whose life is not in danger should, if it is Shabbath, preferably go to a doctor who observes the Torah and its mitzvoth, and thus avoid unjustified violation of the Shabbath. *doctors who do not observe Shabbath*

b. 1) If

   a) it is not possible to go to an observant doctor or

   b) there is a non-observant doctor with greater professional expertise,

   he should go to the non-observant doctor.

---

*Using the services of a non-Jewish doctor is discussed in Chapter 32, paragraphs 1, 6, 21, 45 and 51, Chapter 33, paragraph 2, and Chapter 38, paragraphs 1, 3 to 6, 12, 14 to 17 and 19 to 23.

2) This is so even if he knows that the non-observant doctor will, for instance,
   a) turn on a light,
   b) note down the name and details of the illness and so forth on his medical-record card and
   c) write him out a prescription on Shabbath.
3) Likewise, one may summon a Jewish doctor for a patient on Shabbath, even if the patient is not dangerously ill and even if one knows that the doctor will come in his car.
4) In any event, if one can prevail upon the doctor not to violate Shabbath or Yom Tov, one is, of course, definitely obliged to do so.

c. However, one must not call or go to a non-observant doctor for purely financial reasons, as would be the case if, for example,
1) there is indeed a doctor in the neighborhood who observes the Shabbath, but one would have to pay him for visiting the patient, whereas
2) a doctor of equal competence who violates the Shabbath and lives far away would answer the call without payment (because, for example, he works for a health plan to which the patient belongs).

d. 1) If a Jewish doctor writes out a prescription on Shabbath for a patient who is not dangerously ill (as in the situation described above), the medicines should not be collected from the pharmacy until after Shabbath.
2) This is because one is not allowed to benefit on Shabbath from a forbidden activity performed by a Jew on Shabbath (the writing out of the prescription).

the doctor's telephone

9. a. When the telephone rings in a doctor's house, it is permissible to lift the receiver off the hook (in the manner described below), as long as there is any chance that a dangerously ill patient is calling
1) for advice or

2) to request an urgent visit.

b. 1) If possible, the receiver should be lifted in an unusual manner.

2) For instance,

    a) one should remove it with one's elbow or wrist or

    b) lift it up together with another person.

c. Chapter 32, in paragraphs 40 to 42, contains further details with regard to lifting and replacing the receiver and speaking on the telephone.

10. a. In a place where there is no *eiruv* (and carrying articles about is forbidden), a doctor visiting a patient's house should not take medical instruments with him, unless he has been called out to see a patient whose life is, or could possibly be, in danger. *[carrying medical instruments]*

b. When it is reasonable to expect that the doctor may need the instruments later for another dangerously ill patient, he may take them back with him afterwards.

c. If he can, the doctor should carry the instruments in an unusual way, in accordance with the principle set out in Chapter 32, paragraph 28.

11. a. When washing his hands before or after attending to a patient, the doctor should use liquid soap. *[washing hands with soap]*

b. If there is none available, he should use a bar of soap, but, where possible, only under the running tap.

12. a. 1) A doctor, a nurse or any other person who is called on to render assistance to a patient on Shabbath may be paid after Shabbath. (See Chapter 28, paragraph 67.) *[paying for medical attention]*

2) This is an exception to the rule against receiving remuneration for services rendered on Shabbath. (Compare Chapter 28, paragraph 51.)

b. 1) In the event that immediate payment is demanded, it is desirable instead to give the doctor (or other person) as security some item bearing one's name and address, to prevent him from unnecessarily writing on Shabbath (if he is Jewish).

2) a) However, should one have no such item, one may give him something else as security.

b) This is so despite the fact that the doctor will note down one's name, although one must, of course, try to dissuade him from violating the Shabbath.

c. 1) When

a) one has nothing one can give as security or

b) the doctor does not agree to accept a security, one may pay him, but

2) it is prohibited

a) to accept change from the doctor on Shabbath and, all the more so,

b) to ask for a receipt

since neither of these actions will help to alleviate the patient's condition, and

3) one must not write a check, unless

a) the patient is, or may be, dangerously ill **and**

b) one has no alternative but to pay by check.

(In connection with writing, see Chapter 32, paragraph 48*b*.)

d. Compare the situation set out in Chapter 32, paragraph 55.

doctor on call at home

13. a. A doctor who is on call at home need not stay in the house throughout the hours of Shabbath.

b. In the event of an emergency involving danger to life, one is allowed to contact him wherever he happens to be, even if he will have to come home by car.

c. This case must be distinguished from that in paragraph 22 below, since here there is as yet no dangerously ill patient requiring attention.

non-Jewish patients

14. a. When a Jew is required to violate Shabbath for a non-Jewish patient whose life is in danger, he may do so if the activity he is required to perform is the subject only of a Rabbinical prohibition.

b. If Torah prohibitions are involved, he would be well advised to seek detailed instructions from an expert authority on the laws of Shabbath.

THE HOSPITAL

15. a. It is permissible for a patient to stay in a hospital where Shabbath is violated (for example, by Jewish nurses writing down the patient's temperature). *staying in a hospital where Shabbath is violated*

b. This is so even if the patient is not dangerously ill.

c. Of course the patient must try to minimize the extent to which Shabbath is violated for him.

d. He should bear in mind that this is more likely to be achieved by a soft-spoken request than by a peremptory demand.

16. a. 1) If a patient who is not dangerously ill is staying in such a hospital, he should take care on Shabbath not to eat food which Jews cooked on Shabbath. *food cooked on Shabbath*

2) This is the case

a) even if his food is cooked together with food for a dangerously ill patient and

b) even if the actual food he is given was cooked by Jews for a dangerously ill patient who, for some reason, did not eat it.

3) See further Chapter 32, paragraph 78.

b. The position with regard to a light turned on in the ward by a Jew is as follows: *light switched on on Shabbath*

1) The patient who is not dangerously ill may benefit from the light if

a) the ward also contains a person who is dangerously ill **and**

b) it was permitted to turn on the light for that person's urgent needs, as specified in Chapter 32, paragraph 63.

2) Otherwise,
   a) while he is not obliged to leave the room to avoid benefiting from the light,
   b) he should not do, by the light switched on in violation of the Shabbath, anything which he would not have done without it.

bringing in food

17. *a.* One may bring kosher food to a dangerously ill patient on Shabbath, even through *r^{e}shuth ha-rabbim*, if
   1) he is in a hospital where the food is not kosher **and**
   2) he does not have any kind of kosher food available sufficient to meet his needs.
b. Were this forbidden, the knowledge that he has to eat non-kosher food could result in a disturbance of the patient's mental equilibrium and so bring about a deterioration in his condition.
c. When bringing the food, one should try to carry it in a different way from that which one would use on another day of the week, as explained in Chapter 32, paragraph 28.
d. One should not bring food through *r^{e}shuth ha-rabbim*
   1) for a patient whose condition is such that he does not know what kind of food he is eating or
   2) if the patient is a child too young to appreciate that there is anything wrong with the hospital food.
e. In any event, one must do whatever is possible before Shabbath to have the necessary food available and should not rely on the fact that one will be permitted to violate Shabbath if one will not have made the necessary preparations beforehand.

separating t^{e}rumoth, ma'asroth and challa

18. *a.* A person who is ill in a hospital in Israel on Shabbath may be in the awkward position that
   1) he knows *t^{e}rumoth* and *ma'asroth* have not been separated or may not have been separated from the food he is given and
   2) he does not have sufficient food available from

which *t^erumoth* and *ma'asroth* have been separated.

b. It is better for a person faced with such a difficulty to separate *t^erumoth* and *ma'asroth* from the food he receives on Shabbath, rather than to eat it without making the required separation.

c. This applies to any patient ill in a hospital, whether or not his life is in danger.

d. Similar considerations govern the separation of *challa.**

e. *T^erumoth*, *ma'asroth* and *challa* separated on Shabbath are *muktzeh* and may not be moved. (See Chapter 11, paragraph 19c.)

19. a. 1) A patient who is confined to his bed may use a bell which is not electrically operated to ring for assistance.

ringing a bell for assistance

2) This is the case
   a) even if the patient's life is not in danger and
   b) whether the patient is hospitalized or confined to his bed at home.

b. 1) Except in the circumstances mentioned in c and d below, he may not use an electric bell (like those installed at bedsides in hospitals), unless
   a) he is sure that ringing the bell will not make a light come on **and**
   b) he needs immediate attention to his medical needs.

2) Even then, he should, if he can, ring the bell in an unusual manner, for instance by pressing the button with his elbow. (See Chapter 33, paragraph 2c.)

c. 1) However, an electric bell may be used, even where a light will come on when it rings, if

---

*For the separation of *challa* outside what the Halacha regards as the Land of Israel, see Chapter 31, paragraph 41.

a) the patient is dangerously ill **and**

b) ringing the bell may help to save or prolong his life.

2) The bell should be rung in an unusual manner, unless this could be detrimental to the patient's condition or its treatment. (See Chapter 32, paragraph 28.)

d. 1) If a patient confined to bed needs to relieve himself,

a) he should try to find somebody who can call for assistance or

b) he should ask a non-Jew in the room to ring the electric bell for him.

2) When

a) neither of these possibilities is open to him,

b) his need is very urgent **and**

c) no light will come on,

he may ring the electric bell himself, even if he is not dangerously ill, but, if he can, he should do so in a manner which differs from that usually adopted.

3) Where a light will come on, he may, nonetheless, ring the bell (since there is no other course open to him and the need is very urgent), but **only** in an unusual manner — unless he is dangerously ill, in which case the variation of manner is desirable but not essential.

4) This was permitted by the Rabbis due to the importance attached by them to the preservation of human dignity.

bedsores **20.** Regarding treatment for the prevention of bedsores see paragraph 5 above.

signing before urgent surgery **21.** *a.* One may sign a consent to the performance of an urgent operation, but only if

1) the patient's life is, or may be, in danger,

2) the hospital management makes the performance of the operation conditional on the prior consent of the patient or his relatives **and**

3) the hospital management will not be satisfied with an oral consent given before witnesses.

b. 1) Similarly, one may sign when required to do so by a doctor before he will give urgent treatment to a dangerously ill patient, if indeed he cannot be persuaded

a) to forgo his demand or

b) to accept some kind of pledge or security until one comes in the evening to sign.

2) In these circumstances one may sign even though the doctor needs the signature for his own purposes and not for reasons connected with the patient's welfare.

3) When trying to convince the doctor to drop his demand for an immediate signature, one should remember that gentle though firm persuasion is likely to prove more effective than strident protest.

c. 1) In any event, if one must sign, one should try to do so in an unusual way, for example with one's left hand.

2) In addition, one should try to sign as briefly as one can, in order to write as little as possible, for instance by signing just one's initials, or, better still, with a mere, meaningless mark.

d. It is of course forbidden to sign on Shabbath purely to save money, as where one wishes to be exempt from paying for an operation or for treatment.

22. a. A doctor who is on duty or on call in a hospital where there is a dangerously ill patient should not leave the hospital to go home, knowing that, due to the distance, he will have to drive on Shabbath in order to come back on duty. *doctor on duty leaving the hospital*

b. 1) He may, however, go home if he will be driven back in time for his spell of duty by a non-Jew and,

2) furthermore, he may be driven back home by the non-Jew (whether before or after his duty).

(For details see the comparable situation in paragraph 69 below.)

avoiding Shabbath duty

23. *a.* 1) A Shabbath-observant doctor who is on duty in a hospital may well be apprehensive about performing acts which would normally be forbidden on Shabbath, but

2) he should not exchange his duty with a Jewish doctor who does not observe Shabbath.

3) On the contrary, he should conscientiously carry out his duty, in accordance with the Halacha, and will receive his just reward from the Almighty. (See Chapter 32, paragraph 6.)

b. 1) A doctor who is on duty in a hospital where all the patients are non-Jews must exchange his duty and entrust his patients over Shabbath to the care of a non-Jewish doctor, who will be able to do freely whatever their welfare requires.

2) He should not work on Shabbath, even if

a) he has to pay the non-Jew who takes his place or

b) he will have to be on duty for twice as long during the week.

keeping to routine on Shabbath to avoid dangerous delays after Shabbath

24. *a.* Even inessential treatment may be given to patients in a hospital on Shabbath if

1) the work of the nurses is organized in shifts,

2) treatment not administered by the day shift (on Shabbath) will have to be administered by the night shift (after Shabbath),

3) there will be a consequent delay in the treatments programmed for the night shift **and**, as a result,

4) dangerously ill patients will not receive proper attention.

b. Nevertheless, hospital managements would do well to consult a halachic authority for his advice on how to avoid this situation, in which the holy Shabbath is turned into just another day of the week.

25. *a.* One may donate blood on Shabbath for a patient who *donating* is in urgent need of a transfusion, if it is not available *blood* from a blood bank.

    b. In these circumstances, one may donate blood even if this will necessitate one's having to sign one's name or have one's name noted down. (See paragraph 21 above.)

    c. When necessary, one is allowed to use a vehicle to bring donors or the equipment required.

26. *a.* 1) It is the responsibility of the hospital management *prepara-* to make suitable arrangements for preserving the *tions for* sanctity of the Shabbath. *Shabbath*

       2) It should see to it that, as far as possible, whatever *to be made* the patient will need on Shabbath is made ready *by manage-* before Shabbath begins. *ment*

       3) The management should not rely on the fact that it will be permissible to violate Shabbath for dangerously ill patients if adequate preparations are not made before Shabbath.

       4) See also Chapter 32, paragraph 34.

    b. Thus, the management should have prepared, prior to Shabbath, a sufficient quantity of

       1) boiled water for drinking,

       2) hot water for washing patients,

       3) sterile syringes and needles,

       4) cotton (cotton wool) tufts and swabs, and

       5) plasters and dressings cut to various sizes.

    c. Lights should be left on in corridors and rooms near patients who may need attention during the night.

    d. There should be a supply of suitably adapted record cards and auxiliary symbols for the temporary notation of temperatures, doctor's instructions and so forth, without having to write on Shabbath.

    e. 1) At a hospital which is open for the admission of patients on Shabbath, several numbered files should be prepared in advance before Shabbath.

       2) Each file should contain forms with directions for

the various tests and examinations which may
have to be carried out on Shabbath.

3) Each form should be marked with the number of
the file in which it is contained.

4) In this way, on admission, the patient's name and
other essential information will only have to be
written on the file and not repeated on each form
which may be required.

drawing off **27.** When taking blood for a number of different tests from
blood a dangerously ill patient, one should attempt to draw all of
the blood at once, and not take blood both from a vein and
from a finger.

regular **28.** *a.* Certain dangerously ill patients need to have a blood
blood count taken or their sugar checked several times a
counts week, but not every day.

b. In such cases, one should avoid Shabbath, unless
there is a special reason for performing the tests on
predetermined dates (for comparison of results) and
one or some of those dates fall on Shabbath.

examining **29.** *a.* One may use an autoanalyzer on Shabbath to carry
blood with out blood tests required for a dangerously ill patient.
auto- *b.* This is so even if the autoanalyzer at the same time
analyzer subjects the blood sample to other tests which are not
immediately required.

urine tests **30.** For the examination of a patient's urine (even when he is
not in danger) see Chapter 33, paragraph 20.

use of **31.** *a.* The use of an electrocardiogram to examine the
electro- functioning of the heart is permitted only for a patient
cardiogram whose life is, or may possibly be, in danger.

b. 1) It is desirable, where possible, to use a liquid rather
than an ointment to make a good contact for the
conduction of electricity.

2) The liquid should not be applied with cotton, due to

the prohibition involved in squeezing the liquid out. (Compare Chapter 32, paragraph 59.)

32. a. The use of an X-ray machine is also permitted only for a patient whose life is, or may possibly be, in danger.

  b. The screen should be switched on before Shabbath and left on.

  c. If, however, one forgot to turn it on before Shabbath, one may turn it on on Shabbath (for a patient whose life is, or may be, in danger), but, where possible, in a manner which differs from that usually adopted during the week.

use of X-ray machine

33. a. To operate some instruments, one has to turn on a number of different controls.

  b. In the event that one needs to use such an instrument on Shabbath for a dangerously ill patient, one should
    1) first adjust the various controls and,
    2) only then, connect the instrument to the current.

adjusting controls before turning on instrument

34. a. In order to identify material sent for laboratory examination, the test request form should be attached to the tube or jar containing the specimen with a rubber band.

  b. This will avoid the need for sticking on a label.

attaching details to specimens for examination

35. a. Test results are often returned by hospital laboratories in batches containing the results of a number of different patients.

  b. One may not sort them according to the patients to whom they relate. (Compare Chapter 3, paragraphs 62, 69, 76 and 84.)

  c. One should
    1) examine each result separately, inserting it into the patient's file* as soon as one has finished reading it, or

checking results of laboratory tests

---

*It is of course forbidden to punch holes.

2) insert all the results into their appropriate files and, immediately afterwards, read them, or

3) check the results and leave them unsorted until the termination of Shabbath.

experimental treatment

36. A doctor may administer treatment of an experimental nature to a dangerously ill patient, even if

a. the efficacy of the treatment for the patient in question is a matter of doubt **and**

b. the treatment involves the violation of Shabbath by the infringement of Torah (and not just Rabbinical) prohibitions.

miscellaneous types of treatment

37. a. In connection with medicines and injections required by dangerously ill patients, see Chapter 32, paragraphs 52 to 62.

b. With regard to patients who are ill but not dangerously so, see Chapter 33, paragraphs 4 to 22.

postponing treatment: general rule

38. a. Operations on a dangerously ill patient should be postponed until after Shabbath if there is no risk of an aggravation in his condition which could further endanger his life.

b. The same applies to all other treatment involving the infringement of Torah prohibitions.

c. Similarly, one should not, on Shabbath, perform laboratory tests or radiography needed for surgery to be carried out on the following day, unless the operation is urgent and might otherwise be delayed.

postponing radiation treatment

39. If a patient receives radiation treatment once every day, but it makes no difference at what time of the day it is administered, it should, where possible, be postponed until after the termination of Shabbath. (See, however, paragraph 24 above.)

postponing second stage of treatment

40. a. 1) Sometimes a dangerously ill patient needs to be treated twice during the day, in a way which involves the infringement of a Torah prohibition.

   2) For example, a patient may need to receive radiation twice a day.

   3) In such a case, the second treatment should be left (if possible) until after Shabbath.

  b. 1) The same applies in the case of a single treatment

     a) which comprises several activities,

     b) which can consequently be performed in two stages and

     c) the second stage of which could be carried out after Shabbath.

   2) In these circumstances, there is no justification for the inessential infringement of a Torah prohibition, and the second stage must be left until after the termination of Shabbath.

   3) For an example, see Chapter 35, paragraph 4.

41. *a.* A dangerously ill patient may be transferred from one floor to another by means of an elevator, if he cannot easily be taken up or down the stairs. *use of elevator*

  b. Furthermore, a friend or relative is allowed to accompany him in the elevator. (Compare paragraph 70 below.)

42. *a.* One may open a folding partition on Shabbath and erect it around the bed of a patient *opening partitions*

   1) so as to enable him to rest undisturbed or

   2) so that he can be privately examined and treated in a ward containing other patients.

  (See Chapter 24, paragraph 27.)

  b. One may not open a partition on Shabbath with the intention of screening the patient off from uncovered excrement, so that he can pray (without infringing the principle set out in paragraph 89 below), unless

   1) the partition has been opened or unrolled to the extent of at least a *tefach* since before Shabbath, in which case one may open it further on Shabbath, **or**

2) the partition is attached to the wall, in which case it may be opened on Shabbath even though it has been completely closed since before Shabbath. (See Chapter 24, paragraphs 32, 34 and 35.)

c. Once a partition has been erected to give the patient privacy, there is nothing wrong with his taking advantage of its presence to pray. (See Chapter 24, paragraph 37.)

going home upon discharge

43. a. A patient who is discharged from a hospital on Shabbath or is released after treatment in the emergency room, and cannot walk home, is not permitted to go home in a car driven by a Jew.

b. He may go home in a car driven by a non-Jew, provided that

1) his condition places him (at least) within the category of persons who are ill, even if not dangerously so (as defined in Chapter 33, paragraph 1),

2) it is impossible for him to stay in the hospital until the end of Shabbath and have all his wants supplied there, **and,**

3) his home is within the distance he is allowed to walk on Shabbath.

c. It is highly desirable that hospital managements should

1) set aside a room where patients can wait until the termination of Shabbath and

2) refrain from discharging patients on Shabbath.

writing certificate of discharge

44. a. When a patient is discharged from a hospital on Shabbath, it is forbidden to write out, or to request a Jew to write out, a certificate of discharge on Shabbath.

b. One may request a non-Jew to write out the certificate, if

1) the patient is still ill, even though not dangerously so (as in Chapter 33, paragraph 1),

2) the patient needs further treatment, as specified in

the certificate, **and**

3) it will not be possible to obtain the certificate after Shabbath, or waiting will cause a delay in the treatment.

EATING BEFORE PRAYERS AND MAKING KIDDUSH WHEN ILL,
VISITING THE SICK AND PRAYING FOR THE SICK
ON SHABBATH AND YOM TOV

45. a. A person who is ill and must eat on Shabbath before his morning prayers should recite *kiddush* before he eats.

b. He should preferably first say at least the *birchoth ha-Torah* and the first paragraph of the *Sh^ema*.

c. On weekdays, too, a person who has to eat before morning prayers ought first to say at least *birchoth ha-Torah* and the first paragraph of the *Sh^ema*.

d. Someone who is not feeling well may take medicine or pills (with water if necessary) before saying his morning prayers, even if he is only suffering from a slight indisposition or a minor ailment.

e. 1) It is better for somebody who is weak
    a) to say his morning prayers by himself and eat later **rather than**
    b) to eat before his prayers, so that he can say them with a congregation, but
2) he should go to the synagogue afterwards in order to participate in *kaddish*, *Bar^echu* and *k^edusha* and to hear the reading of the Torah.

eating before morning prayers

46. a. A person who is ill and cannot drink wine, or is forbidden to do so, should preferably not recite *kiddush* for a number of individuals with the intention that another of the company should drink the wine in his stead.

b. Rather, one of the following courses should be adopted:
1) another of the company (even the patient's wife)

making kiddush with others

should make *kiddush* for them all, or

2) the patient himself should recite *kiddush*, taste at least a drop of the wine and then pass the cup to another of the company to drink the prescribed quantity, or

3) the patient should make *kiddush* over bread and the company should make *kiddush* separately over wine.

c. A different, though less preferable, solution is for the patient to make *kiddush* over bread for the whole company.

making kiddush by oneself

47. a. Sometimes, a patient cannot eat enough bread or drink enough wine to make *kiddush* (and has no one to make *kiddush* for him).

b. Such a person should have the intention of fulfilling his obligation to make *kiddush* by the very recital of the Friday night *Sh^emoneh Esrei* prayer.

c. He may then eat his meal without making the usual *kiddush*.

d. If he is able to eat enough bread or drink enough wine on Shabbath morning, he should recite the usual Friday night *kiddush* then, omitting, however, the verses which precede the blessing on the wine.

visiting the sick

48. a. It is permitted to visit the sick on Shabbath and Yom Tov.

b. Although one should not simply wish the person who is ill a complete recovery, one should encourage him by telling him, "One may not cry out on Shabbath (Yom Tov), but a cure is near at hand."

c. 1) On Rosh Hashana and Yom Kippur, one may wish an ill person a complete recovery and pray for him in the same way as on any other day, despite the contents of the next paragraph.

2) This is so even if they occur on Shabbath.

3) The reason is that these days are in their very essence days of repentance and prayer.

49. *a.* With the exceptions mentioned below (and in the *praying for* preceding paragraph), one should not pray for the *the sick* recovery of a sick person on Shabbath, since the sadness engendered detracts from the spirit of the day.

b. An individual, or even a congregation, may pray and recite Psalms on Shabbath or Yom Tov for an ill person whose life is in immediate danger.

c. The same applies in the case of a person who is dangerously ill even when the danger is not immediate, but only if he asks that one should pray for him.

d. A person who is ill, even though not dangerously so, may pray for a recovery and recite Psalms privately on Shabbath and Yom Tov.

USE OF MOTOR VEHICLES IN CONNECTION WITH
DANGEROUSLY ILL PATIENTS

50. *a.* As is apparent from Chapter 32, paragraphs 36, 52 and *general rule* 53, one is allowed to drive a car on Shabbath when this may be instrumental in saving the life of a patient.

b. Thus, one may, for example,
1) drive the doctor to the house of a dangerously ill patient, or
2) drive a dangerously ill patient to the doctor's house or to the hospital, or
3) go by car to bring essential medicines.

c. One should, of course, refrain, during the course of the journey, from any act
1) which involves a violation of the Shabbath,
2) which is not essential to save the patient's life **and**
3) whose omission will not be detrimental to one's efforts to save the patient.

(See also paragraph 62 below.)

51. *a.* 1) One must take the shortest route.
2) One must not diverge from it, except where a *taking the shortest route*

diversion could be of assistance in saving the patient's life.

b. Where the shortest route leads the wrong way up a one-way street, it is better to take a longer route, if there is a risk that

1) going the wrong way up the one-way street may cause an accident **or**

2) a delay may be caused by a car coming in the opposite direction.

c. 1) One may drive the patient to a hospital which he knows, or which he thinks is more desirable from the point of view of medical expediency, even if there is a nearer hospital within walking distance.

2) Needless to say, one may not do this out of purely financial considerations.

(Compare Chapter 32, paragraph 38.)

stopping unneces- sarily on the way

52. a. One may not stop on the way, except for the purposes of the dangerously ill patient, if stopping will cause the brake lights to come on.

b. Therefore, if one sees from a distance that the traffic lights are at red, one should try, if possible, to travel slowly, so as to avoid having to brake at the traffic lights. (See further paragraphs 58 and 61.)

c. Naturally, one may stop at the traffic lights if one has to do so in order to prevent an accident. (Compare paragraph 51b above.)

signaling

53. a. As far as signaling during the course of the journey is concerned, in the daytime, one should use hand signals, rather than the indicator lights, whenever one can.

b. If one must turn on the indicator lights, one should reduce their use to a minimum.

interior light operated by car door

54. a. 1) Sometimes, one knows in advance that one may be called upon to drive one's car on Shabbath for the purposes of a dangerously ill patient.

2) In those circumstances, one would do well to take steps, before Shabbath commences, to ensure that no unnecessary lights will be turned on when the car is being used.

b. Of course, even where these precautions have not been taken

1) one may, nevertheless, use the car on Shabbath when the emergency arises and

2) one may, for instance, open the car door, despite the fact that this will cause the interior light to come on.

c. 1) However, having opened the door and entered the car, one should not just close it and drive off, as the closing of the door would turn the interior light off again.

2) While the door is still open, one should adjust the light switch (in a different manner from that which one would normally adopt), so that the light remains on even after the door has been closed.

d. 1) It may happen that one does not adjust the switch, either

    a) because one forgets to do so, or

    b) because it is nighttime and having the interior light on would interfere with the driver's vision.

2) In that case, the closing of the door will have turned off the light.

3) One should consequently take steps, while sitting in the car, to prevent the light from coming on again when the door is re-opened at the end of the journey.

4) One can do this either

    a) by turning off the switch or loosening the bulb in its fitting (in a manner one would not normally adopt), or

    b) if neither of these methods is possible, by taking the bulb out of the fitting altogether (also in a manner one would not normally adopt).

e. 1) It may happen that one does not take any of these steps while sitting in the car, either
   a) because one forgets to do so or
   b) because the switch cannot be adjusted to keep the light from coming on when the door opens, and one is also unable either to loosen or to remove the bulb, or
   c) because one will need the light for the patient when he leaves the car.

2) In that case, the opening of the door at the end of the journey will turn on the light.

3) Therefore, one should not just close the door after leaving the car, as
   a) closing the door would again turn off the interior light and
   b) this is in no way necessary in connection with saving the life of the patient.

4) What one should do is to adjust the switch (in a different manner from that which one would normally adopt), while the door is still open, so that the light remains on even after the door has been closed (as in *c*2 above).

turning on and adjusting exterior lights

55. *a.* When driving at night, one may adjust the lights as necessary to avoid danger.

b. Where possible, when one first turns on the lights, one should do so in such a way that one will not have to adjust them when faced with another vehicle coming in the opposite direction.

c. It is advisable not to turn on the headlights at all, insofar as this is compatible with safety.

d. Any inessential operation which would activate an additional light on the control panel should be avoided.

turning off exterior lights

56. *a.* Except in the circumstances mentioned below, one may not turn off the lights at the end of the journey, because this is in no way necessary for the patient's needs.

b. 1) One should on no account turn off the lights in order to avoid a fine.

2) If the law of the land forbids one to leave them on, one should cover them with blankets (in a place where there is an *eiruv* and taking the blankets out of the car is permitted).

c. 1) An exception occurs in the case of a vehicle designated for use in emergencies (such as an ambulance).

2) The headlights of such a vehicle may be turned off after use if leaving them on would drain the battery and make it difficult to start the engine a second time.

57. *a.* A driver who has brought a dangerously ill patient to *parking* the hospital should leave his car parked at the spot where it has come to a halt at the end of the journey, unless it could be a potential source of danger in that position.

b. He must not drive the car further than is essential for the welfare of the patient, merely in order to avoid the risk of being fined for parking in a forbidden area. (Compare paragraph 51 above.)

c. On the other hand, he should not leave the car right in front of the hospital entrance, where it could obstruct the access of other drivers bringing emergency cases for treatment.

d. What he should do is to stop before actually reaching the hospital entrance, or beyond it.

e. If he cannot do so, he should

1) stop in front of the entrance to allow the patient to get out, and then

2) push the car to a suitable parking place, without using the engine.

f. If this too is impossible, he should, after dropping the patient off, drive a sufficient distance beyond the entrance to avoid interfering with the traffic to the hospital.

stopping at **58.** *a.* 1) Pressing the brake pedal turns on the brake lights.
destination 2) Consequently, one should try to stop without using
without use the brake pedal.*
of brake
pedal *b.* 1) To accomplish this, when approaching one's
destination one should cease all pressure on the
accelerator pedal.

2) In this way, when the destination is reached, one
will be traveling slowly enough to bring the car to a
halt with the hand brake.

c. 1) Another course, and one which may be expedient if
one is not going slowly enough to stop with just the
hand brake, is

a) to turn off the ignition while the car is still
moving** and **then**

b) to change into a lower gear, thus making the
car travel slowly enough to stop with the hand
brake.

2) a) One should not slow the car down by changing
into a lower gear before turning off the ignition.

b) This would increase the number of combustions and the amount of fuel consumed until
the car came to a halt.

c) On the other hand, turning off the ignition
merely prevents further new combustion from
taking place.

d) Once the engine is turned off, changing gear
has no effect on fuel consumption, since none is
being consumed.

3) A practical advantage of this course is that the car
will stop with the engine already switched off.

---

*Of course, if non-operation of the brake lights is liable to cause an
accident, one should use the brake pedal, even though this will
make the brake lights come on.
**This course cannot be adopted if turning off the ignition locks the
steering, reduces braking power or could be otherwise dangerous.

d. 1) If
   a) one is driving a car with a manual gearshift
      and
   b) the patient's condition will not be aggravated
      by a jerky stop,
   a further possibility may be open to one.
2) One may be able to apply the hand brake without
   using the clutch, thus automatically stalling the
   engine.
3) In some cars,* the panel lights do not come on as
   soon as the engine stalls, and one might therefore
   be able to turn off the ignition in the brief interval
   which elapses after the extinction of the engine,
   before the panel lights come on. (See paragraph 60*e*
   below.)

59. *a.* If one is unable to adopt any of the courses mentioned
   in the previous paragraph, one may have to stop the
   car by braking in the ordinary way.
   b. This may be the case, for example,
      1) if one is transporting a patient who could be
         harmed by a sudden stop, such as
         a) someone suffering from a fracture or
         b) a woman about to give birth to a baby, or
      2) if one is unable to concentrate on one's driving and
         at the same time pay attention to all of the details
         mentioned above. (See paragraph 62 below.)
   c. If the engine is still operating after one has come to a
      halt, one may ask a non-Jew to turn it off (but it is

when engine may be turned off after stopping

---

*a. Variations in design can radically effect the prohibitions and
   practicalities involved in any given act, such as accelerating,
   braking, changing gear or switching off the engine.
*b. In many modern cars, nearly every operation entails the
   ignition or extinction of a light on the panel or elsewhere.
*c. As a result, a person who is in a position where he may have to
   drive on Shabbath should consult a duly qualified halachic
   authority for detailed advice related to the particular vehicle
   he would be driving.

better just to tell him that the engine is still on and let him draw his own conclusion as to what he ought to do).

d. If there is no non-Jew available, then, subject to the contents of paragraph 60 below, there is room for taking a lenient attitude and

1) having the engine switched off by a boy under thirteen or a girl under twelve, or,

2) in the absence of a minor, turning the engine off oneself, preferably in an unusual manner.

when engine may not be turned off after stopping

60. a. Often, switching off the engine will cause lights (for instance, panel lights or outside lights) to come on or go off.

b. Where that is so, there is no justification, in the circumstances described in the previous paragraph, for having the engine turned off by a minor or for turning it off oneself (except in the cases of danger set out below).

c. This is because the engine is not being turned off as part of the effort to save the patient's life.

d. An exception occurs, and one may have the engine turned off by a minor or even turn it off oneself (if no non-Jew is available), when leaving the car with the engine running would create a public danger, as where

1) there is a reasonable fear that the continuous running of the engine will make it overheat, causing the radiator to explode and injure passersby, or

2) there is a risk of children playing with the car.

e. 1) Even after the engine has stopped (for instance, as the result of stalling), one may not turn the ignition key to the off position if, as a result, lights will go out on the instrument panel. (See paragraph 58*d* above.)

2) In this case too, one would turn off and take out the key if there was a risk that children might see the key in the ignition and switch on the engine.

61. *a.* 1) When possible, it is preferable for a driver who has *stopping at* to stop at traffic lights to stop in neutral by means *traffic* of the hand brake.* *lights*

    2) In this way, the engine will continue running, and he will not have performed any forbidden act.

  b. Failing this, he should act as recommended in paragraph 58 above and not tread on the brake pedal. (See paragraph 52 above.)

  c. Even if the engine will stop operating and he will subsequently have to switch it on again, it is preferable to do this rather than to turn on the rear lights at the initial stage by depressing the brake pedal.

62. *a.* As has been seen above, a number of stipulations *when one* require one to take care during the actual course of *should* driving not to violate Shabbath unnecessarily. *drive*

  b. These stipulations only apply to an experienced driver *normally* who has already practiced driving in conformity with them on an ordinary weekday.

  c. One can reasonably fear that an insufficiently experienced driver will endanger human life if, while driving, he concentrates his attention on the fine details of Shabbath observance.

  d. Such a driver

    1) should be warned to devote all his thoughts solely to the saving of the patient whose life is in jeopardy, and

    2) should drive in exactly the same manner as he would on an ordinary day of the week, **but**

    3) should observe the stipulations set out

      a) in paragraph 54 above, regarding the loosening or removal of the interior bulb or the adjusting of its switch, and

---

*Even if use of the hand brake is accompanied by the ignition of a panel light, this is preferable to the ignition of two or more rear warning lights through use of the foot brake.

b) in paragraphs 56, 57, 59 and 60 above, which relate to the period after the vehicle has come to a halt.

handling car keys

63. Concerning the handling of car keys, see Chapter 20, paragraphs 77 and 83.

removing unnecessary heavy baggage

64. *a.* Before driving the doctor to the house of a dangerously ill patient, or the patient to the hospital, one should, if time is not of the essence, try to remove unnecessary heavy objects from the car.*

b. One should remove the objects even if they are *muktzeh.*

c. The reason for this is that any substantial increase in the weight of the load causes one to exert additional pressure on the accelerator, bringing about an increase in the number of combustions produced.

removing inessential items before driving beyond permitted walking distance

65. *a.* 1) It may be that the hospital to which a dangerously ill patient has to be driven is past the limit to which one is permitted to walk on Shabbath (usually two thousand *amoth* beyond the boundary of the *eiruv* or, if there is none, two thousand *amoth* beyond the last house of the town).

2) Where this is so, the driver should try not to take along any items which do not belong to him and are not essential on the journey or for the patient.

3) Such items should be removed from the car before the journey, provided that
   a) there is time and
   b) carrying is permitted in the place where the car is parked.

taking food for the driver

b. 1) Subject to what is said below, the driver may take food with him in the car, not only
   a) for the dangerously ill patient, but also

---

*Provided there is an *eiruv* or the car is parked in a garage or some other *r^eshuth ha-yachid.*

b) for himself.

2) He may do this

    a) even if he will be driving through an area where there is no *eiruv*, and carrying articles about is forbidden, and

    b) even if he will be traveling beyond the permitted walking distance.

3) a) However, when the point of departure is in a place where it is prohibited to carry, one should not take food from the house to the car for the use of the driver.

    b) What the driver may do, in case of need, is put his food with that of the patient and carry the food for both of them out together, but

    c) he may do this only if the car is not parked in a place which strictly fits the definition of r*e*shuth ha-rabbim (as set out in Chapter 17, paragraph 3).

4) If, when the driver arrives at the hospital, he parks the car in a place where it is not permitted to carry, he may not take his food out but must eat it inside the car.

66. *a.* Even if the car is parked in a place where one is not allowed to carry, a driver who is about to take a dangerously ill patient to the hospital on Shabbath may bring with him, from the house to the car, *taking along vehicle licence, etc.*

1) the vehicle license,

2) his driver's license and

3) any other documents which he ought to have with him when driving.

  b. Where carrying is not allowed, he should try to take them out in an unusual way; that is to say

1) he should not carry them in his hand or in his pocket, but

2) he should, for example,

    a) slip them between his belt and his trousers or

    b) put them under his hat.

c. 1) If he parks the car, at his destination, in a place where carrying is forbidden, he must not remove these documents from the car.

2) He must leave them there, together with the car keys* and any other items which are not required for the purposes of the patient.

driver generally forbidden to return

67. *a.* 1) Someone who has justifiably driven as far as required for the purposes of a dangerously ill patient is not allowed to drive back on Shabbath except in the circumstances specified below.

2) If he has traveled beyond the limit to which he would normally be permitted to walk, he may not even walk back.

3) In this latter case, the distance he may walk from the place where he now finds himself is the same as that permitted to the local inhabitants, namely up to two thousand *amoth* beyond the *eiruv* (if there is one) or the last house.

when driver may return

b. 1) A driver may drive back on Shabbath, after completing a journey for a dangerously ill person, only if

a) he is required to make another journey for a person whose life may be in danger, or

b) there is a reasonable likelihood that he will be required to make another such journey.

2) Thus, the driver of an ambulance in a settlement where there is an insufficient number of other ambulances to deal with potential emergencies may drive back to the settlement.

how to drive back

c. Even when he is allowed to drive back, the driver may not

1) stop on the way or make a detour from the shortest route back to his base, except for reasons connected with the saving of human life (as explained in paragraphs 51 and 52 above), nor

---

*See, however, paragraph 60*e*2 above.

2) when he reaches his base, travel further than is essential to enable him to fulfill his duties in the event of a fresh alert.

68. a. Generally, an ambulance which maintains radio contact with its base may not be driven back after a call. *ambulances in radio contact*

b. Its radio receiver should be left on the whole time, so that, in case of need, contact can be made with it wherever it happens to be.

c. If, however, the ambulance comes from a distant settlement, where there are no other ambulances or where the number of ambulances is insufficient to cope with a potential emergency, it should be driven back to its base, even if it is linked by radio.

69. a. 1) A doctor who has traveled to see a dangerously ill patient is in a position analogous to that of the driver described in paragraph 67 above. *when doctor may return*

2) He may not drive back home, unless there is a reasonable likelihood that he will be needed there to treat another dangerously ill patient.

b. 1) The doctor may go back home with a non-Jewish driver, as long as his home is within the permitted walking distance from the place where he is now (two thousand* *amoth* from the last house, or from the *eiruv*, if there is one).

2) He may do this even if he is returning solely in order to suit his own convenience.

3) What is more, he may, from the first, telephone a non-Jewish taxi driver to take him to the patient, in

---

*In case of great personal hardship, he should consult a qualified authority on the Halacha, since, in certain limited circumstances, it may be permissible for him to return even if the distance between the place where he now is and his home is over two thousand *amoth*, as long as it is not more than twenty-four thousand. (See paragraph 71 below, where the possibility of being driven back by a Jewish driver is also discussed.)

preference to driving himself,* even if he does so
only because the non-Jewish driver will be able to
bring him back home afterwards.

4) With further reference to the use of transport
operated by non-Jews, see Chapter 38, paragraph
13.

relatives or   **70.** *a.* A relative, or any other person in whom the patient
friends   has confidence, may accompany him in the vehicle to
accompany-   the hospital.
ing patient   *b.* He may do so even if there is already someone in the
vehicle who is capable of extending aid in case of need.

c. This is permitted out of fear that the patient's mental
equilibrium might be disturbed if he is not accompanied to the hospital by somebody he knows.

d. The relative or friend may go along even if the patient
himself does not request it.

e. The patient may take with him to the hospital
anything which could possibly be required on
Shabbath

1) to save his life or

2) to keep his mind at rest.

nurse   **71.** *a.* 1) Some places (for instance, kibbutzim) have a nurse
accompany-   whose duty it is to accompany patients to the
ing patient   hospital.

2) If a seriously ill patient or a woman about to give
birth has to be driven to the hospital, the nurse may
accompany him or her even on Shabbath (as in
paragraph 70 above).

b. If

1) there is no one else in the place where she was on
duty who can stand in for her and

2) there is a reasonable possibility that she will be

---

*Provided, of course, that the delay does not further endanger the
patient.

needed there to attend to another dangerously ill patient,
then she may also travel back.

c. If there is another nurse, or someone else who can take her place, she may travel back only in the circumstances mentioned below.

d. It is desirable to arrange in advance for a room to be available in the neighborhood of the hospital, so that a nurse arriving on Shabbath with a dangerously ill patient can stay there until Shabbath is over.

e. A nurse who has delivered her patient to the hospital may travel back with a non-Jewish driver in the same circumstances as those described in paragraph 69b above.

f. Under those same circumstances, she may also be able to go back with a Jewish driver, but only if
    1) the ambulance or car in which she is traveling is allowed to be driven back (as in paragraph 67 above), and
    2) the capacity of the vehicle is such that the weight of an additional passenger will not cause an increase in the number of cylinder firings during the course of the journey.*

g. 1) If she returns with a Jewish driver, he must be extremely careful not to perform any forbidden activity for her which he would not have to perform otherwise.
    2) Thus, there is no justification for him
        a) to go out of his way or
        b) to travel to his destination by a longer route in order to suit her convenience, nor even
        c) to stop specially for her at her house if he would normally have to drive straight on.

h. 1) Where she would otherwise have to endure great hardship, the nurse may return (subject to the

---

*It is understood that fulfillment of this condition is extremely unlikely in the current state of vehicle design.

various other conditions referred to above), even if the distance between the town where she is now and the place to which she wishes to return is more than two thousand *amoth*, as long as it is not more than twenty-four thousand.

2) Examples of great hardship are
   a) that she has nowhere to stay until after Shabbath or
   b) that she has nothing to eat.

i. 1) When human life would not be threatened by the delay, she would do well, on the facts of her case, to ask a qualified halachic authority how to proceed, rather than rely on her own judgment.

2) Indeed, it is highly advisable to obtain guidance from such a halachic authority before an emergency actually occurs.

choice between ambulance service and Shabbath-observant driver

72. *a.* As will be seen in paragraph 73 below, it is in general preferable, when a dangerously ill patient needs to be taken to a hospital, to use a driver who observes Shabbath rather than one who does not.

b. Nevertheless, should the need arise, one may phone for an ambulance on Shabbath and is not obliged to trouble a Shabbath-observant neighbor who drives a car,

1) if the neighbor will have to remain cut off from his family for the whole of Shabbath (due to his inability to return home) or

2) if he is in bed and has to be awakened for the purpose.

c. Moreover, despite the desirability of transporting the patient by means of a Shabbath-observant driver, a Shabbath-observant car owner is not, strictly speaking, obliged to accede to a request for his services at the cost of suffering either of these two inconveniences, provided that the patient can be taken to a hospital, without any delay, by the usual ambulance service.

d. The rules relating to payment on Shabbath of a charge

demanded by members of the ambulance service are analogous to those set out in Chapter 32, paragraph 55.

73. *a.* If the patient is taken to a hospital by a driver who does not observe Shabbath, the driver will almost certainly drive back, or drive on, usually without any justification.

choice between driver who is Shabbath-observant and one who is not

  b. 1) As a result, it is preferable to use
      a) a Shabbath-observant driver* who will not drive back on Shabbath, or,
      b) when none is available, an ambulance which is allowed to return to its base (as specified in paragraphs 67 and 68 above).
    2) However, if one cannot easily find a Shabbath-observant driver or an ambulance, one may of course use the car of someone who does not observe Shabbath, even though he will continue to drive afterwards, in violation of the Shabbath.

  c. 1) a) It is better to phone a Shabbath-observant driver and ask him to take the patient to the hospital than to look for a taxicab driven by a non-observant Jew, who will continue to drive afterwards in violation of the Shabbath.
      b) This is on the assumption that one is sure the Shabbath-observant driver will answer the phone and comply with the call, either because of his function or because it has been pre-arranged.
    2) However, if a car driven by someone who does not observe Shabbath is available and ready for use, and one does not have to look for it, one should transport the patient in that, rather than telephone to a Shabbath-observant driver.

---

*One need not bother him if he will be subject to the inconveniences mentioned in paragraph 72*b* above.

d. It goes without saying that one is not at all obliged (or indeed permitted) to weigh the considerations mentioned in this paragraph unless time is not of the essence and one is absolutely sure that there is no need to rush.

PESACH

taking
medicines
containing
chametz

74. *a.* 1) All medicines which
    a) contain *chametz*, however little, **and**
    b) taste pleasant, even slightly,
    are forbidden on Pesach, except to patients who are dangerously ill.

2) One may not even keep them in one's possession on Pesach.

3) Examples of such medicines are
    a) lozenges or syrup prepared from ingredients which include *chametz* and
    b) preparations containing glucose made from wheat.

b. 1) Medicines which
    a) contain *chametz*, **but**
    b) taste bitter (to the extent that a dog would not eat them),
    may be swallowed even by a patient who is not dangerously ill.

2) He should not, however, dissolve them in water before taking them, since the *chametz* may separate out and become edible.

3) It goes without saying that one is allowed to keep such medicines in one's possession on Pesach.

powder
sometimes
preferable
to pills

75. *a.* Someone who has to take medicine for a slight pain should not take it in tablet form if there is any fear that *chametz* may have been used in the composition of the tablet.

b. He should take it in the form of a powder, with no admixture of *chametz*.

c. He should see to it that the pharmacist
1) prepares the powder from pure ingredients, free from the admixture of any extraneous substance,
2) does not merely grind down tablets which have already been made up and
3) uses vessels, instruments, scales and weights which are absolutely *chametz*-free (according to the rules pertaining to Pesach).

76. *a. Chametz*-free pills made up with cornstarch or with kosher-for-Pesach matza meal may be taken on Pesach. *permitted pills*

b. 1) Pills coated with a substance which is *chametz* may on no account be swallowed on Pesach (by a person who is not dangerously ill). *coated pills*
2) One may not even keep them in one's possession on Pesach.
3) This is because the actual *chametz* which forms the coating is in a palatable state.

77. It is rare nowadays for medicines to be contained in cachets made from *chametz*, but, in places where this could still be a possibility, the nature of the materials used in the manufacture of the cachets should be investigated. *cachets made from chametz*

78. *a.* Capsules, suppositories, injections and ointments do not usually contain *chametz*. *capsules, supposi- tories, injections and ointments*
b. Nevertheless, it is desirable that a halachic authority should consider each case separately.

79. One may buy medicines containing *chametz* after Pesach, *buying medicines after Pesach*
a. even for a patient who is not dangerously ill and
b. even from a Jew who is suspected of not having sold his *chametz* before Pesach in accordance with the Halacha.

use of rice
and
cornstarch

80. *a.* Even Ashkenazi Jews, whose custom it is not to eat rice or cornstarch (cornflour) on Pesach, may cook them

    1) for a person who is ill, though not dangerously so,

    2) for a child suffering from severe diarrhea or

    3) for a baby who for some reason requires them.

b. The rice should be checked before use, to make sure it does not contain any grains of wheat, barley, rye, oats or spelt.

c. The rice or cornstarch should be cooked by boiling the water first and pouring the rice or cornstarch into the boiling water.

d. When Ashkenazi Jews cook rice or cornstarch, it is better for them to do so in vessels kept especially for this purpose.

VARIOUS LAWS RELATING TO ILLNESS (OTHER THAN PROHIBITIONS APPLYING SPECIFICALLY TO SHABBATH AND YOM TOV)

prayer
before
receiving
medication
or
treatment

81. *a.* 1) Before taking any medication or medical treatment, one should pray to God to cure one from one's illness.

    2) The words of the prayer are as follows:

"יְהִי רָצוֹן מִלְּפָנֶיךָ ה' אֱלֹקַי שֶׁיְּהֵא עֵסֶק זֶה לִי לִרְפוּאָה שְׁלֵימָה, כִּי רוֹפֵא חִנָּם אָתָּה."

"May it be Your will, Lord my God, that this treatment bring me a complete cure, for You cure without recompense."

b. Afterwards, one should thank the Almighty and say, "בָּרוּךְ רוֹפֵא חוֹלִים" "Blessed is the Healer of the sick."

doctor's
prayer

82. It is also fitting that the doctor, before he begins his medical work in the morning, should pray to God to help him, so that he can faithfully carry out his duty to heal the Almighty's creatures.

drinking
milk after
meat

83. *a.* A patient who has eaten meat and needs to drink milk need not wait longer than an hour, even though he is used to waiting six hours when he is healthy.

b. He is, however, first required to recite grace after eating the meat, so that the meat and milk should not appear to be consumed at the same meal.

c. It is also proper for him, before drinking the milk, to clean and wash his mouth by eating some other food and drinking something else.

d. 1) In general, a person who regularly follows a commendable practice is treated as if he has made a vow to adopt that practice.

2) Consequently, if he wishes to cease following the practice, he must obtain a release from his "vow."

3) a) The case under discussion in this paragraph is not quite in the same category, as the patient does not desire to abandon his practice of waiting six hours between meat and milk.

b) He merely wishes to suspend it until his health improves.

4) Therefore, if there is no one available to release his "vow," he may, nonetheless, drink milk after only one hour, as above.

84. a. 1) The appropriate blessing said before eating food *should* be recited over a medicine if
   a) it is not bitter, but palatable, **and**
   b) one chews, sucks or drinks it.

   2) One should *not* recite the blessing over medicine
   a) which is bitter **or**
   b) which is not a liquid and is swallowed without chewing or sucking (as in the case of most pills).

reciting blessing before taking medicine

b. 1) One should *not* recite a blessing over water which one drinks *solely*
   a) to weaken the bad taste of medicine **or**
   b) to make it easier to swallow medicine.

   2) One *should* recite the appropriate blessing before drinking
   a) liquids other than water for these purposes or

b) water for these purposes if one also has the intention of thereby quenching one's thirst.

medication with forbidden ingredients

85. *a.* One should not chew or suck medication (such as iron tablets) containing ingredients made from a substance one is forbidden to eat.

b. However, even a patient who is not dangerously ill may swallow them straight down.

fish oils for children

86. *a.* The authors of most of the later halachic works take a lenient attitude with regard to children drinking fish oil made from forbidden fish.

b. In places where a stricter view is prevalent, one should consult the opinion of a qualified halachic authority.

salting meat

87. *a.* 1) Since meat which has been cooked with the blood still inside may not be eaten, the blood is extracted before cooking.

2) The process by which this is done generally includes salting the meat and leaving the salt on for a complete hour.

b. 1) If meat is required for a patient who is on a low-salt diet, one may avoid the necessity for covering it with a great deal of salt by roasting (grilling) the meat instead of cooking it.

2) Once the meat has been roasted, it may subsequently be cooked, provided not more than seventy-two hours have elapsed between slaughter and roasting.

c. In the event that

1) the patient is on a low-salt diet and

2) roasted meat is not good for him, one may cook the meat for him after leaving it salted for only twenty-four, or at the very least twenty-three, minutes.

d. One may also salt the meat one is preparing for him with dietetic (sodium-free) salt.

e. If the doctor has ordered him to be on a totally salt-free diet, one may, when one has to, be so lenient as to kosher the meat (after washing it) by scalding, that is to say, by putting it into boiling water which is still on the flame (and one may then let it cook).

88. *a.* One must separate *t^erumoth* and *ma'asroth* from medicines containing ingredients which
  1) grew in what the Halacha regards as the Land of Israel **and**
  2) are still sufficiently palatable to be eaten, and not just swallowed without chewing or sucking.
  b. *T^erumoth* and *ma'asroth* need not be separated from medicines which taste bitter.

separating t^erumoth and ma'asroth from medicines

89. *a.* Even a person who is ill should not pray or put on *t^efillin* in a place where there may be excrement, an uncovered bedpan or the like.
  b. It is better not to pray or put on *t^efillin* at all rather than to do so in such a place.
  c. This problem frequently exists in hospitals, and one should ask a duly qualified halachic authority how to conduct oneself in the circumstances.
  d. See also paragraph 42 above.

prayer and t^efillin in hospital

90. *a.* Since one's body must be clean when wearing *t^efillin*, a person who is suffering from a stomach disorder and cannot control his bowel movements, is not allowed to put them on.
  b. He should ask a qualified halachic authority what to do with regard to prayer.
  c. A patient whose illness causes him a great deal of pain is not obliged to put on *t^efillin*.

ill persons who may not, or need not, put on t^efillin or pray

91. *a.* Sometimes a dangerously ill patient is advised to undergo an operation or treatment which, if successful, is likely to cure him, but which, if unsuccessful, may shorten his life.
  b. In such cases,
  1) if the weight of expert medical opinion is in favor of

undergoing dangerous treatment

the treatment, one would be justified in proceeding with it, notwithstanding the risk, but

2) one should also consult the advice of a rabbi steeped in the wisdom of the Torah, and ask him to pray to the Almighty God to work His wonders in the patient's favor.

doctor
treating his
parents

92. *a.* Although a son must be careful not to inflict a wound on his father or mother, he may, if he is a doctor, treat them, even to the extent of, for instance, administering an injection or removing a thorn, as long as

1) they agree and
2) there is no one else available who can do what is required (as well as the son can).

b. If there is someone else available, but he demands remuneration for his services, the son may do what is required, subject to the parent's consent.

persons
who have
difficulty in
eating
matza on
Pesach
night

93. *a.* A person who is unable to eat a *ka-zayith** of matza on the night of Pesach within the space of two, or at most four, minutes should eat as much as he can, but

1) he should not recite the special blessing normally said before fulfilling the obligation to eat matza on the night of Pesach and
2) he should try to eat a *ka-zayith** within a maximum of nine minutes.

b. He should not recite *birkath ha-mazon* unless he has eaten a *ka-zayith** within a period of four minutes or less.

c. In order to make the matza easier to eat, he may

1) crumble it into small pieces and even
2) wet it a little with cold water (but not to such an extent that it loses its characteristic appearance).

d. If he cannot eat the matza in any other way, he may

---

*In practice, the definition of a *ka-zayith* is not the same for all of the purposes mentioned in this paragraph. See Glossary.

dip it, or even soak it a little, in some other liquid or in
warm water (but not in a k^eli rishon or a k^eli sheini).

94. In the Babylonian Talmud, Tractate Sanhedrin 101a,   *the merciful*
we find Rabbi Abba asking about the apparent *Healer*
contradiction at the end of Exodus 15:26, "All the
illnesses which I put upon Egypt I shall not put upon you,
for I am the Lord your Healer." Since He does not put the
illnesses upon us, why do we need to be healed? To this,
Rabba the son of Mari, to whom the question was put,
replies with an explanation given by Rabbi Yochanan:
The verse must be understood in light of its opening
words, "If you will listen to the voice of the Lord your
God..." [That is to say,] if you will listen, I shall not put
the illnesses upon you. If you will not listen, I shall put
them upon you; however, I am the Lord your Healer.

Chapter 41

Laws Applicable in Various Emergency Situations

PUTTING OUT A FIRE WHERE THERE IS DANGER TO HUMAN LIFE

doing all one can to put out the fire

1. *a.* If a fire breaks out and there is even the remotest fear that human life may be in danger, one must do all one can to see that it is put out.

   b. This would be the case if, for example, there were a fear that the fire could spread to a nearby house where there is an elderly or sick person, or a baby, who cannot be taken out in time.

   c. In such circumstances, one may

      1) put out the fire oneself, doing whatever is necessary to that end, such as disconnecting the electricity supply, or

      2) telephone the fire department.

   d. Even if it afterwards transpires that ten different people have separately telephoned the fire department, each of them is assured of a worthy reward from the Almighty for his good intentions. (See Chapter 32, paragraph 7.)

   e. The rule set out in this paragraph ought to be given the widest publicity.

attendance of the police

2. *a.* One may call out the fire department when there is a fear of danger to life, even if one knows that Jewish police officers will come with them to investigate the cause of the conflagration and will make a note of their findings on Shabbath.

   b. 1) Notwithstanding this, where it is possible to object and to persuade the police officers not to violate the Shabbath, one is of course definitely obligated to do so.

2) One should take into account that a soft-spoken request is likely to prove more effective than a peremptory protest.

PUTTING OUT A FIRE AND SAVING PROPERTY WHERE THERE IS NO DANGER TO HUMAN LIFE

3. If a fire breaks out in a place where there will certainly be no danger to human life, *general rule*
   a. it is forbidden to extinguish it on Shabbath,
   b. one must not transgress even a Rabbinical prohibition in order to save property and
   c. one must certainly not call out the fire department. (See, however, paragraph 14 below.)

4. a. An exception occurs in the case of a fire which, while not presenting the slightest danger to human life, does expose three or more people to the risk of injury. *fires which threaten injury, but do not endanger life*
   b. In such a case, in line with the rule set out in Chapter 25, paragraph 8,
      1) one may extinguish the fire (since only a Rabbinical prohibition is involved), but
      2) one may not alert the fire department (since this would involve Torah prohibitions and there is no danger to life). (See, however, paragraph 14 below.)
   c. This could apply, for example, to the remains of a brushfire or of a bonfire whose embers are still hot, if the circumstances are such that
      1) there is no risk that the fire will spread or grow and become a threat to human life, but
      2) there are children in the vicinity whom it is impossible to keep at a distance, giving rise to a fear that one of them might burn himself.

5. a. When fire breaks out in a house on Shabbath, the general rule is that it is forbidden to save property *saving property: general prohibition*
      1) by taking it out of the house into a common courtyard or the street, or

[677]

2) by taking it out of one's own private courtyard into another courtyard or the street.

b. This is so even if there is an *eiruv*, so that it is permitted to carry articles about.

c. 1) The prohibition is a Rabbinical one, imposed because people tend to lose their presence of mind when faced with the sudden prospect of a financial calamity.

2) If there were no restrictions, then, in the panic of the scramble to rescue as much as one can, one might well forget that it is Shabbath and come to put out the fire.

3) Consequently, the Rabbis restrained one's freedom of action in the manner already mentioned, while allowing one to save limited quantities of food, eating utensils and clothing, as detailed in paragraphs 7 to 11 below.

4) Having resigned oneself to one's loss, one will not come to extinguish the fire.

to where property may be moved

6. One may save all of one's property from a fire if one can do so by moving it

a. from one part of one's house to another,

b. from one part of one's courtyard (even if it is not covered by a roof) to another,

c. from one's burning house to one's own private courtyard (which one does not share with anyone else and to which one can carry without the need for an *eiruv*, as stated in Chapter 17, paragraph 11a), or

d. from one's apartment to the common staircase, or to the apartment of a friend in the same house (as long as there is an *eiruv* permitting one to carry there).

saving food and eating utensils: basic principle

7. a. As mentioned in paragraph 5 above, even under the circumstances outlined there, one is allowed to rescue a limited quantity of food and eating utensils, but only in a place where there is an *eiruv*, so that carrying is permitted.

b. The basic quantity (subject to what is stated below) that one may save is sufficient food and utensils for as many of the three Shabbath meals as one has not yet eaten.

c. One may save this quantity even if one has food to eat and eating utensils elsewhere.

d. Likewise, one may rescue food and eating utensils for members of one's household and guests, as well as for one's animals.

e. The amount and type of food and utensils one may rescue for each Shabbath meal are such as would normally be required by an average person, including *lechem mishneh* for each meal.

f. Notwithstanding that one has already rescued food and utensils for the members of one's household and guests, each of them may also separately rescue as much as he needs for the Shabbath meals he has not yet eaten, as above.

g. Despite the fact that one has already rescued sufficient food, as above, one may save more food, but of a different variety, on the grounds that one now prefers this variety for one's Shabbath meal.

h. Since the amount a person drinks during the course of the day is not a fixed quantity, one may save as much drink and as many drinking utensils as one thinks one needs for the whole day.

8. a. The restrictions set out in the preceding paragraph as to the quantity of each kind of food and utensils one may rescue apply only if one takes them out in a number of separate containers.

b. If large quantities of food or utensils are in one big container, one may take the container out, with the food or utensils still inside, despite the fact that there is more than required for the Shabbath meals.

c One may even empty a number of small containers into a large container, so that one will be able to save more by taking out the latter.

saving quantities of food and utensils in one large container

d. One may not, however, save more by putting the smaller containers themselves into the larger container.

carrying out clothing

9. In the same way as one may rescue food, one may also pick up and take out a sufficient quantity of clothing for oneself and the members of one's household to wear that Shabbath.

saving clothes by wearing them

10. a. Furthermore, one may save articles of clothing from the fire by putting them on and going out wearing them.

b. In doing so, one may
   1) put on as much as one can, even one garment over another,
   2) go out even into *r^eshuth ha-rabbim* wearing the clothes, and take them off there, and
   3) go back after taking the clothes off, in order to put on more and save them too from the fire.

inviting others to save property

11. a. The owner of a burning house who is restricted as to the property he may save, in accordance with the rules set out above, may not, once he has rescued as much as he is allowed, tell other people to rescue more for him.

b. 1) Yet, he may tell them to save things for themselves.
   2) In that event, each of them may save whatever he would be permitted to save if the house were his.
   3) What they save belongs to them, and they need not return it to the owner of the house, since he told them to save it for themselves.

c. 1) If, however, the rescuers do not want to keep what they have saved, they may return it to its owner.
   2) After Shabbath, they may also take a fee for their trouble, and this does not fall within the pro-

hibition against taking remuneration for services rendered on Shabbath.

3) Nevertheless, a person who wishes to distance himself from anything savoring of a transgression would give back what he has saved, without asking to be paid for his exertions.

d. It can be argued that if somebody, of his own accord, comes to rescue property for the owner of a burning house, without having been requested by him to do so, he may save whatever he can.

12. a. The inhabitants of nearby houses who fear that the fire may spread to them are allowed to take anything out of their houses, as long as it is to a place to and in which one may carry.

neighbors who fear spread of fire

b. 1) Since the fire has not yet reached their houses, they are not likely to be so alarmed as to lose their presence of mind.

2) Consequently, one need not be afraid that they will come to put the fire out during the course of the rescue operation.

13. a. Everybody, including the owner of the burning house, is permitted to take out sacred writings which are liable to be burned.

saving sacred writings

b. Sacred writings include *sifrei Torah*, the Pentateuch, the Prophets, the Talmud, halachic works, prayer books and other Torah-study books, as well as *t^efillin*, even though they are *muktzeh* and there are restrictions on moving them. (See Chapter 20, paragraph 14.)

c. Sacred writings may be taken out even to a place where there is no *eiruv*, as long as the place has the requisite partitions for an *eiruv* to have been made. (See Chapter 17, paragraphs 2, 12, 21 and 25a.)

USING THE SERVICES OF A NON-JEW TO PUT OUT A FIRE

rules
applicable

14. *a.* 1) One need raise no objection if a non-Jew comes of his own accord to put out a fire, without having been told to do so (by a Jew).

   2) One may even call a non-Jew when there is a fire and say to him,
      a) "Whoever puts out the fire won't lose by it", or,
      b) outside Israel, where the firemen are not Jewish, "Whoever calls the fire department will be rewarded."

   3) In other words, one may hint to the non-Jew as to what one wishes him to do. (See Chapter 30, paragraph 13.)

b. 1) On the other hand, it is forbidden to tell the non-Jew directly that he should extinguish the fire, in order to avoid material loss, unless
      a) there is a possibility of danger to human life or
      b) there are three or more people about and one of them might be physically injured.

   2) Even if the non-Jew comes to put out the fire of his own accord, one may not urge him to speed up his fire-fighting efforts.

c. Nonetheless, a Jew may tell a non-Jew to put out a fire in the non-Jew's house, or in that of another non-Jew, even if the Jew's intention is to avoid the spread of the fire to his own house, with resultant damage to property there. (See Chapter 30, paragraph 33.)

saving
sacred
writings

15. *a.* One may tell a non-Jew to put out a fire in order to save sacred writings from being burned.

b. One may likewise tell him to take them out of the burning house, even if he will have to take them through an area which fits the strict description of a *r^eshuth ha-rabbim*.

c. See also Chapter 30, paragraph 12.

INDIRECTLY BRINGING ABOUT THE EXTINCTION OF A FIRE

16. *a.* Although it has been stated above that one is not *putting* allowed to put out a fire merely in order to save *water* property, one is permitted to perform an act which will *where the* indirectly result in its extinction, as illustrated in the *fire has not* examples below. *yet reached*

    b. Thus, if one side of a cupboard catches fire, one may
       1) pour water over the side which is not burning or
       2) cover the side which is not burning with wet cloths*
       so that the fire will die out when it reaches there.

    c. One may also put plastic bags filled with water near the fire, with the object that they should burst in the heat, releasing the water and so extinguishing the flames.

    d. If one end of a tablecloth has caught fire, one may pour liquid (other than water) onto the part which is not yet burning.

17. *a.* 1) If a burning candle falls onto the tablecloth and *burning* there is no non-Jew at hand to remove it, the Jew *candle* himself should *falling on*
        a) carefully remove the cloth,** with the burning *table* candle on it,
        b) lower it till it is near the floor and then
        c) gently tilt the cloth so that the candle rolls off.
      2) This may be done despite the possibility that the candle may go out when it falls onto the floor.

    b. 1) Where there would otherwise be a risk of a conflagration, the Jew may pick up the candle and take it away.

---

*If one has no wet cloths, one may wet cloths on Shabbath, but not with clean water.

**From Chapter 20, paragraph 60, it can be seen that, in time of need, one can rely on the more lenient view to the effect that the tablecloth does not become a *basis la-davar ha-assur.*

2) He must not, however, extinguish it unless
   a) there is fear of danger to human life or
   b) there are three or more people in the vicinity and one of them might suffer physical injury.

sparks falling on table 18. A spark which falls onto the tablecloth may be shaken off to prevent the cloth from being burned.

defective paraffin stoves or heaters 19. For the rule with regard to paraffin stoves or heaters which are emitting smoke or soot, see Chapter 13, paragraph 18.

ACCIDENTS AND HAZARDS TO LIFE

general rule 20. a. The situations described until now are illustrations of the principle that the saving of human life overrides the laws of Shabbath.

b. The more diligent a Jew is in saving the life of even just one of his fellows, the more praiseworthy are his actions.

c. Consequently, upon the occurrence of any disaster, accident or hazardous situation, one should violate Shabbath if there is any hope of thereby saving human life.

d. For examples, see below.

exposed electric cables in the house 21. a. When
   1) there are exposed electric cables or wires in the house and
   2) there is a danger of someone's touching them, one should act as follows.

b. If possible, it is best
   1) to leave the house for the duration of the Shabbath,
   2) to lock it up, so that no one can enter, and
   3) to delay effecting the repair until after Shabbath.

c. 1) Sometimes it is impossible to leave the house.
   2) This could be the case if there are children or sick

people in the house who cannot be taken out.

   3) In such a situation, one should cut off the electric current by taking out the fuse.*

d. 1) Sometimes this too is impossible.

   2) An example would be if one had to leave the electricity on for the sake of a person who is dangerously ill.

   3) In that event, since the exposed cables or wires comprise a hazard to human life, one would be allowed to repair them oneself or to call in a professional electrician to repair them.

22. *a.* When

   1) electric cables have fallen in the street and

   2) there is a fear that somebody may touch them, one may alert the corporation or authority which supplies the electricity, so that they should cut off the current.

fallen electric cables in the street

  b. 1) The violation of the Shabbath which this entails could be avoided if one stood near the cables for the duration of the Shabbath in order to warn people of the danger involved in touching them, but

   2) the strict letter of the Halacha does not oblige one to adopt this course.

   3) Nevertheless, if one wishes to take it upon oneself to wait near the cables and warn passers-by, there is merit in doing so.

23. *a.* 1) The bite of a dog with rabies can endanger human life.

   2) As a result, if one fears that a stray dog is infected with rabies and is liable to bite someone, one may

     a) catch it or even

     b) kill it.

stray dogs and poisonous snakes

---

*Where practicable and safe, the fuse should be removed in a different manner from that which one would normally adopt.

b. 1) a) Similarly, one may catch a dog which has bitten someone, so that one can investigate whether it is healthy or has rabies.

 b) Otherwise, one would not know how to treat the victim, since unnecessary treatment for rabies is in itself dangerous.

 2) Likewise, one may catch a snake which has bitten someone, so that one can classify its venom.

floods and **24.** Whatever property one is permitted to rescue in the case
other perils of a fire (as specified in paragraphs 5 to 13 above) one may also save in the eventuality of a flood or any other peril which threatens loss.

CALLING THE POLICE

burglars **25.** *a.* 1) a) Usually, when a burglar breaks into an apartment, there is a fear that he will attack anyone he finds inside.

 b) In view of this danger, the occupant, a neighbor or anyone else may telephone the police (but only if he cannot chase the burglar off without endangering himself).

 2) This applies even when one sees a burglar breaking into an empty apartment, if it seems likely that he will also break into another apartment, which is occupied.

b. 1) a) Where there is no fear of a dangerous attack, it is prohibited to call the police.

 b) This is so even if, as a result, one will lose one's whole fortune.

 2) Thus, one may not telephone the police if one sees a thief breaking into a place where there are no people around, such as a bank or a store.

fights **26.** *a.* A person witnessing a quarrel which is liable to degenerate into a fight and lead to bloodshed is allowed to alert the police (even by telephone).

b. The same applies upon the occurrence of any event which is liable to bring about danger to human life.

27. One may catch and hold a dangerous thief or violent combatants, with a view to handing them over to the police. *arrest*

28. One may notify the police (even by telephone) if *lost*
a. a small child is lost or *children*
b. a small child is found wandering about, in a distraught condition, and the only way one can calm him is by asking the police to find his family.

29. It is forbidden to give or take fingerprints on Shabbath or Yom Tov. *fingerprints*

SECURITY AND DEFENSE

30. One is permitted, and indeed obliged, to stand on guard in the war against hostile infiltrators and terrorists in their various guises, even if they only come to steal. *infiltrators and terrorists*

31. In the course of his duty to guard against danger, a soldier may go out, even where there is no *eiruv*, wearing around his neck a chain with an engraved disc bearing his name, his military number and his blood group. *wearing identification discs*

32. a. 1) A member of the home guard, the civil defense or the security forces who has to stand guard or is on active duty may, if the potential danger warrants it, take a gun or other weapons with him, *carrying weapons*
   a) even to a place where it is forbidden to carry and
   b) even beyond the limit to which it is permitted to walk on Shabbath.
   2) If he has to go out with a gun, he should, as much as he can, mitigate the violation of the Shabbath by

wearing it slung over his shoulder, instead of carrying it in his hand.

3) See also paragraph 34 below.

carrying and using a flashlight

b. 1) He may also take a flashlight with him, wherever he has to go, if there is a possibility that he may need it for an essential purpose, such as looking for suspicious objects.

2) a) If he has to use the flashlight, he may switch it off afterwards.

b) Otherwise, the batteries may run out and the flashlight will not be fit for use again that night.

minimizing degree of Shabbath violation

c. 1) In any event, he should minimize, as much as possible, the severity of the prohibitions he has to infringe.

2) Thus, if he can do what is required in a manner which differs from that normally adopted on another day of the week, he should do so.

3) See further Chapter 32, paragraph 28.

signing for mobiliza-tion order or equipment

33. a. A person receiving a mobilization order on Shabbath may be required by the military authorities to sign for it.

b. The purpose of the signature is twofold:

1) to inform the authorities that the messenger who delivered the order has performed his duty and

2) to prevent the recipient from evading mobilization by claiming that he has not received the order.

c. Both of these objects could be achieved without signing, for example, by the recipient's giving the messenger his reserve-duty passbook for retention until after the termination of Shabbath.

d. The signature itself has no practical effect whatsoever on the life-or-death situation which has necessitated the mobilization.

e. Therefore, the recipient is not allowed to sign for the order, even if, as a result,

1) the messenger will

a) sign himself or

b) write down that the recipient of the order has refused to sign, or

2) the recipient will be put on trial for his refusal.

f. 1) The same applies when clothing or equipment is issued upon mobilization and a signature is required to ensure that all the items are returned at the end of the period of service.

2) This signature too has no practical bearing on any risk to human life and so must not be given on Shabbath.

34. a. A soldier who is ordered to report for duty on Shabbath at a time of emergency may of course take with him all vital items he is required by the military authorities to have for the safeguarding of human life. *mobilization: what to take with*

b. In addition, he may take with him his *tallith*, his *t^efillin*, a prayer book and other essential personal effects, such as toilet paper.

c. He should put his personal effects into his kit bag together with the other items.

d. 1) If he has to go through an area where carrying is prohibited, or beyond the limit to which he would normally be permitted to walk, then he should try to put the kit bag into a vehicle and not carry it himself.

2) The vehicle should be one whose journey is justified by the aim of saving human life and not, for instance, a press car.

35. a. A Shabbath-observant soldier whose turn for standing guard comes out on Shabbath should not exchange his duty with a soldier who does not keep the mitzvoth, since the latter is also under an obligation to observe Shabbath. *guard-duty roster*

b. On the contrary, if the observant Jew stands guard, he may well be able to avoid superfluous violation of the Shabbath.

[689]

<table>
<tr>
<td>*reaching
one's place
of duty*</td>
<td>**36.** *a.*</td>
<td>1)</td>
<td>A member of the security forces who has to be on essential duty in another part of town on Shabbath should go there on foot (or before Shabbath).</td>
</tr>
</table>

36. *a.* 1) A member of the security forces who has to be on essential duty in another part of town on Shabbath should go there on foot (or before Shabbath).

reaching one's place of duty

2) He should not travel by car, even if the vehicle is in any event being driven to the same destination.

b. 1) If it would be impossible for him to walk all the way to his place of duty, he must ensure that he is within its vicinity when Shabbath commences.

2) He must not rely in advance on the fact that human lives may be dependent on the fulfillment of his duties and that, as a result, he will be permitted, in the last resort, to travel to his place of duty in a vehicle.*

reporting suspicious movements

37. If somebody sees suspicious movements or individuals on Shabbath, and there is a fear that there may be terrorists around, he is permitted, and indeed obligated, to inform the police immediately.

finding suspicious objects

38. *a.* 1) A person finding a potentially dangerous, suspicious object on Shabbath in a place where there may be people, or where people may pass, should alert the police immediately.

2) He should do so even if a violation of the Shabbath is involved.

b. 1) The strict letter of the Halacha does not oblige him to avoid this by staying where he is for the whole of Shabbath to warn people not to come near, and

2) indeed, he must not do so unless he can be certain

---

*The position here must be distinguished from that of the doctor in Chapter 40, paragraph 13.

a. In that case, the doctor need not stay near his place of duty (at home), as he might not be called upon to attend a dangerously ill patient at all during Shabbath.

b. In the present case, the member of the security forces knows perfectly well, before Shabbath, that he will have to report at his place of duty on Shabbath. (Compare Chapter 40, paragraph 22.)

a) that nobody is endangered by the risk of an imminent explosion **and**

b) that there are no additional explosive charges in the vicinity.

39. *a.* The following should eat or drink enough to satisfy their essential needs on Yom Kippur, but only in *shi'urim*, as explained in Chapter 39, paragraphs 18 to 26: *military service on Yom Kippur*

1) a soldier who is in a state of full alert, if there is a danger that abstention from food and drink will make him too weak to carry out his duties properly when the need arises;

2) a soldier who is in a region where extreme conditions of heat prevail, if there is a fear that failure to drink will result in dehydration of his body, with all its consequent dangers.

b. A soldier who may find himself in these circumstances would be well advised to ask a competent halachic authority, before the arrival of Yom Kippur, how he should conduct himself.

40. *a.* 1) The situations which an emergency is liable to bring in its wake are many and varied, and it is impossible to predict them in advance. *the guiding principle in all situations*

2) Sometimes a given action is prohibited and sometimes the circumstances are such that one is not only permitted, but obliged, to perform the selfsame action.

3) The great rule which guides us is that the Torah lays down laws "which a person shall perform and by which he shall live" (Leviticus 18:5) and not by which he shall die.

b. 1) Man was created, put into this world and charged with the obligation of observing the six hundred and thirteen mitzvoth of the Torah.

2) However, the Torah does not require him to observe

these mitzvoth if their observance could endanger his life.*

3) Quite the reverse! The Jew is commanded by the Torah to transgress the commandments of the Torah in order to avoid danger, or the risk of danger, to his life or to the life of his fellow-Jew.

c. Notwithstanding the foregoing, the Jew should always remember the words of the Rabbis (expressed in the Sifra on the above verse) as to the purpose of life in this world: "'...and by which he shall live' [means] in the world to come; for, if you say it means in this world, does his life here not end in death? So, what meaning can I give to the words, 'and by which he shall live'? [It must refer to life] in the world to come. [And the verse concludes,] 'I am the Lord, I am Faithful to pay rewards.'"

In brief, we are given life and put into this world to offer us the opportunity of performing the mitzvoth of the Torah. The reward for the performance of the mitzvoth in our transient life here is eternal life in the world to come. Hence, the vital importance of preserving our lives in this world!

---

*There are three exceptions to this rule, namely those offences broadly classed under the headings of bloodshed, idolatry and forbidden sexual relations, which are so serious that one must lay down one's life rather than commit them.

Glossary

(Please note: This Glossary is not intended to give an exhaustive and precise definition of each expression which it contains. It is designed merely to help the reader obtain a *general* idea of the meaning of unfamiliar words he may find in the text. Its use for any other purpose may well be misleading.)

al ha-michya: The blessing recited (in most cases) after eating cake or cookies (biscuits).

al ha-peiroth: The blessing recited after eating grapes, figs, pomegranates, olives or dates.

amah (plural *amoth*): A measure of length, 22.7 inches (57.6 centimeters) by one halachic view, 18.9 inches (48 centimeters) by another. In any given instance involving this measure, that view is followed which makes for greater stringency.

aravoth: Willow twigs, used on Sukkoth.

arba kanfoth: A four-cornered garment with a prescribed tassel (*tzitzith*) at each corner, worn to fulfil the biblical injunction to wear fringes on the corners of one's garment.

arba'a minim: Collective name for *ethrog, lulav, hadassim* and *aravoth*.

Av: The month of the Jewish calendar in which the Temple was destroyed.

Bar^echu: The first word (literally "Bless") of the phrase calling upon the congregation to bless God.

basis la-davar ha-assur: An article which the Halacha subjects to the same restrictions on handling as a *muktzeh* object that has been placed or hung on it.

birchoth ha-Torah: Blessings recited before the study or reading of the Torah.

birkath ha-mazon: The blessing recited after eating bread or a meal including bread (Grace after Meals).

birkath ha-zimun: The form of introduction to, and commencement of, *birkath ha-mazon* used when three or more people have eaten together.

carm^elith: An area which is not *r^eshuth ha-rabbim*, but to which the Rabbis applied rules similar to those applying to *r^eshuth ha-rabbim*.

challa: A proportion of the dough which has to be removed once it is kneaded and which, in Temple times, was given to a *kohen*.

chametz: Food which is made from, or contains, flour and which is leavened. It may not be eaten or kept on Pesach.

Chanuka: The Feast of Lights.

charoseth: A mixture of nuts, wine, cinnamon and apples eaten on Passover night.

cholent: A stew, normally containing meat, potatoes, barley and beans, put on the fire before the commencement of Shabbath and left there all night, so that one should be able to have a hot meal during the day.

chol ha-moed: The intermediate days of Pesach and Sukkoth, between the first and last days of Yom Tov.

day: Unless otherwise indicated, or inconsistent with the context, a day, for the purposes of the Halacha, is regarded as commencing and terminating at what can colloquially be called nightfall.

dreidel: A spinning-top used for playing a Chanuka game.

eiruv: An abbreviation for *eiruv tavshilin* or for *eiruv chatzeiroth*; often used as a general term including both *eiruv chatzeiroth* and *shitufei m^evo'oth*.

eiruv chatzeiroth: The arrangement for permitting the transfer of objects on Shabbath from one *r^eshuth ha-yachid* to another, or within a *r^eshuth ha-yachid* which belongs to two or more adjoining occupiers in common. The expression is often used as a general term including also *shitufei m^evo'oth*.

eiruv tavshilin: The arrangement whereby one is permitted on Yom Tov to make preparations for Shabbath occurring on the following day; also, the food set aside before Yom Tov for this purpose.

Eretz Yisrael: The geographical area of the Land of Israel within the boundaries defined by the Halacha. In case of doubt, a competent halachic authority should be consulted.

ethrog (plural *ethrogim*): Citron, used on Sukkoth.

hadass (plural *hadassim*): Myrtle twig, used on Sukkoth.

Halacha (adjective: halachic): Jewish religious law.

havdala: The blessings recited at the termination of Shabbath or Yom Tov.

kaddish: A prayer in sanctification of God's name recited after certain other prayers or after studying Torah when ten or more male adults are present.

ka-zayith: A measure of volume, concerning whose size there is considerable controversy. The two most commonly accepted views equate it to 49.8 cubic centimeters and 28.8 cubic centimeters. In practice, the size attributed to the *ka-zayith* varies with the purpose for which it is required, and a competent halachic authority should be consulted when the quantity involved is between these two figures.

*k*e*dusha*: A sanctification of God's name recited by the congregation, in conjunction with the person leading prayers, when the latter repeats the *Sh*e*moneh Esrei*.

*k*e*li rishon*: The pot or other vessel in which food has been cooked, so long as it retains a temperature of 45 degrees centigrade (113 degrees Fahrenheit) or more, even if it is no longer on the fire.

*k*e*li sheini*: A pot or other vessel into which food is transferred from the vessel in which it was cooked.

*k*e*li sh*e*lishi*: A pot or other vessel into which food is transferred from a *k*e*li sheini*.

*k*e*li she-m*e*lachto l*e*-issur* (plural *keilim she-m*e*lachtam l*e*-issur*): An object which is *muktzeh* because it is used for performing an activity that is forbidden on Shabbath.

kiddush: The blessings recited in sanctification of Shabbath and Yom Tov; often colloquially used for a snack which follows.

kil'ei kerem: Produce which grows from seeds sown within a given distance of vines; the grapes which subsequently grow on those vines.

kohen (plural *kohanim*): A priestly descendant of Aaron, the High Priest.

Kosher: To make meat fit for a Jew to eat, by removing the blood from it in the manner prescribed by the Halacha.

lechem mishneh: Two whole loaves with which one begins each Shabbath meal.

lulav: Palm branch, used on Sukkoth.

ma'aser sheini: The Second Tithe removed from food grown in Eretz Yisrael. At the time when the Temple stood, it was eaten in Jerusalem; today, one must redeem it in the prescribed manner and may then eat it anywhere.

ma'asroth: The various tithes removed from food grown in what the Halacha regards as Eretz Yisrael.

matza (plural matzoth): Unleavened bread.

m^ekom p^etur: An area which is neither *r^eshuth ha-rabbim,* nor *r^eshuth he-yachid,* nor *carm^elith.*

m^ezuzoth: Parchment scrolls inscribed with extracts from the Pentateuch, in accordance with halachic requirements, and affixed to the doorposts.

mikveh: A ritual bath complying strictly with the requirements of Jewish religious law.

mitzva (plural mitzvoth): A religious obligation or duty.

mohel: A person who performs circumcision in accordance with the Halacha.

muktzeh: A term describing objects whose handling is subject to restrictions of various kinds on Shabbath and Yom Tov.

muktzeh mei-chamath chesron kis: Denotes an object, having an appreciable value, which is *muktzeh* because its owner is particular not to use it for other than its intended purpose, lest it be damaged. In most cases, the object's intended use is one that is forbidden on Shabbath.

muktzeh mei-chamath gufo: Denotes an object which is *muktzeh* because it is neither designed nor designated for any use, and is not fit for either human or animal consumption.

muktzeh mei-chamath mitzva: An object which has been set aside for use in the performance of a mitzva, and from which it is forbidden, as a result, to derive a benefit.

orla: Fruit which grows on a tree in the first three years after planting.

parve: Refers to food which contains neither meat nor dairy products; also, to a utensil which is used exclusively for food which is neither meat nor dairy.

Pesach: Passover.

Purim: The day on which one celebrates the deliverance of the Jews, some 2,500 years ago, from death and destruction, as described in the Book of Esther.

r^eshuth (plural *r^eshuyoth*): A term used to denote one of the four categories of place: *r^eshuth ha-yachid, r^eshuth ha-rabbim, carm^elith* and *m^ekom p^etur.*

r^eshuth ha-rabbim: A public thoroughfare meeting criteria laid down by the Halacha; such an area is subject to restrictions with regard to the moving of objects into, out of or within it.

r^eshuth ha-yachid (plural *r^eshuyoth ha yachid*)· A place which is enclosed in a manner complying with the Halacha, and within which one may carry, but which is subject to restrictions with regard to the moving of objects into and out of it.

Retzei: An additional prayer inserted into *birkath ha-mazon* on Shabbath.

Rosh Hashana: New Year.

s^echach: The roofing material of a *sukka*.

sefer Torah (plural *sifrei Torah*): A scroll containing the Pentateuch.

sha'atnez: A combination of wool and linen.

Shabbath Shira: The Shabbath on which the regular weekly portion read from the Torah includes the song sung by Moses and the Children of Israel at the crossing of the Red Sea.

Shavuoth: The Festival of Weeks.

Sh^ema: Extracts from the Pentateuch whose recital is obligatory twice every day and commences with an acceptance of the sole sovereignty of God.

Sh^emini Atzereth: The Eighth Day of Solemn Assembly.

Sh^emoneh Esrei: The principal of the prayers, recited in a standing position at least three times every day (with variations on Shabbath and other special days).

shitufei m^evo'oth: The arrangement by which it becomes permissible to transfer objects in, to or from the street on Shabbath.

shi'urim: Prescribed quantities forming the limit of what may be eaten over short periods of time on Yom Kippur by a person whose life would otherwise be in danger (and who is not in need of more).

shofar: Horn blown on Rosh Hashana.

Simchath Torah: The Festival of the Rejoicing of the Law.

siyata di-Shmaya: Help from Heaven.

sukka: The booth in which one resides during Sukkoth.

Sukkoth: The Festival of Tabernacles.

tachshit (plural *tachshitim*): An ornament, or an object which is not an article of clothing but is worn for the purposes of the body.

tallith (plural *tallitoth*): A prayer shawl.

tefach (plural *t^efachim*): A measure of length, 3.8 inches (9.6 centimeters) by one halachic view, 3.15 inches (8 centimeters) by another. In any given instance involving this measure, that view is followed which makes for greater stringency.

t^efillin: Phylacteries.

t^eruma (plural *t^erumoth*): That part which is initially removed from food grown in what the Halacha regards as Eretz Yisrael, and which, in Temple times, was given to a *kohen*. The plural form, *t^erumoth*, is often used to denote *t^eruma* and *t^erumath ma'aser*.

t^erumath ma'aser: A tenth part which is removed for the tithe designated for the Levite out of food grown in what the Halacha regards as Eretz Yisrael, and which, in Temple times, was given to a *kohen*.

Torah: The Pentateuch; the whole body of Jewish law and learning; a *sefer Torah*.

tzitzith: Fringes which the Halacha requires to be worn on the four corners of a garment.

Ya'aleh Ve-yavo: An additional prayer inserted into *birkath hamazon* or *Sh^emoneh Esrei* on special days such as Yom Tov.

Yom Kippur: Day of Atonement.

Yom Tov: The first and last days of Pesach and Sukkoth (that is to say, including Sh^emini Atzereth and Simchath Torah), Shavuoth and the two days of Rosh Hashana. The rules which apply to Yom Kippur are by and large those which apply to Shabbath and not those which apply to Yom Tov.

yom tov sheini shel galuyoth: The second and eighth days of Pesach, the second day of Sukkoth, the day after Sh^emini Atzereth (known as Simchath Torah) and the second day of Shavuoth, which have to be observed as Yom Tov by Jews living outside the boundaries of Eretz Yisrael.

Comprehensive Index

Index

when permissible, 33:19; 35:34, 35
Concrete, fresh
watering, 23:43
—hinting to non-Jew to water it, 30:13
Condensation on windowpane
wiping off, 23:37
writing in, 23:37
Construction toys, playing with, 16:18,
20
Contact lenses
going out wearing, 18:17
soaking soft, 15:82
Contagious disease, preventing spread
of, 32:13
See also illness
Containers
using to save food or utensils from
fire, 41:8
See also Opening containers
Contraceptive drugs, 34:19
Cookies
crumbled, mixing with soft cheese,
8:15
crumbling, 6:11; 7:5(YT)
cutting or breaking lettering, 11:8
extracting water or milk from, 3:52
grating, 6:11
putting in hot tea, 1:59
Cooking, Chapters 1; 2(YT)
adding water to pot on covered flame,
1:16
baked products, 1:11, 59
by non-Jew, 38:3, 11
definition, 1:1-4
for medicinal purposes, 33:24, 25(YT)
for sick person
—who is dangerously ill, 32:72-79
—who is not dangerously ill,
33:24(YT), 25(YT); 38:11
fried products, 1:11, 59, 61
hot solid treated as k^eli $rishon$, 1:58
of fully cooked liquids, 1:7, 8, 9, 15, 55
of fully cooked solid food, 1:10, 15
of inedible products, 1:1n
of partially cooked food, 1:6
on Yom Tov for non-Jew, 2:5(YT),
6(YT)
on yom tov $sheini$ $shel$ $galuyoth$,
31:34-36, 38(YT)
preparing meat for patient on low-salt
diet, 40:87
rice or cornstarch on Pesach, 40:80

roasted products, 1:11, 59
See also Fire; Food; Gas; K^eli $rishon$;
K^eli $sheini$; K^eli sh^elishi; Pots;
Stove; Water
Cooking utensils, moving, 20:7-10, 15
Cooling
drinks, 1:74; 10:1, 2, 13
fruit, 10:1
using water cooler, 10:13
warm food, 1:73
See also Air conditioner
Coop. See Poultry
Copper, worn to alleviate rheumatic
pains, 34:15
Copperware, polishing, 12:24
Copy, carbon: non-Jew making for Jew
on Shabbath, 31:15
Cord
used to form notional shelter ("$ohel$"),
24:12
See also Cutting; Knot
Cork, removing from bottle, 9:20
Cornflour. See Cornstarch
Cornstarch
cooking on Pesach, 40:80
See also Cereal
Corpse, human: moving a, 20:39
Correspondence. See Reading
Cosmetics, using, 14:57-61
Cost. See Price
Cot. See Crib
Cotton, absorbent
applying
—eye medication with, 34:8
—oil to baby's body with, 14:28; 37:7
cleaning
—nipples with before feeding baby,
36:17
—skin before injection with, 33:10
—thermometer with, 40:2
—wounds with, 35:2, 11; 37:8
in aching ear, 18:20; 34:9
making wicks from, 13:21(YT)
preparing tufts or swabs, 14:29, 39;
34:9; 35:19
—in hospital before Shabbath, 40:26
using as ear plug, 14:39
wiping away ointment with, 35:30
Cotton (wool). See Cotton, absorbent
Coughs, treating, 34:10
Counting
floor tiles, 29:33

Index

Finding
   money in street, 22:34
   suspicious objects, 41:38
Fingernails (and toenails)
   cleaning, 14:56
   cutting, trimming or filing, 14:54, 55;
     35:17
   polishing, 14:57
   removing polish, 14:61
   thorns or splinters under, 32:11; 35:17
Fingerprinting, 41:29
Fingers, removing stains with lemon,
   14:17
Fire
   burning
     —*challa*, 11:19; 13:5 (YT)
     —*chametz* on Pesach, 13:5 (YT)
     —*muktzeh* object, 22:32 (YT)
     —with magnifying glass, 13:1, 2 (YT)
   burning candle falling onto table-
     cloth, 41:17
   covered, moving pots on, 1:22
   covering on Shabbath, 1:18n, 23
   department, calling out, 41:1-4
   extinguishing
     —after cooking for dangerously ill
       person, 32:77
     —by letting water boil over,
       13:13 (YT)
     —by non-Jew in non-Jew's house,
       30:33; 41:14
     —by putting water where fire has not
       yet reached, 41:16
     —by turning off hot water tap, 13:15
     —hinting to non-Jew, 30:13; 41:14
     —non-Jew saving sacred writings by,
       30:12; 41:15
     —scope of prohibition, 13:1, 8 (YT),
       9 (YT)
     —to save property, 41:3
     —when human life endangered, 41:1,
       2, 14
     —when people may be injured, 41:4,
       14
     —when telling non-Jew is forbidden,
       30:15; 41:14
   flame
     —extinguished, what to do, 1:23, 28;
       13:14 (YT)
     —lowering, 13:1, 9 (YT), 10 (YT); 32:77
     —raising, 13:3 (YT), 5 (YT), 17 (YT)
     —transferring pot to larger, 1:21

lighting
   —for dangerously ill person. *See*
     Cooking; Heating
   —matches, 13:2 (YT), 3 (YT); 21:5 (YT)
   —on Yom Tov, 13:2-7 (YT)
   —scope of prohibition, 13:1, 2 (YT)
replacing pot on, 1:18-20, 32
saving property from, 41:3, 5-16
   —*m^ezuzoth*, 30:12, 15
   —through agency of non-Jew, 30:12,
     15; 41:15
spark falling onto tablecloth, 41:18
transferring food from one pot to
   another, 1:16
uncovered, using, 1:63
urn on, taking water out and putting
   it back, 1:33, 34
See also Candles; Cigarettes and
   cigars; Gas; Kerosene; Pots
Firewood, moving, 21:6 (YT)
First-born, redemption of, 29:31
Fish
   aquarium
     —changing or adding water, 27:27
     —moving, 27:27
     —removing dead fish, 27:29
     —removing newly spawned fish,
       27:58
     —returning fish to, 27:28
   boning, 3:11-13
   catching, 27:31, 32, 33
   chopping or mincing, 6:14; 7:6 (YT),
     7 (YT)
   eating "gefilte" (stuffed), 3:15
   removing skin of, 3:30
   salted
     —putting into vinegar, 11:3
     —washing to remove salt, 11:4
   selecting from mixture of boiled and
     fried, 3:64
   selecting from mixture of same
     variety, 3:24
Fish oil, giving to children, 37:4; 40:86
"Five-stones," playing, 16:11
Flame. *See* Fire
Flashlight, operating when standing
   guard, 41:32
Flavoring
   measuring, 11:30 (YT); 29:41 (YT)
   with juice, 5:7; 8:14, 15; 11:38
Flies
   killing, catching or driving away, 25:4

Index

Honey
mixing with soft cheese, 8:1, 13
spreading on bread, 11:33
Honoring Shabbath, general rule,
29:1, 2
Hood
of baby carriage. *See* Baby carriage
shaking snow off, 15:36
wearing coat with hood attached,
18:31
wearing in rain, 18:10
Hook
attaching or detaching, 23:39
hanging picture on, 23:39
Hopscotch, playing, 16:40
Horse, placing rope of halter on, 27:17
Horseradish, preparation of, 7:3(YT)
Hospital
accompanying patient to, 36:11;
40:70, 71
ambulance
—payment for, 36:6; 40:72
—radio-linked, use of, 40:68
—returning after emergency, 40:67, 68
—telephoning for, 36:8; 40:72
—use by women about to give birth,
36:6, 8
—*See also* Car
arriving at too early for childbirth,
36:10
discharge from, 36:10; 40:43, 44
eating food cooked by Jews on
Shabbath, 40:16
letter referring patient to, writing,
32:48
light switched on in ward, using,
40:16
patient separating *t*^e*rumoth* and
ma'asroth and *challa*, 40:18
praying in, 24:30, 37; 40:42, 89
preparations for Shabbath by
management, 40:26
putting on *t*^e*fillin* in, 40:89
traveling to for childbirth, 36:6, 8
washing floor in, 23:6
where Shabbath is violated, staying
in, 40:15, 16
See also Doctor; Illness
Hotel, paying for, 28:62
Hothouse, opening and closing door of,
26:9
Hotplate, electric. *See* Electrical

appliance; Stove, electric
Hot spring, therapeutic: bathing in, 14:6,
10(YT); 34:14
Hot-water bottle
as bed-warmer, 1:71; 34:11
heating water for, 33:26(YT)
to assuage pain, 33:15; 34:11
Humidifiers
hanging on radiators, 23:27
improvising in dry weather, 25:10
Hydrogen peroxide, to wash wounds,
35:11
Hygiene, 23:10-17

Ice
disposing of, 10:1
making, 10:4
melting, 10:1, 2, 3
putting in drink, 1:74; 10:2
putting in empty cup, 1:74; 10:3
scattering sand or cinders on, 23:17;
25:9
Ice cream
melting, 10:8
preparing from liquid, 10:7
preparing from powder, 10:6
Icing, squeezing onto cake, 11:14
Identification
card or certificate
—carrying in time of emergency,
18:22
—handling, 28:6
disc, soldier wearing, 18:22; 41:31
tags or discs on animals, 27:9
tags or labels on clothing, 18:25, 44
Ignition. *See* Car
Ill, care of. *See* Illness
Illness
alerting relatives of patient, 38:3
bathing person who is ill, 14:1, 14;
32:81, 82
carrying medical instructions, 40:7
determining whether dangerous,
32:8-13
disabilities, 34:26-30
eating before prayers during, 40:45
extracting blood from meat for sick
person, 40:87
kiddush when ill, 40:46, 47
lights, turning on and off for sick
person. *See* Lights

Lights (*continued*)
electric bulbs, removing, inserting
and handling, 13:29; 32:66, 71
—by non-Jew in refrigerator, 31:1
—in car, 40:54
hinting to non-Jew to turn off, 30:5
hinting to non-Jew to turn on, 30:7,
58n
in refrigerator, 10:14-16; 22:16; 31:1;
32:71
kerosene lamps, 32:63n, 68; 33:6
memorial. *See* Memorial lights
moving, 32:65; 33:6
of car. *See* Car
telling non-Jew to turn off, 30:5
—so that sick person can sleep, 30:11;
38:2, 5
—so that small child can sleep, 38:26
telling non-Jew to turn on, 30:7
—between sunset and nightfall on
Friday evening, 30:24
—for sick person, 30:11; 38:5
—for small child, 38:26
turned on by non-Jew, benefitting
from
—in apartment building, 30:51
—scope of prohibition, 30:7, 37, 38
—when non-Jew turned on for himself, 30:52
—when there was already light
before, 30:58
—when turned on for small child,
38:26
turned on by non-Jew incidentally,
30:23, 52; 31:1
turned on for dangerously ill person,
use by other people, 32:69; 40:16
turned on in hospital ward, 40:16
turning on for patient who is not in
danger, 33:3, 6
turning on or off for dangerously ill
person, 32:63-70; 38:2
—choice between larger and smaller
bulbs, 33:67
—minimizing number of lights,
32:66
—varying manner of turning on or
off, 32:64, 70; 38:2
used to examine baby with earache,
37:14
See also Candles; Lamp
Limb, artificial: going out with, 18:15

Limits to which one may walk, 16:41;
27:13
driving beyond, 40:65
Lining, detachable. *See* Raincoat
Lips
applying lipstick to, 14:58; 34:13
furuncle on, 32:11; 35:16
smearing margarine or butter on,
11:33
smearing oil on, 34:13
Liquefying fruit, 5:2
Liquids. *See* Cooking; Kneading;
Mixing; Pouring; Spilled liquid;
Straining; Water
Lock
combination, 23:54
"keyhole lock," 23:32
Logs (small), moving, 21:6(YT)
Loofah, using, 12:12
Loop of garment
inserting belt, ribbon or thread. *See*
Inserting
torn, going out with, 18:41, 43
Loose-leaf file, using, 28:9
Loquat, removing pits from, 3:17
Loss, hinting to non-Jew to prevent,
30:13
Lost child, violating Shabbath for, 32:15;
41:28
Lost property, picking up and keeping,
29:30
Lotteries, conducting, 16:47
Lulav. See Arba'a minim
Lying on grass, 26:20

Ma'aser sheini. See T^erumoth and
ma'asroth
Ma'asroth. See T^erumoth and ma'asroth
Maggots in beans, lentils, etc., checking
for, 4:5(YT)
Magnifying glass, burning with, 13:1,
2(YT)
Mail
delivered by non-Jew, 31:20, 21, 23
opened by non-Jew, reading, 30:57
opening, 28:4, 5
—through agency of non-Jew, 30:10,
57n; 31:22
sending, 31:20
signing for, 31:21
See also Commerce; Letter

Index

Index

Oatmeal. *See* Cereal, cooked
Obituary notices, prohibition on reading, 29:48
Occupational therapy, 34:23
"Odds or evens," playing, 16:32
"*Ohel.*" *See* Protective shelter
Oil
  applying
  —to baby's body, 14:27, 28; 37:6, 7
  —to hair, 14:48
  —to hands, 27:50; 34:13
  —to lips, 34:13
  —to skin irritation, 34:12
  —to skin on Yom Kippur, 39:33
  —to sprain, 35:35; 38:20
  —to squeaky hinges, 23:38
  —to squeaky wheels, 28:47
  —to thermometer, 40:2
  of lamp
  —moving, 20:32; 22:2
  —using, 21:3(YT)
  patches, scattering cinders or sand over, 20:44; 25:9
  pouring
  —into *keli sheini*, 1:53
  —on eggs and onions, 8:23
  —on vegetables, 8:4
Oilcloth. *See* Tablecloth, synthetic
Oil lamp
  attending to wick of, 13:21(YT)
  considered as *keli she-melachto le-issur*, 20:16
  See also Oil
Ointment
  applied by non-Jew, 38:19
  containing *chametz*, 40:78
  for inflamed nipples, 36:22
  for prevention of bedsores, 40:5
  on dressing, 33:14; 35:8, 27
  on skin irritation, 34:12
  on superficial wound, 35:20
  rubbing on baby, 14:27; 37:6, 10
  smearing on thermometer, 40:2
  to soothe pain, 33:13; 35:8
  wiping away, 35:30
Olives
  pitting, 3:55
  pouring salt water off pickled, 3:19
Onions
  chopping fine, 7:2(YT)
  eggs and, 3:73; 8:23
  removing from mixed salad, 3:23

salting, 11:1
skins or peels, removal of, 3:31
Opening. *See individual items*
Opening containers, Chapter 9
  bottles
  —caps which break open, 9:17
  —corks, 9:20
  —crown caps, 9:20
  —paper seal over top, 9:11
  —slicing off plastic spout, 9:7
  boxes
  —taped or gummed closed, 9:10
  —tied with string, 9:14
  cans, 9:1-3, 22(YT), 23
  —if sealed by metal strip, 9:18
  —through agency of non-Jew, 30:57n; 31:3
  cartons
  —by perforating, 9:3, 5-7
  —normally used to retain contents after opening, 9:3; 16:18n
  —previously marked or perforated, 9:8
  —stuck closed, 9:10
  if normally re-used, 9:2; 16:18n
  if normally used to retain contents after opening, 9:3
  in forbidden manner, using contents after, 9:23; 30:57
  jars, 9:21
  on Yom Tov, 9:22(YT)
  packets thrown away on opening, 9:4
  parcels tied with string, 9:14
  preferable course, 9:1
  sealed bags. *See* Bags
  seals, 9:11, 12
  See also Perforations; Wrappings
Operation
  after Shabbath, preparing for, 40:38
  assessing risk of, 40:91
  non-urgent
  —performed by non-Jew, 38:3
  —postponing, 40:38
  signing consent to, 40:21
  to save life of fetus, 36:3
  See also Doctor; Hospital; Illness
Oranges
  cutting
  —letters or designs into peel, 16:27
  —lines to ease peeling, 11:15
  —through markings on peel, 11:10
  peeling. *See* Peeling and shelling

Index

[737]

Index

Index

Index

Sweating, sprinkling with talc, 34:12
Sweeping
    carpets, 23:4
    muktzeh objects, 22:36
    when forbidden, 23:2
    when permitted, 23:1
Sweets. *See* Candy
Swelling, preventing or reducing, 35:34
    See also Compresses
Swimming, 14:12; 16:38
Swing, using, 16:16; 26:16, 17
Switch, turning on or off, 13:28
    See also Car; Electrical appliance
Synthetic materials
    washing. *See* Cleaning, clothes;
        Tablecloth, synthetic
    which give off sparks, wearing, 15:72
Syphon, preparing soda-water in, 11:35
Syringe. *See* Injections

Table
    cleaning, 12:40
    —removing liquid spilled on, 12:37,
        38, 39; 23:7
    clearing
    —of dirty dishes and cutlery, 12:36;
        28:79
    —of refuse, 12:32, 33; 22:36
    dismantling, 24:22
    erecting, 24:19-23
    extending and decreasing size of,
        20:59; 24:23
    folding table, opening and closing,
        24:23
    laying, 3:79
    legs, fixing or detaching noise
        absorbers, 23:42
    pulling out and inserting drawers of,
        24:24
    —if containing *muktzeh* object, 20:65,
        66, 69
    —if *muktzeh* object is on table, 20:59,
        69
    spreading cloth over, 24:25
    tilting to remove *muktzeh* object from,
        20:61; 22:9
    with candlesticks on it
    —moving, 20:52, 59, 61; 22:37, 52
    —using, 20:59
    with drawer containing *muktzeh*
        object, moving, 20:65, 66

with low-denomination coin on it,
    moving, 20:54
Tablecloth
    folding, 15:45, 46
    moving with candlesticks on it,
        20:52, 60, 63
    shaking out, 12:32; 22:36
    —crumbs where birds will eat them,
        27:21
    —through window, 12:30
    shaking sparks off, 41:18
    synthetic
    —cleaning, 12:39, 41, 42
    —folding, 15:46
    See also Table
Table-napkins. *See* Napkins
Table-tennis, playing, 16:6
Tablets. *See* Medicine
Tableware. *See* Cutlery; Dishes
Tachshit, definition, 18:11, 12, 24
    See also individual items under Going
        out with
Tacking, temporary: removing, 15:65
Tag
    animal wearing, 27:9
    going out with, 18:25, 44
    removing from clothing, 15:79
Tailor's chalk marks, rubbing off, 15:65
Talcum powder, 34:12
Talking. *See* Speaking
Tallith
    folding, 15:45
    going out wearing
    —at commencement of Yom Kippur,
        18:38
    —to synagogue, 18:6
    —with broken silver chain, 18:41
    taking to synagogue and back, 28:81
Tampon, going out wearing, 18:20
Tank, water: opening lid of, 23:40
Tap. *See* Gas; Heating
Tape, adhesive: playing game with, 16:28
Tape measure, *muktzeh*, 29:43
Tapping. *See* Clapping or tapping
Taxicab, ordering, 29:52
Tea
    bags, 1:53; 3:58; 4:14 (YT)
    essence
    —pouring from *keli rishon* onto, 1:56
    —pouring out of teapot, 3:57
    —preferred way of making tea with,
        11:38

[748]

Index

Index

Watch
  electronic, 28:24
  going out wearing
  —as pendant, 18:26
  —on wrist, 18:27
  —pocket watch on chain, 18:27
  stopwatch, 28:30
  which stops working
  —automatic, 28:28
  —shaking, 28:22
  —when *muktzeh*, 28:24, 28
  —while being worn, 28:25
  See also Clock
Watchman, hiring for Shabbath, 28:59
Water
  adding to pot on covered flame, 1:16
  bottle. *See* Hot-water bottle
  changing or adding in aquarium,
    27:27
  coloring. *See* Coloring
  discharging over sown ground, 12:18;
    26:7
  draining away, 23:10, 11
  filtering, 3:56
  for washing hands in morning, dis-
    posal of, 14:40
  heating. *See* Heating, water
  hot, use of. *See* Heating, water
  keeping *arba'a minim* in, 26:27; 28:81
  keeping flowers or twigs in, 26:26
  mixing hot and cold, 1:51, 52; 14:3, 5
  removing from *keli rishon* with ladle,
    1:16, 33, 34, 48
  scenting, 14:15
  shaking out of garment, 15:6, 16, 33,
    34
  squeezing out of hair. *See* Hair
  standing dirty dish or pot in, 12:2, 3, 8;
    28:81
  transferring from one vessel on fire to
    another, 1:16; 8:21
  turning on metered supply, 12:19
  See also Spraying, water; Urn;
    Washing
Water coolers, electric, using, 10:13
Water heater (boiler). *See* Heating
Watering
  freshly poured concrete or plaster,
    23:43; 30:13
  See also Irrigation
Watermelon
  removing seeds from, 3:16

  seeds of, moving, 20:27
Waterproof pants or sheets
  cleaning, 15:5, 8
  drying, 15:11
Water tank, opening lid of, 23:40
Wax
  modeling with, 16:13
  putting receptacle under candle to
    catch, 13:38; 22:26
  removing from candlestick hole,
    13:43(YT)
Wearing. *See* Clothing; Going out with
Weaving, 16:36
Weighing. *See* Measuring or weighing
Wet. *See* Cloth; Clothing; Diapers; Hair;
    Laundry; Radiators; Raincoat;
    Warming, hands
Wheelchair, 34:27
Wheels, oiling, 28:47
Whey, separating, 3:19, 20, 51; 4:1(YT)
Whipping food, 11:31, 32
Whistling
  kettle, 28:40(YT)
  with one's mouth, 16:2; 28:37
  with whistle, 16:2
  See also Musical sounds
White coat, wearing over clothes, 18:5
Wick
  cleaning, 13:20(YT)
  making, 13:21(YT)
  raising, 13:17(YT)
  replacing
  —of oil lamp, 13:21(YT)
  —of paraffin lamp or stove, 13:22(YT)
  trimming, 13:20(YT), 21(YT)
Wig
  brushing or combing, 14:46
  going out wearing, 18:7
  perfuming, 14:51
  spraying with hair spray, 14:50
  styling, 14:50
Winding
  clocks and watches. *See* Clock
  toys, 16:14
Window
  broken pane
  —covering, 23:36
  —removing, 23:35
  —replacing, 23:34
  curtain, hanging, 24:29
  opening or closing
  —near burning candle, 13:33

The Distributors' Foreword to the second Hebrew edition

Translation of the Distributors' Foreword to the second Hebrew edition

שמירת שבת כהלכתה

כולל

דיני שמירת שבת ויום טוב
בשים לב לבעיות שהתעוררו בזמננו
(לאלה הנוהגים לפסוק כשיטת הרמ״א)

מאת
יהושע ישעיה נויבירט

מהדורה חדשה, מתוקנת ומורחבת

בית מדרש הלכה — מוריה
ירושלם עיה״ק תובב״א
אך את שבתתי תשמרו כי אות הוא

The title-page of the second Hebrew edition